The Idols of Death
and the God of Life

PABLO RICHARD ET AL.

The Idols of Death
and the God of Life

A THEOLOGY

Translated from the Spanish by
Barbara E. Campbell
and
Bonnie Shepard

ORBIS BOOKS
Maryknoll, New York 10545

The Catholic Foreign Mission Society of America (Maryknoll) recruits and trains people for overseas missionary service. Through Orbis Books Maryknoll aims to foster the international dialogue that is essential to mission. The books published, however, reflect the opinions of their authors and are not meant to represent the official position of the society.

First published as *La lucha de los dioses: los ídolos de la opresión y la búsqueda del Dios Liberador,* by DEI (Departamento Ecuménico de Investigaciones), Apdo. 339, San Pedro Montes de Oca, San José, Costa Rica, and CAV (Centro Antonio Valdivieso), Apdo. 2339, Managua, Nicaragua. Copyright © 1980 DEI-CAV

Except where noted, all biblical quotations are from the *New English Bible*

Manuscript Editor: William E. Jerman

Library of Congress Cataloging in Publication Data
Main entry under title:

The idols of death and the God of life.

  Translation of: La lucha de los dioses.
  Includes bibliographical references and index.
  1. Liberation theology—Addresses, essays, lectures.
2. Church and the poor—Addresses, essays, lectures.
3. Idolatry—Latin America—Addresses, essays,
lectures. I. Richard, Pablo. II. Campbell, Barbara E.
(Barbara Ellen), 1926-   . III. Shepard, Bonnie.
BT83.57.L813   1983   261.8'098   83-6788
ISBN 0-88344-048-2 (pbk.)

Contents

Contributors

Pablo Richard, Chilean, biblist and sociologist; professor at the National University of Costa Rica; member of DEI (Departamento Ecuménico de Investigaciones, San José, Costa Rica) staff.

J. Severino Croatto, Argentinian, biblist; professor at the Instituto Superior Evangélico de Estudios Teológicos (ISEDET), Buenos Aires; author of *Exodus: A Hermeneutics of Freedom* (Orbis).

George V. Pixley, born in Chicago, reared in Nicaragua, biblist; professor at the Baptist Seminary of Mexico; author of *God's Kingdom: A Guide for Biblical Study* (Orbis).

Jon Sobrino, Spaniard, longtime resident of El Salvador, theologian; professor at the José Simeón Cañas University of Central America and at the Center for Theological Reflection, San Salvador; author of *Christology at the Crossroads: A Latin American Approach* (Orbis).

Victorio Araya G., Costa Rican, theologian; professor at the Latin American Biblical Seminary and the National University of Costa Rica; member of the DEI staff.

Joan Casañas, Spaniard, longtime resident of Chile, theologian; member of the Agermanament group, Barcelona.

Javier Jiménez Limón, Mexican, theologian; staff member of the Center for Theological Reflection, Mexico City.

Frei Betto (Carlos Alberto Libanio Christo), Brazilian, theologian; pastoral advisor for Christian base communities in various dioceses of Brazil; author of *Against Principalities and Powers: Letters from a Brazilian Jail* (Orbis).

vii

Franz Hinkelammert, German, longtime resident of Latin America, economist; director of postgraduate economics at CSUCA-UNAH, Honduras; member of the DEI staff; author of *The Ideological Weapons of Death* (Orbis, forthcoming).

Hugo Assmann, Brazilian, theologian and sociologist; professor at the University of Costa Rica and the National University; member of the DEI staff; author of *Theology for a Nomad Church* (Orbis).

Introduction

This collective work poses the question of God in Latin America. It approaches this complex subject from the point of view of one of the enduring biblical traditions: the battle of the gods—that is, Yahweh's struggle against false gods. From this perspective, the question of God acquires a radically different dimension from what might be expected.

The central question in Latin America today is not atheism—the ontological question of whether or not God exists. To be or not to be: that is *not* the question. The following discussion does not take place within the metaphysical frame of reference; it does not take on the ontological, universal, and abstract characteristics that traditionally surround this topic. The central issue is linked neither to the connection between atheism and secularism, nor to the crisis that marks the West European modern age.

The central issue is *idolatry*—a worship of the false gods of the system of oppression. Even more tragic than atheism is the faith and hope that is put in false gods. All systems of oppression are characterized by the creation of gods and of idols that sanction oppression and anti-life forces.

Much to the contrary of what might be supposed, false gods not only exist today, but are in excellent health! Many are the worshipers who invoke their mercy, their love, and their power, and theologies abound to rationalize a false practice of liberation.

The search for the true God in this battle of the gods brings us to an anti-idolatrous discernment of false gods, of those fetishes that kill with their religious weapons of death. Faith in God as a liberator, who reveals his face and mystery through the struggle of the poor against oppression, necessarily entails repudiation and removal of false gods. Faith becomes anti-idolatrous.

Last but not least, it is well to point out the great importance of this discussion in our Latin American context, with its past of religious and political domination, and its present of repression and misery. We believe that, in these times, the problem of the idols of oppression, and of the search for God

1

the liberator, has taken on a new dimension, in evangelization as well as in political involvement. It is here that liberation theology finds one of its most fruitful challenges.

The Staff,
DEI, Departamento Ecuménico de Investigaciones
San José, Costa Rica

* **|** *

PABLO RICHARD

Biblical Theology of
Confrontation with Idols

In an oppressed world, evangelization must direct its attention mainly to idolatry, not to atheism. The oppressive world of today is a world of fetishes and idols, of clerics and theologians. The modern capitalist system is growing more religious and pious by the day. Heightened scientific and technical production has been accompanied by an even greater production of gods, cults, temples, and religious and theological symbols. Atheism has become a serious problem for the capitalist system: it is an obstacle to the production, circulation, and consumption of idols and fetishes.

When the modern world became emancipated from Catholic and monarchal feudalism, atheism was necessarily given a social, political, technical, and scientific dimension. There was once a bourgeoisie that was revolutionary *and* profoundly atheistic. Today, however, atheism is an obstacle to the development of the modern world. It acts as a brake on consumption, and as an active resistance to the creation of mechanisms of political, cultural, and ideological domination.

Capitalism is terrorized by and obsessed with the problem of atheism. For this reason economists, politicians, business executives, journalists, artists, professors, and others pursuing the limitless growth of capitalism are increas-

3

ingly preoccupied with religion and theology. The economist Milton Friedman is also an em·nent theologian. The political reasoning of North American presidents and of the Trilateral Commission is also religious and theological reasoning.

The more repressive and militarized the secular state is, the more it needs to
create a magisterium to pass judgment on matters of dogma and morality.
Religion is an obligatory theme in any journal of international importance.
The entertainment industry makes great profit by treating theological
themes, one example being the version of the life of Jesus in *Jesus Christ
Superstar*. Even the CIA and the counterinsurgency apparatus are interested
in religion as a problem.

Atheism is definitely the greatest threat to the continued growth of the
modern capitalist system. The often-proclaimed secularization of modern
life and the provocative announcement of the "death of God" have only
served to uncover new ways to produce religious goods, and to expand the
market for the consumption of new theologies.

Faced with this modern capitalist world threatened by atheism, the poor
and oppressed world, itself threatened by underdevelopment, discovers that
its political struggle for liberation has acquired a new atheistic and anti-idolatrous dimension. Political confrontation has turned into theological confrontation, and theology has become a new arena for struggle. Liberation
praxis now demands liberation theology. The poor no longer fight solely
against the oppressing classes and their mechanisms of exploitation; now the
poor also fight against fetishes, idols, and all sorts of mystical, spiritual, and
theological forces.

In this context, evangelization—the search for and proclamation of the
God of Jesus Christ—acquires a new dimension. For the capitalist system,
this proclamation represents a subversive and irrational atheism, whereas for
Christians it represents an anti-idolatry and anti-fetish practice. Thus it is, in
today's oppressed world of the poor, that evangelization faces the problem of
idolatry. In these times it is impossible to seek the God of Jesus Christ
without coming directly face to face with the idols and fetishes of the dominant system. Christians can theologically analyze the question of God only
from a political perspective that confronts the religious system of modern
capitalism. The poor can seek the visage of the real God only by working
within a political praxis of liberation. Likewise, class struggle has been transformed into a struggle of the God of Jesus Christ against the Olympus of the
gods of the capitalist system.

This study seeks to clarify the question of idolatry in Old and New Testament texts. It analyzes biblical texts that deal with this theme, placing them in
their context and trying to find a unified interpretation. Our historical situation is different from that of biblical times, but the "sense of faith" *(sensus
fidei)* is the same, especially in view of the discovery that the majority of the
biblical references to idolatry are found within a context of resistance to and
struggle against oppression. The biblical message on idolatry is essentially

one of liberation and of hope in moments of crisis, and of the oppression of the people of Israel and the first Christian communities.

ANTI-IDOLATRY BIBLICAL THEOLOGY IN THE OLD TESTAMENT

In the Old Testament, idolatry has two distinct sources of meanings: one from within the worship of the true God, and the other from outside that worship. In the first case idolatry is linked to the problem of cultic images of Yahweh—"Yahwist" idols. In the second case it is associated with the worship of other gods, false gods.[1] In both cases, idolatry takes on different meanings.

In the most synthetic formulation of Mosaic law, these two meanings are clear:

I, the Lord, am your God, who brought you out of the land of Egypt. . . . You shall not have other gods besides me [different or false gods]. You shall not carve idols for yourselves [Yahwist idols] [Exod. 20:2–4 = Deut. 5:6–8, NAB].

This passage contains a prohibition of idolatry based on the *liberating* deeds of Yahweh. Those who are liberated from slavery cannot be idolatrous. Only the slave and the oppressor are idolatrous.

As will be seen below, two types of idolatry occur outside the worship of Yahweh. The idol assumes a different meaning in each of them. The first type is a worship of "other" or "foreign" gods. In the second type the idols are "false" gods. We shall now treat in turn the biblical texts referring to these three kinds of idolatry (one from within the worship of Yahweh, two from without), and their respective theological meanings.

Cultic Images of Yahweh

The problem of idols in the worship of Yahweh appears very seldom in the Old Testament, although the few texts on it carry enormous weight within biblical tradition. The two certain references are Exodus 32 and 1 Kings 12:26–33. Other possible instances are in Judges 8:22–27 (the ephod of Gideon) and Judges 17–18 (the idol of Micah), but these are more controversial, doubtful, and of less importance.

The Golden Calf of Exodus 32. Chapter 32 of Exodus is a continual point of reference in the Bible and in postbiblical tradition for the purpose of combating idolatry. It would be necessary to analyze the economic, social, political, ideological, and psychological context of the narrative of Exodus 32 to extract all the theological density of this text. It deals with a people recently liberated from slavery, undergoing the harsh tests of the "period of transition" in the desert and marching toward the conquest of the promised land. Under these circumstances, Aaron is told: "Come, make us gods to go ahead of us. As for this fellow Moses, who brought us up from Egypt, we do not know what has become of him" (Exod. 32:1). Thereupon, they resort to the power of gold, and make a calf to worship.

The golden calf did not represent "another god," nor did it purport to be a representation of Yahweh. The Israelites were simply constructing the seat, the throne, the symbol of the presence of Yahweh in their midst.[2] There was no sin here against monotheism, but rather against God's transcendence, which also entails a sin against the people. The meaning of this transcendence, negated by the people of Israel, must be interpreted in the concrete historical context of Exodus.

The problem is not that God is invisible and the Yahwist idol is visible, nor is it that God is spiritual and the Yahwist idol material. The sinfulness of the idol in this case does not lie in the attempt to make God material or visible. The visible/invisible antithesis or the material/spiritual one—as those words are understood today—is foreign to biblical thought.[3] The transcendence of God does not exclude his presence or manifestation on the visible or material plane. In their descriptions of God, biblical authors do not hesitate to use the crassest of anthropomorphisms: God is presented as if he had eyes, hands, and feet, and as someone who becomes angry, who is jealous, who repents, and the like. In Exodus 32 itself, God is revealed through sensible, human, and material images. If God is always revealed through material and visible intermediaries, then he could reveal himself through images or idols as well, without violating his transcendence.

In Exodus 32 it is the transcendence of God that is at stake; it is not that the invisibility or spirituality of God is being replaced by the visibility and materiality of the idol. To understand this transcendence, consider the opposition appearing in the text (v. 1 and v. 23) between the presence of the Yahwist idol and the absence of Moses, who left the people alone so that he could climb Mount Sinai. When the Israelites constructed the golden calf, they wanted God to deliver them from the role that Moses was playing. They wanted a god, instead of Moses, to be their leader. They rejected the liberating leadership of Moses and wanted God to exercise another kind of leadership, in accordance with their desires. In their rejection of Moses, the Israelites were rejecting their role as a people. In their rejection of their leader, they were rejecting their own organization as a people, in a concrete effort toward liberation and the conquest of a new land.

Moses, as the leader of his people, had to win their confidence; no matter how difficult, he had to convince them that liberation was possible. He had to instill hope in them, drive away their fear of the pharaoh and his army, and show them concrete ways to survive and to march forward through the desert. When the people wanted to retreat, to avoid the risks involved in their liberation, Moses pushed them forward mercilessly, obliging them to overcome their weaknesses. In a certain sense, Moses had to exert force and violence on the people in order to liberate them. The whole internal process that a people must undergo in order to establish itself as a people is always reflected in the role of its leaders. A people organizes itself as a people and accepts itself as the subject of its own destiny through gestation of its leaders and then obedience to their commands.

In chapter 32 of Exodus, the people had lost confidence in Moses once more, and in the possibility of liberation and conquest of a new land. Within this crisis of the people, as manifested by the refusal to follow Moses as its leader, there also occurred a crisis of the people's faith in God as a liberator. A political crisis and a crisis of faith occurred simultaneously. The Israelites wanted to retreat, and to force God to lead them, not toward the promised land of liberty, but toward Egypt, the land of slavery. They refused to follow God the liberator any longer; rather they wanted God to follow them in their oppression. They refused a God who would rescue them from slavery; they preferred one who would live with them in their slavery. They wanted God-consoler-in-oppression, and not God-leader-out-of-slavery. The sin against the transcendence of God, therefore, consisted in the people's refusal of its own liberation, and in the construction of a false liberation through the alienating worship of a god who would console them, but not set them free. God the liberator is always a god who transcends human impossibilities, always the god of hope against all hope, always the god who will not tolerate the fear and alienation that the oppressor has instilled in the oppressed people.

The book of Exodus is a violent book—violence against the oppressive pharaoh and his army, but violence against the people of Israel as well. In chapter 32, when Moses returned from the mountain and saw the golden calf, he pulverized it, threw it in the water, and then forced the people to drink the water. Later he knifed all those who had sinned; "about three thousand of the people died that day" (v. 27). This violence in the book of Exodus reveals the uncompromising transcendence of the liberating design of God. Processes of liberation are always violent, not only to the oppressor, but also to the oppressed, who must undergo an internal transformation to liberate themselves from their oppressed and alienated consciousness.

Affirmation of the transcendence of God is, at the same time, an affirmation of the plan to liberate the people. A refusal of this objective is, *eo ipso,* an act of idolatry—not the idolatry of other gods or false gods, but the idolatry that is possible only from within the worship of the true God. In Exodus 32, God reveals his transcendence as God the liberator, and not a God who consoles the oppressed so that they will accept their condition as an oppressed people. The veneration of God as consoler is idolatry. The seat or throne of this god—where he reigns or manifests his presence to the people—is gold, and gold is the symbol of domination.

The Golden Calves of Jeroboam. A different historical situation in 1 Kings 12:26–33 basically poses the same problem as does Exodus 32. In this situation the people of Israel is divided. The schism happened when Rehoboam, son of Solomon, imposed a cruel tyranny over the people. To escape this tyranny, the tribes of the north seceded and proclaimed another king, Jeroboam. Jeroboam reigned from Shechem, and his rival, King Rehoboam, reigned in the south, in Jerusalem, where the temple of Yahweh was located.

Because the northern tribes had to go to Jerusalem to worship Yahweh, Jeroboam feared that his subjects would end up recognizing Rehoboam, his enemy in the south, as the king of the tribes of the north. To obviate this political danger, Jeroboam had two golden calves made in the northern territories, and said to the Israelites: "It is too much trouble for you to go up to Jerusalem; here are your gods, Israel, that brought you up from Egypt!" (1 Kings 12:28). He then put one calf in Bethel and the other in Dan, and constructed two sanctuaries as well, to replace the one in Jerusalem.

These Yahwist idols, like the one in Exodus 32, were not meant to represent Yahweh but rather were a symbol of his presence. There was no question of a sin against monotheism (the Yahwist idol is neither another god nor a false god) but rather a sin against the transcendence of God. Jeroboam was trying to solve a political problem by religious means. God was manipulated to meet a political necessity. Just as in Exodus 32, the symbol of this manipulated god was made of gold. Instead of solving the political problems that were the cause of the division of the people, the Israelites resorted to religious means. Instead of combating the oppression of King Rehoboam and thus maintaining the unity of all the people of Israel, they manipulated the presence of Yahweh in their midst to legitimize their actions. The people refused a liberating confrontation with King Rehoboam and fell into idolatry. Idolatry arose as a false liberation, to justify the people's passivity and submission in the face of a situation of injustice and oppression.

The text shows that the Israelites' sin was against themselves and their designs for liberation, against God as liberator. Worship of God the liberator, who freed them from slavery in Egypt, demanded that the people confront the oppression of King Rehoboam. The people preferred a religious transformation of their worship rather than such a confrontation. Thus, once again, idolatry appeared as the religious expression of the people's submission to a situation of oppression.

The chapters following the story of the construction of the golden calf show how this idolatry led the Israelites to destruction. When they abandoned the true path to liberation and thus sinned against the transcendence of God the liberator, the golden calf became the altar upon which they were sacrificed—victims of their own idolatry (1 Kings 13:2).

Liberative Transcendence. The experience of the people of Israel, as narrated in Exodus 32 and in 1 Kings 26–33, lived on in the tradition of God's people. On the basis of this experience, a whole anti-idolatry liberation theology developed throughout biblical and postbiblical tradition. "Yahwist idols" were strictly prohibited. To avoid all risk of idolatry, in later years the use of any kind of image in the worship of Yahweh was prohibited. Still later the legislation was extended to forbid *all* images and statutes, within and outside the worship of Yahweh. The basic theological reason for this was that only humans are the image of god. "So God created man in his own image; in the image of God he created him" (Gen. 1:27).

When all these texts are compared, one can conclude that, if God reveals himself in the Bible as God the liberator, then only the image of a liberator reveals the transcendence of the true God. Both the oppressor and the oppressed practice an idolatry that deforms and perverts the revelation of the liberating transcendence of God.

The Worship of "Other" or "Foreign" Gods

The problem here is not a distortion of the worship of Yahweh, but rather the worship of other gods, not the true God. This kind of idolatry passed through two historical stages.[4] In the first stage, it was believed that the foreign gods existed and held power in their own lands. At this stage, Yahweh was acknowledged as the supreme God among many other gods (specialists designate this phenomenon "henotheism," as differentiated from monotheism). The battles of Israel against other peoples were also Yahweh's battle against other gods. Submission to another people (a political problem) also entailed recognition of the superiority of the god of this people and submission to this other, or foreign, god (a theological problem). A correspondence existed between the political struggles of the peoples and the battle among the gods. Idolatry was a political and theological problem simultaneously.

In the second stage, idolatry acquired a different character, because there was no longer a belief in the existence of foreign gods. This stage will be discussed in the next section.

The anti-idolatry precepts of the first stage were mostly found in the Mosaic law and in historical texts in general. The basic formulation is: "You shall have no other god to set against me" (Exod. 20:2–3 = Deut. 5:6–7)—literally, "You shall have no other gods before me."

This same datum is formulated in more theological terms in Deuteronomy 6:14–15:

> You must not follow other gods, gods of the nations that are around you; if you do, the Lord your God who is in your midst will be angry with you, and will sweep you away off the face of the earth, for the Lord your God is a jealous god.

In the historical books of the Old Testament, the most notable cases of this kind of idolatry are those involving the kings of Israel. In these cases, wealth, power, and idolatry always go together, entailing injustices against the poor. The deuteronomist (Deut. 16:14–20) forbade the kings to do three things: to build military power, to accumulate silver and gold, and to have many women (explicitly in reference to polytheism, not polygamy; the women posed a theological threat, not a sexual problem).

King Solomon is the typical example of the idolatrous king, transgressing all three laws, but especially the last-named (1 Kings 11:1–13). Other kings who are especially condemned by history and the prophets are Ahab of Israel (874–852 B.C.) and Manassah of Judah (698–643 B.C.).

In Ahab's case the historian describes in great detail how he committed a crime against Naboth in order to rob him of his vineyards (1 Kings 21). In reference to Ahab's crime the historian says: "He committed gross abominations in going after false gods" (v. 26).

The proliferation of Manassah's idolatrous practices is described in 2 Kings 21:1–18, as well as the injustice that followed as a direct consequence: "And this Manasseh shed so much innocent blood that he filled Jerusalem full to the brim" (v. 16).

The biblical authors always maintained an attitude of distrust and rejection vis-à-vis the institution of monarchy. On the one hand, the power of Israel was a manifestation of the divine power of Yahweh over all the other gods of neighboring peoples. The superiority of Yahweh was at stake in the political independence of the people. On the other hand, this political power generated injustice and oppression of the weak, and idolatrous practices. Criticism of the oppressive and idolatrous monarchy was always made from the perspective of the exodus, in that the superiority of Yahweh lay in his role as a liberator. In the history of Israel, Yahweh's power is liberating; hence his transcendence and superiority over other gods.

The people of Israel was born as a people through its liberation from slavery in Egypt, and it was in this liberating action that it discovered its God. Oppression among the people contradicted the intimate and specific nature of the people of Israel and its faith in Yahweh. Injustice and idolatry were not just sins like other sins, but rather the negation of itself as a people. Conversely, its justice and the purity of its faith in God were the source of its strength and superiority over other peoples.

The Worship of False Idols

From the time of the exile onward (sixth century B.C.), idolatry took on a new meaning. Monotheism came into place as one of the spiritual acquisitions of exile. There was no longer a danger of following "other" gods or "foreign" gods, because these were simply nonexistent and their idols were made by humans. The affirmation that there is no other god but Yahweh led to a radical de-idolatrization of personal and social life.

The texts that bear witness to this radical opposition between monotheism and idolatry are found mostly in the following books or biblical passages:

Jeremiah 10:1–16: an original writing of Jeremiah's, and his only one on the subject of idolatry. It was written between 609 and 586 B.C., during a turbulent period when the Israelites were threatened and finally exiled by Babylon.

Isaiah 40–55: prophesies of Deutero-Isaiah, in which the theme of idolatry is central and pervasive. His prophetic ministry took place from 550 to 540 B.C., in the middle of the exilic period: 598(586)-538 B.C.

The Letter of Jeremiah (Baruch 6): written, by an unknown author, to the exiles in Babylon. It was inspired by Jeremiah, especially chapter 29. It is a long text, deeply meaningful theologically, and dedicated entirely to the problem of idolatry in the context of exile.

Daniel 14: a postexilic text, but set in Babylon. It contains two typical accounts of the struggle against idols, and above all against the priestly caste that maintained them.

1 Maccabees: covers the historical period between 175 and 134 B.C., from the reign of Antiochus IV Epiphanes, oppressor of the Jewish people, until the death of Simon, high priest and political chief of the liberated Jews. This narrative deals with the violent confrontation between idolatry and monotheism within the context of a war for liberation. The book was written to venerate the memory of the combatants.

Wisdom 13-15: written in the time of Christ or some decades earlier, it is a treatise on "political theology."[5] This work is addressed to the oppressed Jews of Alexandria, and the main theme is that of justice in government. The choice of topic was inspired by the injustices under which these Jews suffered. In this context, these three chapters present a significant theology against idolatry.

One outstanding aspect of these texts is that they are all situated in a context of oppression. When idolatry appears, it is intimately linked to the situation of political oppression. The prophetic or theological denunciations of idolatry, with the consequent affirmation of monotheistic faith, always occur within a context of hope and liberation.

We shall now sketch a brief summary of the theologico-political content of these biblical texts on idolatry.

Jeremiah and Deutero-Isaiah. The texts of Jeremiah and Deutero-Isaiah are strongly polemical. They are easy and direct arguments for the benefit of the exiled Jews so that they could discuss, understand, and confront a Babylon that was cruelly oppressive and extremely idolatrous. In Jeremiah 10:1-16 and in the text of Isaiah 44:9-20, which was inspired by that of Jeremiah, the starting point of the argument against idolatry is the "production process" of idols. Idols are made by humans, using the same materials and the same techniques as in the manufacture of other products destined to satisfy their necessities:

A man plants a cedar and the rain makes it grow, so that later on he will have cedars to cut down; or he chooses an ilex or an oak to raise a stout tree for himself in the forest. It becomes fuel for his fire: some of it he takes and warms himself, some he kindles and bakes bread on it, and some he makes into a god and prostrates himself, shaping it into an idol and prays to it, saying, "Save me, for thou art my god" [Isa. 44:14-17].

To understand the prophet's thought one must analyze the difference between a *talisman*, a *fetish*, and an *idol*,[6] and the dual reality expressed by each of them. A talisman is a material object with magical properties. A fetish is a material object within which resides a spirit that gives it power. An idol is also a fetish, with the difference that the material object is intended to represent, directly or symbolically, the form and the behavior of the spirit or god residing within it. In each of these there is a dual reality: the material object, and the power, spirit, or god present in the material object. The relationship between the two realities is more direct in the idol than in the fetish, because the idol is intended to represent materially the god that resides within, whereas the fetish can assume any physical form whatsoever.

The biblical author attacks idols, taking as his main point of reference the process of human labor that produces the material part of the idol or fetish. He does not directly attack the power, spirit, or god that might inhabit this material object. In modern terms, one might say that this anti-idolatry polemic of the prophets uses a materialist method of analysis, not an idealistic or ideological method. The direct conclusion of this analysis of idols is that the power or spirit present in the idol is also a human product for the satisfaction of human necessities. The prophet does not deny the existence of this power or spirit present in the idol, but simply denies the transcendent or divine origin of this power or spirit.

Persons who make talismans, fetishes, or idols really do have more power. The opposite is also true: it is because they have more power that they can make talismans, fetishes, or idols. Idolatry bears witness to the power that persons can develop through their human efforts. Furthermore, if they really have power, then all that they produce could be transformed into fetishes or idols. The power of the idol is neither a fiction nor a trick—it is real; but the source of its power is human. Humans have the power to transform nature and thereby satisfy their needs, but through this same power and labor they can also create fetishes and idols.

The biblical texts that we are analyzing are aimed specifically at the idolatry of the Babylonians, the cruel oppressors of the people of Israel. The prophets wanted to demonstrate that the power of the idols of Babylon was in fact the political, military, and cultural power of the Babylonians themselves, not the power of the gods they adored. The idols of Babylon were powerful because the Babylonians had the political power to subject and oppress the people of Israel. Being subjected to that oppressive power should not have meant that the Israelites had to recognize and adore the spirits and gods produced by that same power. In that context, idolatry would have meant not only submission to the oppressive power of Babylon, but also recognition that the power was of divine origin, and therefore a good and redeeming power for the oppressed. Politically and theologically, idolatry implied seeking liberation from oppression through political and religious submission to Babylon's power.

Hence the idolatrous content in the words of Gedaliah, who gave this advice to the exiled Jews: "Have no fear of the Chaldaean officers. Settle down in the land and serve the king of Babylon; and then all will be well with you" (2 Kings 25:24). This is the very essence of the philosophy of idolatry: liberation is found through submission to power. This belief can be imposed and inculcated only by an oppressive power, and it generates—in the oppressed as well as in the oppressor—the idolatrous faith that a divine liberating power exists within oppressing power.

Jeremiah's speech, to these same Jews and in the same context, is radically different:

> Do not be afraid of the king of Babylon whom you now fear. Do not be afraid of him, says the Lord; for I am with you to save you and deliver you from his power [Jer. 42:11].

Gedaliah said, "Serve the king." Jeremiah said, "Do not be afraid of the king." Gedaliah placed his hope for liberation in obedience to the king. Jeremiah placed his hope for liberation in the redeeming presence of Yahweh. Faith in God the liberator is always subversive in the face of power, and subversion is always anti-idolatrous. When salvation is sought through power, the power becomes fetishized; it divinizes itself, expands into a transcendent world. The spirit or god that inhabits power is made visible through idols.

Those who submit to this invisible spirit of a power—a submission made manifest in the worship of the visible idol of the invisible spirit—live in peace with that power, and the power leaves them in peace, be their actions good or evil. Those who do not submit to the invisible spirit of a power live in irreconcilable confrontation with it, even if they always do good and follow all the rules imposed by the power. Thus, anti-idolatrous persons are always subversive, even though they obey all laws and precepts. Those who idolize a power, on the other hand, will always be well thought of and accepted, even though they violate all the laws and precepts imposed by the power.[7]

When the artisans of Babylon made their idols, they knew very well that the idols were a product of their human labor, but through the production of idols they sought to materialize submission to the spirit of liberation, which they recognized as a spirit living in the power of nature or in political power—a spirit in which they put all their confidence. The prophet, by showing that the process of human labor in the production of idols is the same process as in the production of other consumer goods, wished to demonstrate that this submission to the spirit present in idols also corresponds to the satisfaction of a human need. Human beings make idols just as they make dresses, tools, arms, vessels, and anything else. The idol is a consumer good just like any other, for the satisfaction of human needs.

What could this human need be that the idol satisfies? The power to possess an all-powerful, universal, and transcendent good that can be used indiscriminately to satisfy all kinds of necessities. This good is the spirit or god that inhabits the idol. In producing the idol as a consumer good, one also produces a god or universal good that ensures possession of all other consumer goods.

Through his anti-idolatry polemics, the prophet wanted to show that this consumer good—the idol that ensures satisfaction of all human needs—cannot safeguard the life of the producer of the idols, *because the life of the idol itself depends on the process of labor that produces it*. If the producer of idols dies, the process of production of idols is halted, and with the producer's death there also dies the spirit or god created in producing the idol. In a certain sense, the idol functions as a kind of money, the possession of which ensures the possibility of satisfying all human needs *except* the need to maintain one's life in order to keep on producing and accumulating this idol-money.

Hence all the satire in the diatribes of the prophets against idols. Their power is recognized, but humans have to produce them if they are to exist at all. They must be carried if they are to accompany the people; they have to be cleaned, so that moisture and urine will not corrode them. They have to be decorated or disfigured to engender either attraction or fear. They must be taken care of, so that they will not be stolen. Idols are powerful, just as money is powerful today, but the psalmist says of them:

> They have mouths that cannot speak,
>   and eyes that cannot see;
> they have ears that cannot hear,
>   nostrils, and cannot smell;
> with their hands they cannot feel,
>   with their feet they cannot walk,
>   and no sound comes from their throats.
> Their makers grow to be like them,
>   and so do all who trust in them [Ps. 115:4–8].

The prophets counter idolatry with faith in the liberating power of Yahweh. The whole of Deutero-Isaiah (Isa. 40–55) is a message of hope and liberation trumpeted to an exiled and oppressed people. This faith in God's power gave life to the political and religious liberation of the people, but this faith could be expressed only through a radical confrontation with the idols of Babylon. Fear of the oppressive power of Babylon intimidated the Israelites into idolatry as a false practice of liberation. Resistance against the oppressive power and the power of its silver and gold idols allowed the Israelites to strengthen their faith and hope in the liberating and transcendent capacities of God. That faith is given voice by the prophet:

> He reduces the great to nothing
> and makes all earth's princes less than nothing [Isa. 40:23].

I am the first and the last,
and there is no god but me [Isa. 44:6b].
There is no god but me;
there is no god other than I,
victorious and able to save [Isa. 45:21b].

The most striking contrast between God and the idols appears in Isaiah 46:1–7. The whole text is built around the idea "to liberate" and other synonyms: to carry, lift, support, transport, save, or deliver. This concept appears fourteen times in this one passage. The central idea is that the idolatrous have to "carry" their idols, whereas believers are carried, lifted, and liberated by Yahweh:

Bel has crouched down, Nebo has stooped low
[Bel and Nebo are Babylonian gods]:
their images, once carried in your processions,
  have been loaded onto beasts and cattle,
  a burden for the weary creatures;
    they stoop and they crouch;
  not for them to bring the burden to safety;
  the gods themselves go into captivity.
  Listen to me, house of Jacob
  and all the remnant of the house of Israel,
a load on me from your birth, carried by me from the womb:
  till you grow old I am He,
  and when white hairs come, I will carry you still;
I have made you and I will bear the burden,
  I will carry you and bring you to safety.
  To whom will you liken me? Who is my equal?
  With whom can you compare me? Where is my like?
  Those who squander their bags of gold
  and weigh out their silver with a balance
hire a goldsmith to fashion them into a god;
  then they worship it and fall prostrate before it;
they hoist it shoulder-high and carry it home;
    they set it down on its base;
  there it must stand, it cannot stir from its place.
  Let a man cry to it as he will, it never answers him;
    it cannot deliver him from his troubles.

The God proclaimed by Deutero-Isaiah, and in whom the people of Israel believed and trusted, is not a neutral and pacific God, but rather a God who is extremely cruel with the oppressors of his people. Affirmation of monotheism and the struggle against idols entails the harshest condemnation of Babylon:

> Your wisdom betrayed you, omniscient as you were,
>   and you said to yourself,
> "I am, and who but I?"
> Therefore evil shall come upon you,
>   and you will not know how to master it;
> disaster shall befall you,
>   and you will not be able to charm it away;
>   ruin all unforeseen
> shall come suddenly upon you [Isa. 47:10–11].

In other words, Babylon's idolatry cannot save it.

The Letter of Jeremiah. The letter is addressed to an exiled, humiliated, and oppressed people. It explores theological depths beyond those reached in the citations above from Jeremiah and Deutero-Isaiah. The author encourages the people to resist and not submit to domination. To accomplish this, they must destroy the "religious terror" of the "supernatural world" created by those who dominate:

> Now in Babylon you will see carried on men's shoulders gods made of silver, gold, and wood, which fill the heathen with awe. Be careful, then, never to imitate these Gentiles; do not be overawed by their gods when you see them in the midst of a procession of worshipers [Baruch 6:4–5].

Oppressors always seek to convince the oppressed that they can help and save them. To this end oppressors must create idols as a basis of hope. The biblical text destroys this basis, along with the false hope:

> They [idols] will never save any man from death, never rescue the weak from the strong. They cannot restore the blind man's sight or give relief to the needy. They do not pity the widow or befriend the orphan [vv. 36–38] . . . , seeing that they are incapable of pronouncing judgment or of conferring benefits on mankind [v. 64].

Daniel 14. This text illustrates the anti-idolatry theology of the former texts with two simple and popular stories. The stories deal with the question of the life of the gods. The idol is a living god, because the priests give it life. When Daniel destroyed the idols and caused the death of all the priests, he was then accused of subversion: "The king has turned Jew!" (Dan. 14:28). Daniel professed his faith in typically anti-idolatrous terms: "I do not believe in man-made idols, but in the living God who created heaven and earth and is sovereign over all mankind" (Dan. 14:5).

1 Maccabees. In this book the close relationships of oppression/idolatry and liberation/monotheism are clearly apparent. The liberation struggle against Antiochus IV Epiphanes was inspired by monotheism. The king wished not only to subjugate the Jewish people, but to do so in the name of an extremely idolatrous religion. Idolatry deepened and legitimized his political domination. In this situation, the oppressed people could profess its faith in God only by violent struggle against the politico-religious system imposed by Antiochus.

At first, the Jews reacted to oppression with passive resistance and flight to the desert. This method proved to be ineffective, and brought several massacres upon the people (2:27–39). The example of these first martyrs inspired the people to proceed to higher forms of struggle. The martyrs said: "Let us all meet death with a clear conscience . . . ; we call heaven and earth to testify that there is no justice in this slaughter" (2:37). However, the leaders of the people reacted strongly:

> They said to one another, "If we do as our brothers have done, if we refuse to fight the Gentiles for our lives as well as for our laws and customs, then they will soon wipe us off the face of the earth." That day they decided that, if anyone came to fight against them on the sabbath, they would fight back, rather than die as their brothers in the caves had done [2:40–41].

The people struggled for thirty years after that, first in a guerrilla war, and then in total warfare, against domination and idolatry. *The Jewish people recovered its faith in God through a political war of liberation.* This is the central message of the book, which is doubly exciting when read from the perspective of Latin America today. A politico-theological understanding of the passages above will serve as a guide to overcome the historical limits of the account and thus to avoid facile and, in the end, sterile correlations between our historical situation and that of the Maccabees.

Wisdom. Here we arrive at the threshold of the New Testament. The Introduction to this book in the *Nueva Biblia Española* rightly says about it, "This is the last book of the Old Testament, and its most important treatise on political theology."

The book begins by connecting faith with justice: "Love justice, you rulers of the earth; set your mind upon the Lord, as is your duty, and seek him in simplicity of heart" (Wisd. 1:1). The practice of justice and correct thinking about the Lord go together. When practicing injustice, one necessarily thinks idolatrously about the Lord.

As mentioned earlier, this book of the Old Testament is also addressed to an oppressed people. It is a reflection on God and justice in conflict with a practice of injustice and oppression. The book also conveys an anti-idolatry message of hope, life, and liberation:

> God did not make death, and takes no pleasure in the destruction of any living thing [1:13].
>
> But God created man for immortality, and made him the image of his own eternal self [2:23].

Chapters 13 to 15 are especially dedicated to the issue of idolatry. The author resumes the anti-idolatry polemic of the prophets, but delves deeper into the causes and consequences of idolatry:

> The invention of idols is the root of immorality; they are a contrivance which has blighted human life [14:12].
>   So this becomes a trap for living men: enslaved by mischance or misgovernment, men confer on sticks and stones the name that none may share [14:21].

The yoke of power engenders idolatry, and thus corrupts life. Idolatry is a trap, in which oppressive power gains access to a "spiritual" and "transcendent" world that hides and legitimizes oppression. This trap impedes both the oppressor and the oppressed from becoming aware of oppression, and simultaneously acts as an obstacle to knowing God:

> On two counts judgment will overtake them: because in their devotion to idols they have thought wrongly about God, and because, in their contempt for religion, they have deliberately perjured themselves [14:30].
>   Then, not content with gross error in their knowledge of God, men live in the constant warfare of ignorance and call this monstrous evil peace [14:22].

Those who fall into the trap of idolatry, under the yoke of power, pervert their consciences, thus reversing the values of truth, justice, and peace, and simultaneously erring in their knowledge of God. Because idolatry arises from oppression, idols are exposed as gods who cannot redeem:

> The greatest fools of all, and worse than infantile, were the enemies and oppressors of thy people, for they supposed all their heathen idols to be gods, although they have eyes that cannot see, nostrils that cannot draw breath, ears that cannot hear, fingers that cannot feel, and feet that are useless for walking [15:14–15].

ANTI-IDOLATRY BIBLICAL THEOLOGY
IN THE NEW TESTAMENT

The thinking in the New Testament about idolatry is a continuation of the Old Testament tradition. The same themes appear, but now reinterpreted in a much more radical and concrete fashion, in the historical context of the lives of the Christians and their first communities. Following is a brief overview of this anti-idolatry theology of the New Testament, in four groups of biblical passages.

Idolatry as Destructive of Human Beings, Nature, and History

Acts 17:16–34. This passage from the Acts of the Apostles describes Paul's activities in Athens, a "city full of idols" (v. 16), and records his speech in the Areopagus. The speech is a radical critique of idolatry. It is addressed to a crowd of pagan philosophers, but Paul reinterprets the anti-idolatry message of the Old Testament on transcendence, revelation, and knowledge of the true God, radicalizing it in the light of the Christian gospel.

To begin his speech, Paul refers to an altar in the Areopagus that bore the inscription: "To an Unknown God." On this altar, pagans worshiped the true God without knowing it. Paul thereupon announced the presence of the unknown god. Thus he did not hesitate to tackle the problems posed by the Old Testament with regard to "Yahwist idols." The shrine of the unknown god would be an authentic and legitimate "Yahwist idol." The apostle thus recognized the search for the true God in the religious practices of the Athenians.

By the same token, however, Paul's speech radicalized and deepened the Old Testament's criticisms of these "idols," using two arguments. The first refers to God as the creator and lord of history. This God needs no temples, altars, or idols to be revealed. Humans do not need these things either, in order to know God. God is fully transcendent and "indeed he is not far from each one of us, for in him we live and move, in him we exist" (v. 27).

The transcendent presence of God in humans, in nature, and in history is the final and most radical foundation of the anti-idolatry critique. This transcendent and liberating presence of God in history—in humans as well as in nature—is totally antagonistic to all idolatrous practices and all fabrication of idols, because now all God's liberating deeds in history have become an image, a sign, an "idol," through which God is revealed and wherein humans can know him in the light of faith. On the other hand, idolatry is revealed through the destruction of history, of human beings, and of nature, to the extent that human beings make fetishes or idols that allow them to manipulate powers, spirits, gods, transcendencies, spiritualities, and values, to use them against other human beings.

Paul's second argument against idolatry concretizes, radicalizes, and illuminates the first argument. Human beings are made in the image *(eikon)* of God (referring to Gen. 1:27): "As God's offspring, then, we ought not to suppose that the deity is like an image in gold or silver or stone, shaped by human craftsmanship and design" (v. 29). A person is the most perfect "idol" of God, through whom the transcendent creator, God, is revealed and manifested.

All fetishization or idolatrization of history, of nature, and humans is the most radical and profound destruction of human life, of nature, and of history. Likewise, the destruction of human life, of nature, and of history—like the destruction of the transcendent and liberating presence of God—always creates a process of fetishization and idolatrization. If persons are made in God's image, if they are "of the lineage of God," then no transcendence or spirituality can exist and be revealed through the destruction of human life. If God is revealed through human liberation, then everything divine, transcendent, supernatural, or spiritual that destroys human life is pure idolatry and fetishism.

Colossians 1:15. The opposition between transcendence and idolatry as revealed through human life or death is concentrated in this text: Christ is "the image of the invisible God." Herein lies the theological explanation of the radically anti-idolatry strength of the deeds of the historical Jesus and of his resurrection, as well as of the gospel as lived and practiced by the first Christian communities. The three following chapters of Colossians analyze the radical antagonism between Christian faith and the idols of money, law, and oppressive political power. In the texts of the New Testament, these three idols are singled out and unmasked as incompatible with the gospel.

Idolatry of Money

1 Cor. 5:9–13, 6:9–11, 10:14–17; Gal. 5:19–21; Col. 3:5; Eph. 5:5; 1 Pet. 4:3; Matt. 6:24. The general attitude of the New Testament to the problem of idolatry brands it, together with other vices and perversions, as incompatible with faith, the Christian community, and the kingdom of God. The terms "idolatry" and "idolatrous" appear within lists of vices in three passages. The following are all parallel terms with a common meaning:

leads a loose life . . . grasping, or *idolatrous,* a slanderer, a drunkard, or a swindler [1 Cor. 5:9–13].

fornicator or *idolater* . . . adultery . . . thieves or grabbers or drunkards or slanderers or swindlers [1 Cor. 6:9–11].

fornication, impurity, and indecency; *idolatry* and sorcery; quarrels, a contentious temper, envy, fits of rage, selfish ambitions, dissensions, party intrigues, and jealousies; drinking bouts, orgies [Gal. 5:20–21].

Two basic data with which idolatry is linked can be detected in these lists and parallelisms: *sex* and *money.* Taking the latter as a point of reference, the following equivalences can be drawn:

idolater/usurer/swindler/thief;
idolatry/feuding/wrangling/jealousy/belligerence/envy.

Idolatry, like other vices and perversions, appears as a destructive element in personal and social relations.

Idolatry is defined in reference only to *greed* in Colossians and Ephesians:

No one given to fornication or indecency, or the greed which makes an idol of gain, has any share in the kingdom of Christ and of God [Eph. 5:5; cf. Col. 3:5].

Here, greed and idolatry are synonymous. The word "greed," in Greek *pleonexia* (literally, "wanting more"), means having or desiring to have more than others; it connotes ambition, avidity, opulence, arrogance. Therefore, the idol would be money—not as a reality in itself, but rather the power that comes from its possession, to desire or extract more money from others, thus creating feuds and discord. Idolatry would be a person's submission to this power of money. Hence the identification of greed with idolatry, and of the idolater with the usurer, thief, and swindler.

All the passages cited above affirm the antagonistic relationship between idolatry and Christian life. In 1 Corinthians 5:9–13, the Christian communities are ordered to exclude idolaters. Idolatry or greed is incompatible with being Christian. The apostle does not order Christians to segregate themselves from idolaters—that would entail leaving this world—but he does order that those who call themselves Christian and yet idolize money be expelled from the community. The texts of 1 Corinthians 6:9–11 and Galatians 5:19–21 state that idolaters "will not inherit the kingdom of God." In 1 Corinthians 10:14–17, idolatry is excluded from the Eucharist—that is, from solidarity with the body of the Messiah and the community. Money as an idol destroys this solidarity, destroys the body of the Messiah and the Christian community.

This radical antagonism appears strongly throughout the gospels, especially in Matthew 6:24:

No servant can be the slave of two masters; for either he will hate the first and love the second, or he will be devoted to the first and think nothing of the second. You cannot serve God and Money.

It is not just a matter of money, but of being a slave to money. "To serve," in Greek, is *douleuein*—that is, "to be a slave," "to be a servant." An antagonistic parallel is drawn between "serving God" and "serving money." Money is a substitute for God and, as such, is an idol. This fetishization of money is also a fetishization of all human, social, and political relationships. The search for God the liberator cannot go on without a violent, frontal attack against money-as-idol and its fetishization of the whole social and political sphere.[8]

Idolatry of the Law

Galatians 4:8–11, 4:21–5:1. Just as money can be an idol, so also the law can become an idol, and persons subjugated to the law can become idolaters. This idea is made explicit in Galatians 4:8–11:

Formerly, when you did not acknowledge God, you were the slaves of beings which in their nature are no gods. But now that you do acknowledge God—or rather, now that he has acknowledged you—how can you turn back to the mean and beggarly spirits of the elements? You keep special days and months and seasons and years. You make me fear that all the pains I spent on you may prove to be labor lost.

Being a slave to the law is the same as being a slave to idols. Idolatrization or fetishization of the law turns it into a matter of "mean and beggarly spirits." The law in itself is good, but when persons look to the law for their salvation, it turns into an idol that kills. The law has no liberating strength. When persons think according to the law, they do the opposite of what they really think; when the law governs what they desire, they end up doing things that they really do not want to do. When persons are subjugated to the law, they are schizophrenic: they do what they do not want to do, and want to do what they cannot do.

Paul illustrates this predicament in Romans 4:17-25, referring to those who have not been redeemed through faith in Christ. Having insinuated itself into a world of transcendent precepts, principles, and values, the law subjugates persons in the name of this world. It creates a nonliberating hope for salvation.

Mark 2:1-3:12. This passage, which contains Jesus' arguments with the Pharisees, advances an anti-idolatry theology that opposes the law. Salvation as attained and announced by Jesus is antagonistic to the law as fetishized by the Pharisees. This radical critique of the fetishization of the law is summed up marvelously in Jesus' statement: "The Sabbath was made for the sake of man and not man for the Sabbath."

Fetishism of the law is the most oppressive and destructive fetishism possible, because, taking on ethical and religious overtones, it perverts persons' consciences. Like the fetishism of money, it destroys personal, social, and political relationships.

Fetishism of the law is both the cause and the consequence of an oppressive and repressive world. Faith in the God of Jesus Christ confronts this fetishism of the law in a radical and violent manner. Those liberated by Christ can profess, communicate, and celebrate their faith only as part of a practice of continual struggle against false gods—the false transcendental and supernatural divinizations and spiritualizations that wield money and the law as instruments of domination. "Christ set us free, to be free men. Stand firm, then, and refuse to be tied to the yoke of slavery again" (Gal. 5:1).

Idolatry of Oppressive Political Power

Revelation 13:11-18, 14:9-13, 15:1-4, 16:2, 19:20. In this group of passages, idolatry appears as a cult of submission to "the beast." This "beast" makes signs and signals. The subjects of the beast make images of it. The power of the beast is such that these images are living; they speak, and kill those who do not worship them. Those who worship the beast and worship its images are branded. Those who do not submit and do not wear the brand of submission on their bodies cannot "buy or sell anything"—that is, they are excluded from the social structure and condemned to death. The sign of the beast is a number: 666.

Within the historical context of the book of Revelation, the "beast" is the oppressive power of the Roman Empire, and the Christians are those who do not submit to this power, for which they are persecuted to death. The text makes a distinction between the "beast" and the "statue" or "idol" of the beast. The idol has real power: it lives, talks, and kills. But the idol has power only because the beast has power. Without the beast, the idol is nothing, but the beast needs the idol in order to impose and legitimize its power. It is thus that submission to the political power of the Roman Empire could be transformed into religious worship. Within this worship of submission, persons seek salvation and the experience of the supernatural, the transcendent, the divine.

Faith in the God of Jesus Christ was radically incompatible with worship of the beast and its idol. Jesus was confessed as the only Lord, entailing a radical de-idolatrization of the Roman Empire, reduced to the condition of a "beast." Submission to the beast became a question of strength and power instead of a religious worship. Likewise, the de-idolatrization of the Roman emperor entailed the negation of the whole divinized, transcendent, and supernatural world created by the Roman Empire, with all its promises of liberation and its religious values touching on human life and culture. The Christians affirmed their full liberation through Jesus Christ, which did not directly imply political action against the emperor, but only meant his delegitimization, and the negation of the whole transcendent, supernatural, divinized dimension manipulated by the emperor in order to dominate and oppress.

Thus, the anti-idolatry message of Revelation is one of hope and liberation for the Christians persecuted and oppressed by the Roman Empire. It was a subversive message as well, and the oppressed identified with it, and felt that it interpreted their reality. In this context, the gospel as lived and proclaimed by Christians, and their indestructible faith in the God of Jesus Christ, the only lord of history, have acquired their full historical significance.

CONCLUSION

Concluding our analysis of all these biblical texts on idolatry, we must say that the consistency of this theology throughout the development of biblical tradition is impressive. Clearly defined and stubbornly unequivocal, this consistency reveals the people of God's experience of a deep faith at the core of their life. The experience of idolatry, especially in situations of oppression, appears as a great historical obstacle to the revelation of God and faith in him.

It is no accident that today the centrality and importance of the problem of idolatry have been discovered in Latin America. Idolatry is part of our deepest experience when we live, express, and communicate our faith in the God of Jesus Christ, in the present situation of extreme oppression on our continent. We live in a profoundly idolatrous world—economically, socially, politically, culturo-ideologically, and religiously. We live crushed under the idols of an oppressive and unjust system. To live the demands of faith in this context is not simply a "pious" or personal act; it necessarily entails a radical confrontation with that system. Idolatry is a question of politics and a question of faith. If capitalism were atheistic, it is possible that our faith would not have this subversive strength within a practice of political liberation. But capitalism is idolatrous rather than atheistic, which poses a political and theological problem at the same time, especially within the context of Latin American capitalism.

The biblical message against idolatry reaches us very directly and deeply. It is a message that interprets our reality with no major exegetical complications. However, today we are living through a new situation, one that did not exist in biblical times, making this anti-idolatry proclamation even more pressing and radical. This new reality is the *praxis of liberation,* with all its political, organic, and theoretical complexities. In biblical times, the possibility of a radical and conscious transformation of the economic and political structure of an idolatrous system did not yet exist. Today this possibility exists.

Christians who adopt the praxis of liberation also adopt the anti-idolatry proclamation of the Bible within a different historical context. This is not only a reinterpretation within a "hermeneutical circle" (an expression we should eliminate), but rather a "hermeneutical leap" into a new historical situation. In this new situation, faith and the revelation of God in history are more critical and radical than they were in biblical times.

NOTES

1. In German biblical dictionaries, there is a distinction between *Bilderdienst* ("worship of images") and *Gützendienst* ("worship of gods"). But in Greek (the Septuagint), Spanish, and English, the word for "idolatry" covers both categories.

2. See Jean-Jacques Von Allmen, ed., "Idol," in *A Companion to the Bible* (translation of *Vocabulaire Biblique*) (New York: Oxford University Press, 1962); also, the entries "Eidolon" and "Eikon" in Gerhard Kittel, *Theological Dictionary of the New Testament*, Godfrey W. Bromley, trans. and ed. (Grand Rapids: Eerdmans, 1964).

3. See Gerhard Von Rad, *Old Testament Theology*, D.M.G. Stalker, trans. (New York: Harper, 1962), Vol. 1, pp. 212–19. The author insists that the question of the

images of God is not clarified by the visible/invisible, material/spiritual antitheses, which are foreign to biblical thought. No image purports to be a faithful representation of divinity. The image says nothing about the existence or interior life of the divinity. It says only how God is revealed.

4. See "Idoles, idolatrie," in *Dictionnaire de la Bible,* Supplément, Vol. 4, pp. 169-87; also Von Allmen, "Idol," in *Companion to the Bible.*

5. "Introducción al libro de Sabiduría," in *Nueva Biblia Española,* Latin American edition.

6. See "Images and Idols," in James Hastings, ed., *Encyclopedia of Religion and Ethics* (Edinburgh: Clark; New York: Scribner's), pp. 1908-26.

7. Franz J. Hinkelammert, *Las armas ideológicas de la muerte* (San José, Costa Rica: EDUCA-DEI, 1977), p. 64: "The theory of fetishism analyzes institutionalized spirituality in modern society. In this sense, the fetish is the spirit of the institution."

8. Hinkelammert, *Las armas ideológicas,* esp. the chapter "El dinero, la bestia y San Juan: la señal en la frente. El fetichismo del dinero" ("Money, the Beast, and St. John: The Sign on the Forehead. The Fetishism of Money"), pp. 23-33.

II

J. SEVERINO CROATTO

The Gods of Oppression

The Bible records the struggle between the God of Israel, Yahweh, and "foreign gods" *(élohê nekar,* "gods of the foreigner"), or "other gods" *(élohim acherim).* The gods are a tremendously effective symbol of the political strength of a people. It can be said that all the gods are at battle—a projection of the socio-political power conflicts between groups or peoples.

The violence of Marduk in the Babylonian creation epic *Enuma Elis* symbolizes the accession of Babylon, once a minuscule city, to political hegemony over Mesopotamia. An Assyrian version of the same poem cannot accept this symbolic submission; in its account, the god Asur replaces Marduk. Nothing could be more natural. In fact, as the myth emerges and develops from a concrete situation whose meaning we are exploring, when read it acts in the opposite sense—that is, as a symbolico-ideological superstructure that reaffirms and intensifies the underlying situation. This dynamic will be examined in greater detail, but for the moment what will suffice is the simple statement that the gods, as symbols of a totality of meaning, battle among themselves.

Therefore, the opposition between Yahweh and Baal is not a novelty as a religious phenomenon. The books of Joshua and Judges bear witness to the successes and failures of the Hebrews in their attempt to occupy the territory of Canaan; they could not help but hate the god of the settlers there. Later, there was a protracted fight between Yahweh and Dagon—that is, between the Hebrews and Philistines: "The Ark of the God of Israel shall not stay here, for he has laid a heavy hand upon us and upon Dagon our god" (1 Sam. 5:7). When Ben-hadad, the Aramaic king of Damascus, suffered his first defeat from the Israeli army of Ahab, his ministers gave this interpretation of their defeat: "Their gods are gods of the hills; that is why they defeated us. Let us fight them in the plain; and then we shall have the upper hand" (1 Kings 20:23; cf. 20:28). Other biblical accounts could be added to these examples, as well as many more from Assyrian and Hittite annals, which witness to the belief that the outcome of a political or military conflict is *divinely* determined.

How does the struggle between Yahweh and Baal have implications for the issues of oppression and liberation? We want to highlight precisely this issue; the question is quite complex and it is important to single out the threads of significance. The battle of the gods is a universal expression of power conflicts, politics being the natural and most obvious instance of it. In this regard, neither the Bible nor Israel is unique.

But this is not the whole story. On another level, the opposition between Yahweh and the neighboring gods is one of worldview; the latter represent a cyclic and "physical" (from *physis*, "nature") vision of reality, whereas Yahweh represents the call to a historical design. But this may seem an ingenuous oversimplification. Moreover, it is possible to be unfair to nonbiblical worldviews by setting up pairs of exclusive opposites. At any rate, our intention here is simply to pose the problem.

In effect, there are two decisive questions:

• Where did the concept of Yahweh as the god of a historical design originate?

• Inasmuch as historical design can also be oppressive (as history tells us), in the final analysis what is the determining factor in the biblical God as a *liberator*-God?

The following chapters will analyze these questions. In this chapter the nonbiblical obverse of the question will be examined: how the gods "other" than Yahweh did *not* symbolize a historical design for liberation.

Because the intention of this joint work is not to present an academic biblico-theological study, but rather to act as a guide to a reading of our Latin American reality, this preliminary essay takes a critical stance with respect to the history of Latin American Christianity.

The central part of this exposition, divided into two sections, will outline the most significant features of the mythical worldview and its *modus operandi* on the anthropological plane. How do oppressive gods, from Baal to his present-day successors, show themselves?

THE MYTHICAL WORLDVIEW

There is a universal experience of the sacred, of a transcendent-immanent *force* pervading everything that has significance in the world. Human beings confess their contingency and their smallness by their unceasing deferral to this sacred power, be it personified or not; be it named or dispersed among empirical phenomena. Basically, this numinous power is conceived of as *life* (creation, fecundity, sustenance), as *knowledge* (originally the possession of the gods, the source of all revelation or, conversely, of all promethean usurpations, such as that of the biblical Adam), and as *order*, because the world is always understood as structured, functional, not chaotic (creation is often depicted as a struggle to establish the cosmic order). We could add a fifth ontological aspect, that of the sacred as *being*, but the expression of this aspect always revolves around the dynamic and operative meanings of force, life, knowledge, and order.

Gods accrue these qualities. Although there are "specialized" gods appearing in religious myths, as will be seen in the discussion of polytheism, each god attracts to itself all possible divine attributes, as demonstrated by another field of religious expression—prayer to the gods. This centripetal phenomenon is very evident and easily understandable: divinity is either essentially totalizing (even in polytheism) or it ceases to be divine.

The lived experience of the sacred, as personal as it may be, resists confinement to an emotional and silent interior. It is natural that the sacred be expressed through gestures or words. This fact is well known,[1] but important to point out for two reasons: on the one hand, religious experience and its expression are common to all peoples and cultures, and the Bible contains nothing new in this respect. On the other hand, this expression also has a universal language that develops two forms: symbol and myth. It would be more correct to say that the myth takes the symbol further and particularizes it. These are two distinct dimensions of religious language.

The symbol is a reality, or an aspect of the visible world, that refers to something else—a second meaning grasped "in transparency"[2] through the first or natural meaning. Symbols tend to be universal (in every culture, for example, water has the same symbolic meanings, even in their multiplicity and opposition) and permanent: they can be transformed, but never lost. In itself the symbol is not an element of religious language, but it can be said to be *eminently* religious—in its capacity to refer to the transcendent, the mysterious, the ungraspable. In fact, looking at the other side of the coin, there is no religious question that is not predominantly symbolic.

What, then, does the myth add? It does not just add: it is another thing entirely. The myth is an *account* of an act or *event* of the gods at the *beginning* of the physical world, or of history, and reveals the *meaning* of a present reality, institution, or custom. The italicized terms are all part of the definition, and they all differentiate myth from symbol. Nevertheless, the myth has to use symbols, as indispensable elements of its language, to complement its own structural ability to refer to an *originative* transcendence.[3]

In these two pillars of religious language—symbol and myth—lies its perennial force, extending the experience of the sacred that it expresses. Hence one indispensable facet of religious language: it cannot but be mythical and symbolic. This even applies to religious metaphysics, which, when its mythical coefficient is diminished, undergoes an enhancement of the symbolic—for example, in the Upanishads or Vedanta, or the apophatic theology of Christian or non-Christian mysticism. The language of the Bible is symbolic as well, and although it eschews myth as an underlying worldview, it makes extensive use of myth as a structure. Failure to recognize this, through the methodological failure to distinguish between worldview and mythical language, has led theology and exegesis into a number of absurdities. Some examples are: not reading beyond the "first meaning" of symbols; understanding mythical language as a photographic record of events; and, consequently, converting an eminently suggestive, profound language, full of hermeneutical possibilities, into rational gnosis.

These reflections are a helpful introduction to the mythical worldview: if we discover oppressor gods in this vision, we shall expect them to be named and invoked in very penetrating and powerful language, which introjects into the depths of awareness the same oppression that it celebrates. By the same token, recognition of God the liberator, and celebration of him with a new language, although still symbolic and mythically structured, constitutes the most significant phenomenon imaginable.

The "Cosmicization" of the Gods

Among the peoples who influenced the atmosphere that Israel breathed, there was a consensus on the *becoming* of the first gods out of chaos. This is a multivalent symbol of precreation, of that which has no structure or order of itself, but is a symbol of everything that is possible. In India, one would say that Brahma is without *nama-rupa* (without-name-and-form), meaning that he is the boundless Being. The Mesopotamian *Enuma Elish*, at the very start, proclaims the emergence of the gods out of formless chaos, when nothing was as yet "named" either in heaven or on earth, both of which, of course, did not exist yet. The Babylonian theogony, which even had repercussions on the works of Hesiod, was the literary development of a common religious theme.

Symbol, united to myth, in theogony means that the gods are epiphanies of the cosmic and of the tellurian. They become the first forms and the first names of reality. The divine, therefore, is archetypal in that it is among the first things in the world. Sacredness lies in the originative, in cosmogony. Hence, everything that has an origin reflects the divine, and everything that is sacred is related to originations.

Therefore, the gods are part of the cosmos *and* they symbolize its immanent sacredness. The names and the forms are plural; the gods are many. This is the most obvious reason for polytheism, which, far from being a degeneration of a presumed original monotheism, represents a profound grasp of the *meaning* of the world; for each aspect or phenomenon of the world there is a divine hierophantic model.

Theogony becomes theomachy—the battle of the gods—with the elimination of some and the domination of others, generally of one. Celebrated as the hero, the victor creates the present world, with its particular order and functions. A symptomatic occurrence—and here arises the suspicion that ideology is interwoven with myth—is that the triumphant and world-ordering god also happens to be the patron of the ruling dynasty, the protector of the city-state that wields political hegemony. Such is the case of the Babylonian Marduk—with his great prestige throughout the Fertile Crescent—of Amon of Thebes, in Egypt, and of many others. Gods like these easily become archetypes for one people's domination over others. The original event of the triumph over chaos, in turn a symbol of evil,[4] is recorded in the liturgy of the New Year, whose importance will be detailed later in this chapter.

Human Beings as "Strangers in Their Own Land"

If the world began as an epiphany in which the gods occupied the highest places, so to speak, then humans are relegated to secondary status. The world is sacred, and "of the gods." The marginalization of humans is expressed in several ways:

Human beings are created to feed the gods. In some myths, this function is carried out by minor gods (=slaves) for the great gods, the lords of the world and chiefs of the pantheon. In the Ugaritic poem on the construction of the temple of Baal, his enemy Mot pretends to be the sovereign of the gods, and thus to be able to "fatten the gods and satisfy the multitudes of the earth."[5] This is an allusion to sacrifices, with which a people gives sustenance to its gods. The myth of the birth of the "gracious" gods Shahar and Shalem interprets the invention of agriculture as the means to maintain those gods recently created.[6]

Human beings are sometimes said to be created to erect or maintain the sanctuaries of the gods. In the sixth tablet of the Babylonian creation epic mentioned above, Marduk exclaims:

I will gather blood and create bones.
I will make a human being; "man" will be his name.
In truth, I will create a human being
so that, assuming the service of the gods, they may rest. . . .
He assigned them their service, and left the gods free [lines 5–8 and 34].

The minor gods can only celebrate this happy event:

They said to Marduk, their lord:
"Now, O Lord, since you liberated us,
how shall we pay homage to you?" [1:49–50].

In the Song of the Fifty Names of Marduk, one of the liberated gods exclaims:

> May he show the Black Heads [the Sumerians] how to worship him, may humans concern themselves with their God and invoke him, and, at his word, attend to their Goddess. . . . May they make his holy places shine and build his sanctuaries [I:113–18].

Numerous texts refer to this central human function. Its designation by such a major myth as the above is highly significant.

The purpose of service to the gods in worship is complemented by another task, directly related to the economic sphere: the destiny of humans to *work* for the gods. In the ancient Near East, where the economy was centered around the temple, to which the king's palace was attached, the creation of humans for the worship of gods had economic implications. Whereas the *Enuma Elish* emphasizes the cultic aspect, another great myth teaches that the mission of humans is to cultivate the earth for the gods. This is the myth of *Atrahasis,* recently expanded by tablets in the British Museum.[7] It represents the best exponent of social conflicts—a model of "revolution" fomented by forced labor.

Here once again appears the idea of humans as replacing the lesser gods, the former slaves of the three great gods who divided up the world—Anu, the heavens; Enlil, the earth and humankind; Enki, the sea. The lesser gods rebelled, went on strike, and tried to set fire to the palace of Enlil, the tyrant. Their work was hard:

> They suffered their work [*dullu*] with patience, they endured labor [*supsikku*]. The labor of the gods was great, heavy the work, great their anguish [I:2–4].

After several attempts, and an assembly where the lords met with the rebels, a solution was found:

> That the god-of-birth create [*li-ib-ni-na,* from *banû,* "to build"!] humanity; that humans bear the labor of the gods *(supsik ilim awilum lîssi)* . . . that they carry the yoke imposed by Enlil, that humans bear the labor of the gods [I:194–97].

When the goddess finishes her task, she comments to the gods who were formerly slaves:

> I have taken away your heavy work, and your hard labor [*supsikku*], and inflicted it on humankind. I have transferred your screams [*rigmu*] to humanity: I have untied your yoke, I have established your liberty [*andurara askun*] [I:240–44].

Now the gods are all free, and the slaves are human beings, who are born to work for them. The gods rose in social status, leaving humans in their lower place. Only given this information can one understand the first verse of this extraordinary song of rebellion of the oppressed: "When [some] gods were human [*inuma ilu awilum*]."

Although Assyriologists are still discussing the precise meaning of these three words, the context of the poem makes the general meaning evident: before the creation of humans, there were some gods who carried out the tasks that now fall to humans. This is not a matter of an ontological change in the gods, but rather of their liberation from a social condition that is now understood to be specific to humans. The ideological point is made: humans are defined by their forced and enslaving labor:

With picks and hoes they built [*ibnu*] sanctuaries,
They constructed [*ibnu*] huge embankments [for canals].
As food for the peoples, as sustenance for the gods [I:337-39].

A chapter is closed, but the myth of Atrahasis offers other surprises on the same topic (see below). Opposition to the Book of Genesis is clear, in spite of the Mesopotamian coloring of the biblical text. In Genesis, work is not for the benefit of God but rather for the benefit of humans themselves, to make the earth fertile—an earth given to them as their domain.

In general, there is no eschatology in these mythical conceptions. Inasmuch as humans are created to give sustenance to the gods (a divine task, but nonetheless alienating), only their stay in this life is of interest. Neither is there an idea of a historical design of a people to compensate for the lack of individual eschatology.

As lords of the earth, the gods have the king as their deputy here below. Either the king has divine aspects, or he is directly divinized (as among the Assyrians); he possesses a divine "glowing force" (the *melamnu* of Mesopotamian texts).[8] The gods protect him with special predilection. The king monopolizes everything that in any way touches on the divine. In Egypt, only the pharaoh is resuscitated as Osiris.[9] In Mesopotamia, the king does not enjoy immortality (consider the frustration of Gilgamesh, the king of Uruk, in his vain search for immortality, as told in the poem of the same name) but rather his condition as the custodian of the land of his tutelar god is emphasized even more. Here, then, is where the legitimization of oppression begins.

Humans seek to identify with the sacred exactly where it appears, in the phenomena of nature, which are sacred and epiphanic. To receive divine strength, humans must identify with those moments in the cosmos that signal an epiphany of the sacred force, or a rebirth of life. More than any religious rite, this correlation with the physical cosmos imposes a cyclic rhythm of life, with diverse implications. Baal is the most palpable symbol of the alternation of nature cycles. When he is revived, life is re-created on all levels. When summer and the drought arrive, it is because he dies with the season, at which

point the god of death, Mot, becomes the ruler. What was known from polemical texts of the Bible and various inscriptions can now be seen in a very
developed form in the epics of Baal and Anat found in Ugarit.

Myth as Archetypal Thought

Some features of mythical thought that coincide in making constant reference to paradigmatic and originating forces are the following:
* That which originates something else is ontologically perfect and insu-
perable. In effect, cosmogony represents the ultimate ontophany.
* If there are changes, they are regressive rather than innovative; time
brings decadence, and one must return to the source, to perfection.
* The model of praxis lies in "what the gods did" in the beginning, as
described by the cosmogonies or creation myths of a civilization or institution.
* Reality is shaped as it is by the originating gods, and it cannot be
changed. The creator god ordered and structured the world and reality as it
now is.
* Humans do not invent anything, but rather are taught by the gods (Prometheus) or by ancient heroes (lawgivers and others, who usually are semi-
gods and differentiated from the humans around them).
* The archetypal is exemplary. This principle operates in the myth of Atrahasis with respect to the possibility, or failure, of social revolution.
* In all the religions, the feast of the New Year synthesizes all these canons.
Through the force of the rites, renovation occurs at all possible levels: the
divine (the reenthronement of the god of a city), cosmo-telluric, social, and
ethical. All praxis takes on its deepest possible meaning in this rite.
With these descriptive elements of the mythical worldview, we can be more
specific about some of its consequences for human action.

CONSEQUENCES FOR AN ANALYSIS
OF THE "GODS OF OPPRESSION"

This section will expand on the three themes developed in the preceding
section, pointing out incidences of the mythical worldview in human praxis,
in light of the issues discussed in this chapter.

Results of the "Cosmicization" of the Gods

The "cosmicization" of the gods means that humans relate to the gods
through nature and natural phenomena: rains, fertility, the cycles of plant
life, the movements of the stars and the planets, and the like. Although in
itself valuable and profound, human adherence to the cosmo-telluric induces
a deterministic consciousness.
Destiny is a very characteristic element of mythical thought. It is related to

the order of the cosmos as inscribed in the cosmogony itself. *Enuma Elish* describes this cosmogony, stating that Marduk delivered the "tablet of the fates," which he had previously taken away from the conquered god Kingu (IV:12, 18; V:69–70), to Anu, the god of transcendence and the sky. Marduk himself was born in the sanctuary of the fates, "sacred place of the archetypes" (I:79). When proclaiming him sovereign, the gods hailed him:

> O Marduk, you are the most important of the gods,
> your destiny is unequalled, your command [like that of] Anu.
> From now on, may your order be immutable! [IV:4–6].

The myth of Anzu relates how he usurps the "tablet of the fates" *(tûp simâti)* from Enlil to gather the power of all the gods into his own hands. Several times, the text repeats, as in a refrain, "the divine functions were obsolete" (I:ii:21.48; iii:39). The struggle for power among the gods is clear in this myth. Enlil, the symbol of absolute and tyrannical power, reveals his vulnerability, although at the end the hero Ninurta fights for him, recovers the tablet of the fates, and order returns to the universe.[10] This gives food for thought, but for now it suffices to point out that the theme of fate is axial in the Mesopotamian worldview, and that it subjugates the life of human beings even more when linked to the life of the gods.

The biblical Yahweh is different: existing previous to, and creator of, the cosmos and the earth, which are made for humans, he relates to humans more through the historical word than through cosmogonic fate. Freedom is preserved.

It is noteworthy that the mythical religions did not develop the idea of the prophet as the interpretor of events in the light of the people's fidelity to the god of salvation. Likewise, it is remarkable that the apocalyptic works, which lack many of the properties of prophecy, mark a recuperation of mythical elements, above all the idea of diagramming the whole history of humanity since creation (this includes the celestial tablets, revealed by the "apocalyptic" figure of the time).[11]

The "cosmicization" of the gods is closely linked to the freedom of humans; the gods are the lords of the earth, and they leave no place for humans. Humans become totally dependent on the gods. When they plow the earth, they are plowing the breast of Mother Earth, and before they can do this, they must enact a rite of passage.

Divinity and Royalty

The myth of Atrahasis introduced the theme that humans are created for oppressive and hard work, not only to serve the gods, but also *in place of the gods*, so that the gods can have repose. The sequence of the narrative is highly significant. The slaves multiply and become dangerous to Enlil, the lord over humans who had already engaged in a conflict with the lower-class gods:

> One year passed, then 600 and 600 years;
> The country grew larger, the people multiplied.
> The country roared like a bull:
> God was disturbed by their shouting [*juburu*],
> Enlil heard their cry [*rigmu*] [I:352–56].

The two italicized Akkadian words refer to the protest and rebellion of the oppressed people. Enlil has no sympathy. To wipe out the strength of the uprising of the united people, he intends to decimate humanity, first through plague, then through a drought, and then through a flood (in this myth, Atrahasis represents a Babylonian Noah, who is saved thanks to Enki's advice). In these three cases, Enki, the god most friendly to humans and a kind of Prometheus, suggests a stratagem to thwart the tyrannical and homicidal actions of Enlil. Enlil takes his final revenge by sterilizing the women so that humans cannot multiply and once again rebel (compare the similar measures taken by the pharaoh, in Exodus 1:11–21).

In itself, this myth is ambiguous. On the one hand, it suggests the rebellion of the oppressed in two ways: not only did the first humans start a rebellion, but they were also inspired by the struggle of the minor gods, who were the slaves of the major gods. On the other hand, although the rebellion of the gods was successful—they were unburdened of their *kabtu dullu*, heavy labor, by the advent of humanity—humanity's rebellion was unsuccessful. This is the central ambiguity.

The ambiguity of the myth of Atrahasis does not end here; there is much more. Everything depends on who is writing, and for whom. Considering its literary construction, the place where the tablets originated (the royal palace at Nineveh), and its long written tradition (from the period of ancient Babylon, from 1635 B.C., until the Neo-Babylonian period), this epic had to be transmitted in court circles, which could not allow a revolutionary epic. Rather, the Atrahasian tradition was used ideologically to teach the failure of all human rebellions. The outcome is that Enlil controls births so that humans will not multiply in excess. As a symbol of strength, he is afraid of humans, and therefore uses his power tyrannically. Such are all oppressors; they become repressors.

However, without a doubt this long-lived tradition in Mesopotamia must also have been sung in popular circles, as was every great epic. Although, from the viewpoint of the upper classes, the myth of Atrahasis aimed to consolidate the servitude of work as the will of the gods, who allow no rebellion of any kind, nevertheless within the oppressed classes some doubt could have arisen. In the final analysis, rebellion *is* possible. The myth shows that an uprising against an oppressor did take place. Throughout the epic the

philanthropic and Promethean figure of Enki is on the scene, seeking to save
humankind. At one point, the poet repeats this refrain at least twice:

> Wherever Enki went,
> he untied the yoke and established a state of freedom
> [*iptur ulla andurara iskun*] [II:v:18–19; 32:33; vi:27–28].

In addition, the poet unleashes a damaging criticism of Enlil: "The gods
ordered total destruction, Enlil acted wrongly [*sipru lemnu*] against humanity" (II:viii:34–35).

The song ends with praise of Enki for defending humans during the flood.[12]
Therefore, there still exists this ambiguity in the myth with respect to oppres-
sion/liberation. It could help to consolidate oppression, just as it could raise
consciousness for liberation. In a sociological reading of the myth, there is no
doubt that its origin and composition allow one to imagine the experience of
revolution against the slavery of forced labor.

There is no mythical epic that clearly celebrates liberation, as in the case of
the exodus of the Hebrews. If there was no experience of liberation in which a
whole people, or a significant group, participated, neither will there be a song
of liberation.

The institution of the ancient Near East that is most extensively described
in the texts, and receives the most ideological support, is that of *royalty*.
Royalty was ever-present, much more so than the priesthood and the temple,
because these depended on the king, who also acted as high priest. Israel was
the innovator in this regard.

In the Syrio-Palestinian region, where the theology of Baal developed, the
typical form of royalty was that of small feudal estates, independent of each
other. At the most, there were small kingdoms that grouped together several
cities, like that of Yamjad or Amurru in the second millennium B.C. In Mesopotamia, there was also the phenomenon of the city-state. However, com-
munications were easy because of the flatness of the land and the creation of a
homogeneous culture, and a tendency toward universalism arose there.
Translated to the political sphere, this meant that each city-state hoped to
establish hegemony over the others. From ancient times, each king claimed
ecumenical titles such as *lugal Urima* ("king of Ur," the religious metrop-
olis), *lugal Kalama* ("king of the whole country"), or *lugal Kish* (the city
from which royalty had descended since the deluge, according to Sumerian
tradition). However, *Kish* also means "totality."

Royalty was seen as a gift of the gods. As pointed out previously, earth was
the property of the supreme god Enlil, who in turn represented the god of the
sky, Anu, symbol of hierarchy and authority, essential—as was royalty—to
the Mesopotamian worldview. Enlil divided the earth among his divine subordinates. Thus the idea of the *divine state* was formulated. In fact, this was
the structure of Mesopotamian society transferred to the realm of the gods.

The tutelar god of a city-state had a huge number of divine ministers at his command. According to Cylinder B of Gudea (the famous Sumerian king at the end of the third millennium B.C. in Lagas), the god Ningirsu, lord and protector of the city, had a house in Lagas with his ministers: the doorkeeper of the sanctuary, the shield bearers, the personal guards, the carriage driver, the prime minister, the keeper of the goats and all the livestock of the temple, the musicians, those in charge of the canals and granaries, and the fish and forest inspectors. This arrangement of the pantheon of the gods evidently reproduces the structure of the human city-state.

The king is the concessionaire of divine rights on earth. The king of a city-state and his tutelar god are structural equivalents, although they exist on different planes, and their functions are parallel. In both cases, power accumulates and is redistributed among subordinates in measures descending to the level of the slave. Once the current social order is accepted because of tradition (and therefore internalized) as a copy of the divine model, then it is perceived as perfect and eternal. This is a thinly disguised manner of justifying the absolute power of the king, who can then dispose of the riches of the country as he wishes, exact heavy tributes and taxes, or draft workers for his necessities.

This mythological method of justifying the social order through reference to the world of the gods is replaced in Greek philosophy by the idea of the world of the senses as a copy of the eternal (Plato, *Timaeus*), and in India by the belief that the four castes originated in the dismembering of Brahma (Rig Veda X.90:11–12):

> The Brahmans [the priestly caste] were his mouth, his two arms became the Rájanya [the warrior caste], his two thighs are the Váisya [the artisan class], and the Sudra [slaves] came out of his feet.

Brahma is the absolute beginning, and each social caste represents him in some way, but on different levels.

The metaphysical nature of this representation does not make it any the less ideological; on the contrary. Besides justifying social differences, it prohibits all change as a transgression against the immutable metaphysical order. Hence the Bhagavad-Gita, the apex of Hindu thought, attributes the better virtues and qualities to the first two social categories (always joined together!) when it sets down the duties of each one of the castes (priests, warriors, farmers, and slaves):

> Calm, self-control, asceticism, purity, endurance, rectitude, knowledge, awareness, orthodoxy is the Duty of the Brahman, born from his very nature. Bravery, energy, constancy, skill in combat, never fleeing, generosity, authority, is the Duty of the warrior. Agriculture, care of the cattle, commerce, is the Duty of the *váisya*, coming out of his very nature. To serve is the duty of the *sudra*, coming out of his very nature [song 18:42–44].[13]

Note the only function assigned to the slave: to serve. All duties *(karma)* are determined "by his very nature" *(svabhava-jam)*. It had already been taught that God himself created the castes (song 4:13). When social reality has a divine model, or a metaphysical or transcendent origin—according to the worldview—then it represents a fixed, immutable order that must be accepted and never transgressed.

Nevertheless, or perhaps for that very reason, this order was seen as natural. Is a rupture possible, then, with the myth that archetypically legitimizes heavy labor of inferiors, differences in social class, and oppression? This question raises certain expectations with regard to the Hebraic worldview, the next to be taken up.

This encirclement of the world by the "gods of oppression" makes it more evident that the real oppressors are humans—specifically, those who hold power. Once again the figure of the king stands out. The gods, masters of the earth and the world, demand services that are performed through labor, through construction of sanctuaries, and through sacrifices.[14] For the masses this service becomes service to the king, who by tradition also assumes the priestly function. Mesopotamia, Egypt, Canaan, Jatti—all the neighboring peoples of Israel—shared this conception of the world without question (and how could they not?). The palaces and temples are ostentatious, grandiose. Texts and other archeological finds hardly talk of anything else. The economic power of the country was concentrated in these royal construction projects. Whoever reads the mercantile tablets of, for example, Ugarit or Mari (fourteenth and eighteenth centuries B.C., respectively) cannot but be impressed by the immense riches of the king's palace.

In archeological excavations of the ancient Near East, magnificent palaces, beautiful temples to the gods, great and opulent tombs for royalty have been found, but few houses for the common people. The case of Nineveh is symptomatic: for a city that stretched out as far as seven miles from its center, the only architectural remains are concentrated in the acropolis, the "official" zone, which takes up a relatively small area. The king possessed everything, and received everything from his subjects.

The Hebrews, when they wanted to be "like the other nations" and have a king, suffered the same consequences. Solomon and, according to the Chronicle tradition, David erected a temple of great magnificence for the God of Israel, and a no less worthy palace for themselves:

All these were made of heavy blocks of stone, hewn to measure and trimmed with the saw on the inner and outer sides, from foundation to coping and from the court of the house as far as the great court. At the base were heavy stones, massive blocks, some ten and some eight cubits in size, and above were heavy stones dressed to measure, and cedar. The great court had three courses of dressed stone all around and a course of lengths of cedar; so had the inner court of the house of the Lord, and so had the vestibule of the house [1 Kings 7:9–12].

The temple took seven years to build, and the palace thirteen! (See the calculation of prices in the narratives of 1 Kings 5–7 and 1 Chron. 21 to 2 Chron. 4.) Besides the residential palace, the king needed "store-cities, and the towns where he quartered his chariots and horses" (1 Kings 9:19).

It is obvious that this expression of grandeur and power could not have been achieved without injustice, without oppressing the people. The deuteronomist editor of the Book of Kings simply mentions (for lack of a critical consciousness?) that Solomon constructed the house of Yahweh, his own palace, and other fortifications through either personal loans or the forced labor of his subjects (1 Kings 9:15; *mas* is the technical word, of Canaanite origin, to designate this kind of work). He had no alternative. (But read Jer. 22:13, in the oracle against Jehoiakim: "Shame on the man who builds his house by unjust means and completes its roof-chambers by fraud, making his countrymen work without payment, giving them no wage for their labor!")

In the worldview of that time, which endured for many centuries, the king could not govern unless he had a "worthy" palace. Consider Jeremiah's irony in his denunciation of Jehoiakim: "If your cedar is more splendid, does that prove you a king?" (22:15).

The Ugaritic poem of Baal is centered upon preoccupation with needing a palace in which to reside if he is to be a real king and govern the earth. "Baal has no house like the other gods do," is the underlying theme.[15] Faced with the demands of suppliants, the god El decides: "May a house for Baal be built, like those of the gods, with an atrium like those of the sons of Atirat" (the mother goddess, wife of El).[16] Baal's palace must be sumptuous:

> That a house of cedar be completed for him,
> that a house of brick be built for him. . . .
> The omnipotent Baal rejoices.
> He has a convoy arrive at his residence,
> the furnishings come to the inside of his palace.
> The mountains bring him silver in bulk,
> the hills the most precious gold,
> caravans carry precious stones to him.[17]

Baal inaugurated his palace with a great banquet for his divine colleagues, in which he sacrificed thousands of animals and gave away thrones and armchairs.[18] Earthly kings did likewise: Solomon (1 Kings 8:63,65), Asurnasirpal, when inaugurating Kalju as the new capital in 879 B.C.,[19] and many other "magnificent" kings. Once more the divine and human planes are equivalent, except that the first legitimizes the second. In this sense, Israel also had its gods of oppression. Recognition of this could have valuable consequences for correct biblical hermeneutics, which cannot treat the Bible as a deposit of truths all of equal value.

In tradition, oppressive features have often been added to the liberator

God of the people. He was burdened with one of these features by pro-Davidic and pro-Solomonic circles: Yahweh resided in an ostentatious temple, like that of Baal in the Canaanite Olympus, thus justifying a practice of social oppression. Luckily, this practice sowed the seeds of rebellion at the same time. Although the deuteronomic tradition emphasizes Solomon's idolatry (imported by his foreign wives and concubines) as the cause of the schism (1 Kings 11:1–13), the source of this tradition attributes the schism to the excessive weight of economic oppression on the tribes, who had to bear the burdens of taxes and forced labor for the house of God and Solomon's own palace (1 Kings 5:6b, 27, 11:26–28, and esp. 12:1–19). "Your father laid a cruel yoke upon us; but if you will now lighten the cruel slavery [abodá qasa] he imposed on us and the heavy yoke he laid on us, we will serve you," was the people's demand of Rehoboam, Solomon's son (1 Kings 12:4). Like Enlil in the myth of Atrahasis, the Israelite king did not accept this plea for justice, so the people had to win its freedom by itself.

Neither the king nor the gods, for that matter, are totally reprehensible. In the royal ideology of the ancient Orient—which can be examined from a broader perspective—the king is the defender of the poor, the orphan, and the widow. Because all power is concentrated in his hands, it falls to him to mete out justice to all who are oppressed, to the helpless. This redeeming function of power [20] has its divine equivalent in the notion of the god of justice and law, which is widespread throughout the Orient.[21] Kittu, mîsaru, day-yânu are all divine attributes that express the function of liberating law, of redeeming justice, and of judgment. These attributes are proclaimed in the epics, in inscriptions, in hymns and prayers, and even in the names of the gods.[22]

As the deputy of the gods, the king assumes the same redeeming function. Thousands of inscriptions or formulas spread throughout the texts document this fact. Some kings were social reformers, such as Urukagina of Sumer, in the twenty-seventh century B.C., of whom it was said that he "reinstated freedom" from social abuses and injustices. Lipit-Ištar, Ammisaduqa, and others are later examples. Myriads of royal epithets or inscriptions testify to this function. Following is a text that is highly significant in that it demonstrates the equivalence of the divine and royal realms, and introduces a very famous juridical text. In the prologue to his Code, Hammurabi introduces himself as chosen by Marduk to govern Babylonia:

When his excellency Anum, King of Anunnaki,[23] and the God Enlil, lord of the heavens and earth who decides the fate of the country, chose the God Marduk, first son of the God Ea,[24] *to carry out the functions of Enlil over the totality [kissatim] of humans,* then he [Marduk] was made to be great among the Igigi. Thus in the center of Babylonia an ever-eternal kingdom was firmly established for him—a reign whose foundations were as solidly cemented together as the earth and the sky. Whereupon Anum and Enlil called me *by my name* to promote the well-being of the people. He called me, Hammurabi, obedient prince and fearful of the gods, to make justice *(mîsaram)* shine forth in my country, to destroy the evil and impious, *and to make sure that the powerful do not oppress the weak.*[25]

It is useful to keep this theological line of thought in mind, to avoid distinctions that are too exclusive. In fact, one finds "gods of liberation" within the horizons of the mythical religions, and "gods of oppression" in Israel who are recognized by the normative tradition. This has an important hermeneutical implication: the biblical "god of liberation" does not correspond to *all* the forms of Yahweh within the tradition. "Yahweh the liberator" displaces other gods little by little, to the extent that an experience of liberation is attributed to him. What is important to discover in the Bible is this semantic axis of liberation, which constitutes the Bible's true "reservoir-of-meaning" and allows one to recognize the specifics of biblical faith.[26]

Implications of Myth as Archetypal Thought

Several concrete implications arise from the analysis of religious myth sketched above.

Culture. Culture does not appear as a human achievement. As an aspect of the reality of the world, it has epiphanic contours. Myths that refer to cultural changes, inventions, the presence of new institutions or laws, are called "myths of origin," which in turn depend on the cosmogonic myth. In Sumer, the gods who most appear on the scene in this kind of cultural myth are Enlil and Enki, the divinities of air and water, respectively. In one famous etiological myth, Enki lets the *mes*—the Sumerian archetypes of civilization—be stolen by goddess Inanna of Uruk. In fact, Uruk had replaced Eridu, the city of Enki, in importance—Eridu being the symbol of the most ancient human achievements. The myth called "Enki and the World Order" dates from the time when Enki still reigned supreme.[27] In every case, it is the gods who transmit this or that cultural innovation to humans. The epiphanization of culture is a universal phenomenon.[28]

On the other hand, the Bible retreats from this vision of the world. Genesis 4:20-22 attributes the origin of architecture, music, metalworking, and the domestication of animals to *humans* (albeit with a certain negative tone). In effect, once God had created the world for humans, it was their responsibility to create all the rest. This is a completely different concept of human culture, one that values human creativity, and is an extension of the theme under consideration: the "gods of oppression" and the "God of liberation."

Social Status. Social situations of human origin are justified archetypically. Some aspects of this influence of the mythical mentality have been dealt with in the discussion of castes in India, or the ambiguity of the myth of Atrahasis. The social inferiority of women is also explained by mythical memory (remember the myths of Prometheus and Pandora in Hellenic tradition). Rabbinism repossesses this mentality. *Berakot*, a Talmudic treatise, lays down the following rule: "Each day we should say three blessings: 'blessed is he who did not make me a pagan, a woman, or ignorant.' "[29] This god has little or nothing to do with the Yahweh of the exodus.

A Nivakle myth from the Paraguayan Chaco links the origin of poverty with the arrival of whites, and concludes with this significant sentence: "It is for this reason that we live now as we do." This etiology implies the internalization of the cultural marginalization of the Nivakle as a situation that was decided in an originative event.[30] It would be easy to draw other examples from the literature of mythology.

Celebration. Holidays, and worship in general, not only have a celebratory significance, but also determine the conditions for praxis. The cyclic holiday of the New Year renews the cosmic order, but in a regressive fashion. Within these limits, it is difficult to develop a historical design. The only country in the ancient Orient to do so, Israel, had a reason for abandoning the New Year celebration. It is this abandonment that is significant, and not the attempts of certain exegetes to reconstruct the festival on the basis of remnants found in the Psalms and other books of the Bible.

The great myth of Baal, found in the Ugarit excavations, probably reflects the Canaanite liturgy of the New Year, which celebrates the resurrection of Baal, god of fecundity and life, through his victory over Mot, god of death and drought. In this atmosphere, it is easy to understand the Hebrews' fascination for Baal, and the prophets' struggle to "conscientize" the people to the true understanding of God the liberator, whom their forefathers had recognized during the exodus.

The importance of the life cycle, and its renewal in the mythical worldview, also explains why the woman is important as a *qadistu* or sacred woman, used by man—above all, the king—to put the fertile and archetypal union between the tutelar god and his celestial spouse into practice on earth. Far from being man's partner in his mission in the world (Gen. 2:18 ff.), woman is an oppressed being.

Authentic Demythologization: "Decosmicization." One final observation: it is common to state that the Greeks were the first to demythologize, because of their criticism of the gods. Pre-Socratic philosophers devoted themselves to nature and its origin *(arche)* without turning to transcendent principles (Aristotle called them *physiologoi,* not *theologoi*). The mythical images became literal; the *logos* followed the myth, and the cosmogonic drama yielded to a natural process. Worship and its rites were no longer of interest. But then the archetypal gods succeeded the primordial elements *(stoicheia)* as the organizing forces of the universe. In general, Greek thought could not detach itself from an archetypification of *physis*, nature. From then on, it could be said that it rationalized (or corrupted!) the myth without outgrowing it. Greek thought continued to be cyclic and ontological, attached to the rationality of nature with all its deterministic weight.[31]

In light of what has been examined in this essay, authentic demythologization (neither a synonym for desymbolization nor a renunciation of the *language* of mythical structure) consists in a "decosmicization" of the divine, leaving the world as the province of humans. To the extent that they are preoccupied with *physis*, humans will continue to be entangled by an oppressive cyclicity that does not allow them to assume their historical destiny. For this reason, the biblical concept of *bará*, creation, presupposes a historical awareness based on a liberating experience of God.[32]

CONCLUDING THOUGHTS

This portrait of the mythical religions that surrounded Israel demonstrates the profound liberating implications of biblical faith. However, as already mentioned, we cannot simply oppose the two worldviews to each other. There are liberating elements in the nonbiblical religions, and there are vestiges of the mythical mentality in certain "zones" of the Bible (for example, the priestly traditions, with their tendency toward the archetypal and the ritualistic, thus retrieving some aspects of the "cosmicization" of the divine; the adaptation of royalty and the temple along mythical lines, etc.). Therefore, it is essential to insist on the *hermeneutical method*, which leads to the discovery of the semantic axis of biblical faith. The nucleus of this axis is the experience of the liberating God of the exodus, and later the experience of Jesus, liberator of the poor.

A disturbing question arises for us Christians. Is it not true that there has been a continual and regressive reassumption of mythical elements throughout the history of Christianity?

With respect to Latin America, this thought is even more dramatic inasmuch as Christianity entered our continent *under the auspices of oppression*. Not only was it *imposed* by force, as the religion of the conquistador, but it also *functioned* as a religion of oppression. If the experience of liberation that allowed the Hebrew people to recognize God as their liberator gave rise to biblical faith, Latin America *could not* be evangelized, because God could not be experienced as a liberator. (To experience him as a "savior of souls, for heaven," or as a savior from *certain* sins, was a deviation from the full truth.) This contradiction was decisive.

Consequently, the indigenous peoples of Latin America were left with their oppressor gods, maybe less oppressive than the god of their conquerors. In spontaneous self-defense, they accepted Christian *forms* for their traditional worldview. Although it could not liberate them, at least their worldview served and still serves as a vehicle for the telling and retelling of their plight. If evangelization (it would be better not to use this word any more) has not brought about an experience of liberation in the economic and social spheres, where it is meant to play a radical and archetypal role, then the possibility of speaking authentically of the "God of liberation" has been lost.

In order that biblical faith—in its liberating, kerygmatic core—may be credible for Latin Americans, some of its historical manifestations must undergo a radical purging. The only way to achieve this is through a new experience of liberation. In other words, there must be a new beginning. Only then will Exodus 14:31 come alive again:

When Israel saw the great power which the Lord had put forth against Egypt, all the people feared the Lord, and they put their faith in him and in Moses his servant.

NOTES

1. See Joachim Wach, *The Comparative Study of Religions*, Joseph M. Kitagawa, ed. (New York: Columbia University Press, 1958); Gerhardus van der Leeuw, *Religion in Essence and Manifestations*, Hans H. Kenner, trans. and ed. (London: Allen & Unwin, 1938; reprint, Gloucester, Mass.: Peter Smith, 1967).

2. Paul Ricoeur, *The Symbolism of Evil*, trans. Emerson Buchanan (Boston: Beacon, 1969), pp. 15–16.

3. On the theme of the interdependence of symbol and myth, see my articles: "El mito símbolo y el mito relato. Reflexiones hermenéuticas," in *Mito y hermenéutica* (Buenos Aires: El Escudo, 1973), pp. 83–95; "Símbolo mítico y creatividad," in *Estudios de filosofía y religiones del Oriente* (Buenos Aires) 1:1 (1971): 31–47. The first publication is a collection of works by SAPSE (Sociedad Argentina de Profesores de Sagrada Escritura, Argentinian Society of Professors of Sacred Scripture).

4. See the typology of "ontological evil" (as it appears in *Enuma Elish*) by Ricoeur, *The Symbolism of Evil*, pp. 163–64, 175–91, 306–10, and which he treats again in Part 4 of *The Conflict of Interpretations: Essays in Hermeneutics*, Don Ihde, ed. (Evanston: Northwestern University Press, 1974), pp. 269–86.

5. Text of Tablet IIAB (= Gordon 51), col. VII:50–52.

6. Text SS (= Gordon 52), lines 60–75. See the French translation and commentary by A. Caquot and M. Sznycer in *Les religions du Proche-Orient asiatique* (Paris: Fayard/Denoël, 1970), pp. 450–58.

7. I have used the original edition (in Akkadian and English) by W. G. Lambert and A. R. Millar, *Atra-hasis. The Babylonian Story of the Flood* (Oxford: Clarendon, 1969). For a history of the identification of the tablets, see pp. 1 ff.

8. On this concept (or rather, symbol) see the excellent study by Elena Cassin, *La splendeur divine. Introduction à l'étude de la mentalité mésopotamienne* (Paris: Mouton, 1968).

9. See the classic study, now in English, by Henri Frankfort, *Kingship and the Gods: A Study of Near Eastern Religions as the Integrations of Society and Nature* (Chicago: University of Chicago Press, 1978). For a study of royal symbolism, see J. Weir Perry, *Lord of the Four Quarters. Myths of the Royal Father* (New York: Braziller, 1966).

10. R. Labat, in *Les religions du Proche-Orient*, pp. 81–92.

11. On the theme of "celestial tablets" in apocalyptic works, see, e.g., Book of Jubilees 5:13, Book of Enoch (Ethiopian 81:1–2) ("Observe, Enoch, these celestial tablets, and repeat what is written on them, noting down each action separately"), 93:2, etc.

12. Lambert and Millar, *Atra-hasis*.

13. I have used the translation from Sanskrit to Spanish of F. Tola, *Bhagavad-Gita. El Canto del Señor* (Caracas: Monte Avila, 1977), pp. 252 ff. For the other passages, see R. C. Zaehner, *The Bhagavad-Gita* (Oxford: Clarendon, 1969), pp. 393 and 186-87.

14. This connection is universal in mythical thought. Compare also the Latin *colere (col-ere)*, which means both "to work the earth" (*cul-tura*, [agri]culture) and "to worship the gods" (*cul-tum*, cult).

15. Tablet VAB (= Gordon *Anat*), col. V:1 ff., 47 ff., and IIAB (= Gordon 51) 1:10 and IV:50 ff.

16. IIAB, col. IV:62 ff.

17. IIAB, col. V:72-73, 97 ff.

18. IIAB, col. VI:36-59.

19. At the banquet, 69,574 guests were fed and feted. See the text published by D. J. Wiseman in *Iraq* 14 (1952) 24-44. Cf. Esther 1 (the banquet of King Ahasuerus).

20. I have developed this topic in "La función del poder: ¿salvífica u 'opresora'?," in *Revista Bíblica* (Buenos Aires) 34 (1972): 99-106.

21. See A. Gamper, *Gott als Richter in Mesopotamien und im Alten Testament* (Innsbruck: Universitätsverlag Wagner, 1966), esp. pp. 65 ff.

22. Ibid.

23. Designation of the major gods.

24. Ea is the same as Enki (the old Sumerian name), who also appears as Nudinmud in the Babylonian creation epic.

25. Code of Hammurabi I (Prologue), words 1-49; italics added.

26. For an attempt to establish some hermeneutical guidelines, see my work *Liberación y libertad. Pautas hermenéuticas* (Lima: CEP, 1978), pp. 25 ff., Eng. trans.: *Exodus: A Hermeneutics of Freedom* (Maryknoll, New York: Orbis Books, 1981).

27. See S. N. Kramer, *Sumerian Mythology* (New York: Harper, 1961) pp. 41-68; C. Benito, *"Enki and Ninmah" and "Enki and the World Order"* (Ann Arbor: University Microfilms, 1969).

28. See E. J. Cordeu, "Aproximación al horizonte mítico de los Tobas," in *RUNA* (Buenos Aires) 12 (1969/70): 67-167, esp. pp. 141 ff.; M. Bormida, "Ergon y mito. Una hermenéutica de la cultura material de los Ayoreo del Chaco Boreal," in *Scripta Ethnológica* (Buenos Aires) 1 (1973): 9-68 (on the origin of different technologies).

29. See the Talmudic treatise on blessings, Berakot VI, 18, trans. J. Bonsirven, *Textes rabbiniques des deux premiers siècles chrétiens* (Rome: Pontifical Biblical Institute, 1954) p. 116 (n. 493). Compare Qidussin 82b: "Happy he whose children are men, and unfortunate he whose children are women" (ibid., p. 419).

30. See *Crisis* (Buenos Aires) 4 (August 1973): 25.

31. For further development of this theme, see my commentary on Genesis 1, *El hombre en el mundo, I. Creación y designio* (Buenos Aires: La Aurora, 1974), pp. 81-87.

32. See *Liberación y libertad*, pp. 53-63, on Genesis 1:1.

III

GEORGE V. PIXLEY

Divine Judgment in History

The topic of God's judgment has become one of great relevance in Latin America, where the poor are crushed by demonic military powers. This topic is central in the Bible, and it is important to revive interest in it for the faithful who live under this dreadful oppression.

There is a strong link between love and justice. Love demands defense of the weak against the violence of their oppressors, even when one must resort to arms to do so. The people of Nicaragua did not hesitate to confront the National Guard of General Somoza, and some Christians interpreted the people's victory as a divine judgment. If we did not labor under a purely individualistic interpretation of divine judgment for centuries, this would seem a completely natural interpretation of the Nicaraguan experience.

Using key biblical texts, this study aims to show how God carries out his judgments in the historical realm. A biblical psalm may serve as an introduction:

> Yahweh[1] takes his stand in the court of heaven
>   to deliver judgment among the gods themselves.
> "How long will you judge unjustly
>   and show favor to the wicked?
> You ought to give judgment for the weak and the orphan,
>   and see right done to the destitute and downtrodden,

46

you ought to rescue the weak and the poor,
    and save them from the clutches of wicked men. . . .
This is my sentence: gods you may be,
    sons all of you of a high god,
yet you shall die as men die;
    princes fall, every one of them, and so shall you" [Ps. 82:1-4, 6-7].

This impressive psalm, with imagery from the mythology of the ancient Near East, establishes that the execution of justice—that is, judgment—is what distinguishes the true God from false gods. Only the God who liberates the weak and the poor from under the fist of their oppressors is truly God. Those who, presenting themselves as gods, favor oppressors will pass away like other mortals: in the execution of divine judgment they are exposed as nongods.

There are many repercussions of this text throughout Latin America. Regimes based on force justify their abuses and their repressive decrees by invoking the name of God against "the threat of atheism." Moved by their God, priests and lay Christians have taken the part of the lowly and have been assassinated as "traitors to authentic Christianity."[2] Basing itself on the Bible, this essay will study divine judgment in connection with the battle against false gods, those known to the social sciences as fetishes.

YAHWEH REVEALS HIMSELF
IN HISTORICAL JUDGMENTS

Liberation of an Oppressed People

For Israel, the knowledge of God was closely linked to liberation from oppression in Egypt. Israel confessed that it did not recognize Yahweh as its God until its liberation from slavery: "But I have been Yahweh your God since your days in Egypt, when you knew no other savior than me, no god but me" (Hos. 13:4). According to the Elohist and priestly writings in Israel's tradition, the people did not know Yahweh by name until their exodus from Egypt:

I am Yahweh. I appeared to Abraham, Isaac, and Jacob as God Almighty [*El Shaddai*]. But I did not let myself be known to them by my name Yahweh. . . . I will release you from your labors in Egypt. I will rescue you from slavery there. I will redeem you with arm outstretched and with mighty acts of judgment [Exod. 6:2-3, 6].

Although it has not been proven that the name Yahweh first appeared in the time of Moses, this traditional belief has always been a basic part of Israel's perception of God.[3]

In the terms in which antiquity understood judgment, Yahweh's intervention against the pharaoh was a classic example of a judge defending the weak against their oppressor.[4] In the words of the Yahwist version:

> The outcry of the Israelites has now reached me; yes, I have seen the brutality of the Egyptians toward them. Come now; I will send you to Pharaoh and you shall bring my people Israel out of Egypt [Exod. 3:9–10].

According to the picture drawn by the psalm quoted previously, Yahweh introduced himself into the lives of the people of Israel as the true God who liberated slaves with a strong hand, crushing their oppressors.

Liberation from slavery became a true confession of faith for the people of Israel. That is to say, Israel professed to be the people who had been rescued by the true God, Yahweh, from slavery (Deut. 26:5–9).[5] The memory of this archetypal event in their national life and their faith was repeated through the generations, becoming amplified and perfected, until it took its form as a confrontation between the sovereignty of the pharaoh—the false god—and the strength and justice of Yahweh—the just and redeeming God.

Using the model of the exodus, the people interpreted other moments in their struggle for national liberty in a similar manner. The pattern of oppression, outcry, plea for a leader, victory, and liberation was repeated several times in the popular stories preserved in the Book of Judges. When faced with the Edomite repression, Yahweh raised up the liberator Othniel (Judg. 3:7–11).[6] During the Moabite oppression, Yahweh raised up Ehud the Benjamite to deliver Israel. At the time of the oppression by Jabin the Canaanite, Yahweh raised up Deborah of Ephraim and Barak of Naphtali, who liberated the people (Judg. 4–5). The outcry of the people against the repeated attacks of the Midianites provoked Yahweh to intervene and raise up Gideon of Manasseh as a liberator (Judg. 6–8). Yahweh acted similarly on other occasions.

Many different experiences of the groups collectively known as Israel served to confirm in the popular memory their belief that Yahweh showed himself as the true God by hearing the outcry of the oppressed and intervening to rescue them.

Upon understanding that the model of the exodus was the utmost revelation of the true God, Israel affirmed Yahweh as a just king and judge. A good king shows his ability to govern by judging righteously—that is, by defending the poor against the rich (2 Sam. 12:1–6, the story of the poor man whose only sheep was taken by his rich neighbor). In the ancient Near East, when a king was crowned it was expected that:

> He shall give judgment for the suffering
> and help those of the people that are needy;
> he shall crush the oppressor [Ps. 72:4].

This link between justice and the true God was not always clearly maintained. In the biased language of the ruling classes, and sometimes in popular consciousness as well, Yahweh's salvation became a family matter, a defense of the people of Yahweh in the same way that Asur defended the people of Assyria, and Kemos those of Moab. Nevertheless, the prophets never tired of reminding the people that the relative strength of the various national gods was not at stake, but rather the proof of who was really God. Yahweh could intervene on behalf of the peoples who did not know him by name, even those who were enemies of Israel:

> Are not you Israelites like Cushites to me?
>   says Yahweh.
> Did I not bring Israel up from Egypt,
> the Philistines from Caphtor,
>   the Aramaeans from Kir? [Amos 9:7].

The Yahwist writer also recognizes that Yahweh intervened on behalf of the oppressed in Sodom and Gomorrah, who are not even identified:

> So Yahweh said, "There is a great outcry over Sodom and Gomorrah; their sin is very grave. I must go down and see whether their deeds warrant the outcry which has reached me. I am resolved to know the truth" [Gen. 18:20].

Rescue of the Innocent

The prayers in the Psalms indicate that the writer hoped that the same God who rescued slaves from their oppressors would intervene as well to save him from those who plotted his ruination. The psalmic prayers appeal to God as judge, king, and savior. Most frequently, the supplicant represents himself as poor, innocent, and oppressed. The third person in these prayers is the iniquitous enemy, portrayed as powerful, wicked, and bloodthirsty. In his misfortune, the supplicant pleads for the just intervention of the divine judge. Knowing the stories of the people, and the attestations of the just who have been redeemed, the supplicant can be confident of a favorable response:

> Give me justice, O Yahweh,
> for I have lived my life without reproach,
> and put unfaltering trust in Yahweh [Ps. 26:1].

> O Yahweh, judge me as my righteousness deserves,
>   for I am clearly innocent.

Let wicked men do no more harm,
establish the reign of righteousness,
thou who examinest both heart and mind,
     thou righteous God [Ps. 7:8b–9].

I will praise thy name in psalms, O thou Most High,
     when my enemies turn back,
when they fall headlong and perish at thy appearing;
     for thou hast upheld my right and my cause,
     seated on thy throne, thou righteous judge [Ps. 9:2b–4].

Hear, Yahweh, my plea for justice,
     give my cry a hearing,
     listen to my prayer,
     for it is innocent of all deceit: . . .
Arise, Yahweh, meet him face to face and bring him down.
     Save my life from the wicked. . . .
But my plea is just: I shall see thy face,
     and be blessed with a vision of thee when I awake [Ps. 17:1, 13, 15].

The righteous shall rejoice that he has seen vengeance done
     and shall wash his feet in the blood of the wicked,
          and men shall say,
     "There is after all a reward for the righteous;
after all, there is a God that judges on earth" [Ps. 58:10–11].

O Yahweh, thou God of vengeance,
     thou God of vengeance, show thyself.
     Rise up, judge of the earth;
punish the arrogant as they deserve.
How long shall the wicked, O Yahweh,
how long shall the wicked exult? . . .
they murder the widow and the stranger
     and do the fatherless to death; . . .
But Yahweh has been my strong tower,
     and God my rock of refuge;
our God requites the wicked for their injustice,
     Yahweh puts them to silence for their misdeeds
                                        [Ps. 94:1–2, 6, 22–23].

These examples from among many more in the biblical psalms make it
clear that the God who revealed himself through his judgments on oppressors
of nations is the same God to whom the supplicant suffering in misfortune
can turn, pleading for justice, for liberation from the wicked. Those in dis-
tress can expect a divine judgment in their favor.

Retribution for the Blood of the Just

The judgment of God is not merely a matter of approval or disapproval. Rather it is a question of rectifying the unjust oppression of the weak and poor by the strong or rich. This is just as true in the case of an oppressed people, of which the archetypal example is that of the Hebrews enslaved in Egypt, as it is in the case of individuals who turn to the divine judge because they are oppressed by powerful and evil persons. The extreme case of this oppression is the murder of the innocent. The theme of Yahweh's retribution for the blood of his servants is so frequent in the Bible that it deserves to be singled out here:

Rejoice with him, you heavens,
Bow down, all you gods, before him;
for he will avenge the blood of his sons
and take vengeance on his adversaries;
he will punish those who hate him
and make expiation for his people's land [Deut. 32:43].

Psalm 79 is a community appeal; the afflicted collectively turn to Yahweh in a moment of national anguish to plead for his intervention. Among other things, they remind him of the blood of those who had fallen in service to him:

Why should the nations ask, "Where is their God?"
Let thy vengeance for the bloody slaughter of thy servants
fall on those nations before our very eyes.
Let the groaning of the captives reach thy presence
and in thy great might set free death's prisoners [Ps. 79:10–11].

A dramatic case that is especially pertinent to the situation in Latin America is the story of Elisha and Jehu. Yahweh sent the prophet to persuade the military officer Jehu to rise up against the king and eliminate the dynasty of Omri. This dynasty was characterized by warfare against the population of its own country, as illustrated by the murder of Naboth so that Ahab could take possession of his vineyard (1 Kings 21). The prophets of Yahweh came out in defense of the lives of the people, denouncing the idolatry with which the kings justified their crimes. These actions brought persecution and death upon the prophets (1 Kings 18–19). In view of this state of injustice, Yahweh commanded Jehu to kill Jehoram, the king, Jezebel, the queen mother, and the whole royal family, "and I will take vengeance . . . for the blood of my servants the prophets . . . and of all the Lord's servants" (2 Kings 9:7).

In the teachings of later prophets, who lived in times of total domination by various powerful empires, God's vengeance for the death of the just takes the form of the Day of Yahweh—an eschatological day of judgment for all the nations of the earth. These prophecies led to apocalyptic literature, a popular protest against the internal domination of a priestly caste, combined with external domination by foreign empires. Given their powerlessness, the masses placed all their hopes in a spectacular intervention by God to right the wrongs that had not been dealt with through the normal interplay of historical forces.[7] In a final act of revenge, Yahweh would resolve the grievances of the people:

> . . . but Egypt shall become a desert
> and Edom a deserted waste,
>   because of the violence done to Judah
> and the innocent blood shed in her land;
>   and I will spill their blood,
>   the blood I have not yet spilt.
> Then there will be people living in Judah forever,
> in Jerusalem generation after generation;
> and Yahweh will dwell in Zion [Joel 3:19–21].

In the extremes of their suffering and impotence, the Palestinian people took solace in the macabre vision of God spattering his garments with the blood of the wicked, while he tramples them in his wrath as if they were grapes (Isa. 63:1–7).

Dispersed throughout the major cities of the Roman Empire, the small Christian church suffered the same experience of oppression and powerlessness. Its apocalyptic visions adopted the same hopes for a final revenge in which God would intervene to remedy the disorder of this world:

> When he broke the fifth seal, I saw underneath the altar the souls of those who had been slaughtered for God's word and for the testimony they bore. They gave a great cry: "How long, sovereign Lord, holy and true, must it be before thou wilt vindicate us and avenge our blood on the inhabitants of the earth?" [Rev. 6:9–10].
>
> The woman, I saw, was drunk with the blood of God's people and with the blood of those who had borne their testimony to Jesus. As I looked at her I was greatly astonished [17:6–7a].
>
> . . . her sins are piled high as heaven, and God has not forgotten her crimes. Pay her back in her own coin, repay her twice over for her deeds! [18:5–6a].
>
> But let heaven exult over her; exult, apostles and prophets and people of God; for in the judgment against her he has vindicated your cause! [18:20].

At the Final Judgment

God's vengeance for the blood of his servants brings us to another grouping of biblical texts, bearing on a divine last judgment, a judgment that ends the oppressions of history once and for all. Although it is always linked with revenge for the blood of the just, the divine judgment goes beyond this theme and therefore merits a separate analysis.

From the times when the masses of Israel took up arms to fight Yahweh's wars, under the leadership of liberators raised up by Yahweh, the militants were accompanied and inspired by prophets, who announced that Yahweh had "delivered the enemy into your hands" (examples: 1 Kings 20:13-14; 2 Chron. 25:7-8). From the eighth through the sixth century B.C., the prophets of Israel carried on this tradition of announcing God's judgment of the nations in their "oracles against the nations" (Amos 1-2; Soph. 2; Isa. 13-23; Jer. 46-51, etc.).[8]

Perhaps the first prophetic work that conceived of a global judgment against all the known nations is Jeremiah 25:13-38, the famous passage about the cup of Yahweh's wrath that makes the kings of the nations get drunk and vomit.[9] According to the Greek text, which seems to be the oldest, a judgment is carried out against Judah, Egypt, Philistia, Edom, Moab, Ammon, Arabia, Elam, and Persia. It is worthy of note that the judgment is carried out against the kings (states), reflecting the popular vision of the origins of injustice.

In the last postexilic part of the book of Isaiah, the meaning that the prophets always gave to judgment is made explicit: both revenge against oppressors and liberation for the just: ". . . to proclaim a year of Yahweh's favor, and a day of the vengeance of our God" (Isa. 61:2). Jesus revived and carried on this prophetic tradition of a judgment against the nations: "When the Son of Man comes in his glory . . . with all the nations gathered before him. He will separate men into two groups, as a shepherd separates the sheep from the goats" (Matt. 25:31-32).

Nevertheless, Jesus' teachings and their development in the synoptic tradition tended to transform the last judgment into an event *outside* history, in which God would distribute to all according to their actions within a history conceived of as a closed era. One example is Jesus' statement that persons would be judged on whether they had declared themselves for him openly to others or not (Matt. 10:32-33). In the parable of the virgins as well, five are received into the Lord's favor, and five are excluded (Matt. 25:1-13). According to the first great missionary to the gentiles, on the day of God's wrath and just judgment, all will be repaid as their works merit (Rom. 2:6). On that day, fire will test the quality of each one's work, to see if it can resist the just anger of God (1 Cor. 3:10-15).

In short, beginning with the oracles of war, the idea developed in Israel of a judgment to end all judgments, in which the nations would get what they deserved for what their kings had done to God's servants—to the poor and humble among his people. In its origins, and in the way it was developed by the prophets, this great judgment would lay the foundations of a new and more just history. But to the extent that the consciousness of a design for God's people *in history* faded out, the last judgment tended to be removed from history, to become both judgment of individual works and judgment of history completed. The idea of the Last Judgment has influenced popular Christian thought from a very early date.

In the Resurrection of Jesus

In the writings of the New Testament, the archetypal story of the rule of evil, and of divine judgment against evil, is the story of the death and resurrection of Jesus. Jesus is the model of the poor and just who suffer in their own flesh the criminality of the powerful; at the same time, he is the Son of God who pays with his blood for his solidarity with the poor. However, the gospels do not glorify his death: Jesus did not live to die, but rather died to defend the right to life. Thus it happens that the savior God—the God of the exodus—carries out his own judgment on Jesus, condemned by the priests and Roman authorities—that is, by the rich and powerful. This new judgment has as its conclusion his resurrection, with chosen witnesses who were to be the apostles of this just Messiah of the poor, executed for defending his brothers and sisters:

> Let all Israel then accept as certain that God has made this Jesus, whom you crucified, both Lord and Messiah [Acts 2:36].
>
> You begged as a favor the release of a murderer, and killed him who has led the way to life. But God raised him from the dead; of that we are witnesses [3:15].
>
> The God of our fathers raised up Jesus whom you had done to death by hanging him on a gibbet. He it is whom God has exalted with his own right hand as leader and savior, to grant Israel repentance and forgiveness of sins. And we are witnesses to all this [5:30–32a].
>
> He was put to death by hanging on a gibbet; but God raised him up to life on the third day, and allowed him to appear . . . to witnesses . . . to us, who ate and drank with him after he rose from the dead. He commanded us to proclaim him to the people, and affirm that he is the one who has been designated by God as judge of the living and the dead [10:39b–42].

The central point of the New Testament profession of faith is that this poor man, whom the powerful of that time declared worthy to die, has been declared *the* just one by God, and through his resurrection he has been appointed the judge of the very ones who condemned him. This is God's archetypal historical judgment in the Christian texts of the Bible; the martyred representative of the people has the last word in history. In the person of the resurrected Jesus, God and his people pronounce the final judgment on the authorities of this world, who would even murder the poor in order to continue in their positions of power.

MOTIVES FOR DIVINE JUDGMENT IN HISTORY

Some of the reasons why God intervenes in history to judge in favor of the poor and helpless have already been mentioned. The limits of this article would have to be redefined to do an exhaustive investigation of the motives for judgment. However, it would be useful to note certain characteristic biblical expressions of this theme, especially to establish the link between idolatry and oppression as motives that provoke divine judgment.

In the Legislation for the New Society

It is well known that, for the Israelites, the high point of Yahweh's revelation to them was their liberation from servitude in Egypt. In popular memory, as preserved in the Pentateuch, the exodus was only the first of several steps that were necessary to get the people of Yahweh established: exodus, adherence to Yahweh's laws, Yahweh's leading them through the desert, and the war to conquer Canaan. In this series of steps, adherence to the legislation takes on the function of creating the institutions that will give structure to their free life as the people of Yahweh. Like all revolutions, the revolutionary change that created Israel exacted the destruction of the old and oppressive order as its first step. The second step was the foundation of the structures for a new and just social life. Legislation enters the scene at the time of the second step.

According to Israelite traditions, the laws that Yahweh gave to the people through Moses on the sacred mountain are found in legal codifications in the books of Exodus, Leviticus, Numbers, and Deuteronomy. They actually came from different periods in the historical life of Israel, but popular memory attributes all of them to the foundational moment on Mount Sinai when Yahweh covenanted with the people to be their God and they his people.

The link between idolatry and injustice is easily discovered in the three fundamental laws of this covenant—the only three that are found in both lists and, according to tradition, were engraved by the finger of Yahweh on the stone tablets delivered to Moses on the mountain (Exod. 20:1–17 and 34:14–26).

Both lists put the prohibition against worshiping other gods in the first place. In the context of the story of the exodus, the god to be rejected was the pharaoh, the king and god of Egypt. Vis-à-vis the pharaoh, whose power was real and undeniable, Yahweh demanded exclusive loyalty; he is the only real God because only he can redeem the people. For the Israelites living in the land of Canaan, the greatest temptation was to adore Baal, the god who legitimized the Canaanite monarchies. This temptation caused crises in the times of King Ahab and the prophet Elias, and threatened to destroy Israel's identity as the people of Yahweh. The first commandment of the Israelite revolution was the basis of the alliance that served as its political constitution:

sovereignty over Israel lay exclusively in Yahweh's hands. To admit another
sovereign would be treason—the most serious offense against the revolution.[10]

The second commandment forbids making images of God. This prohibition tended to become confused with the former, because the most common
images were those of other gods. Nevertheless, the commentary in Deuteronomy 4:15–28 demonstrates that the problem had to do with the fact that
images of Yahweh could be made. According to this passage, the people
heard Yahweh's voice in the Sinai laying down his commandments, but they
saw no image. To avoid the possibility that Yahweh could be manipulated as
could gods made of sticks or stones (Isa. 44:9–20), it was important to maintain his presence as a leading and authoritative voice. Hence the prohibition
of images. To later prophets, even the construction of a temple for Yahweh
made him manipulable; they were proven right when Solomon used the temple he constructed for Yahweh as a legitimization of his exploitive regime.
The second commandment has the purpose of pointing out this temptation to
manipulate Yahweh.

The third commandment appearing on both lists attributed by tradition to
the finger of Yahweh is the law of the Sabbath—the obligation to sanctify the
seventh day by resting and allowing others to rest (Exod. 20:8–11, 34:21).
This law is of benefit to workers, who will then recognize that Yahweh is a
God who looks after their interests. The purpose of this tradition is to affirm
that Yahweh the liberator God is also the founder of a new society that is
organized for the benefit of those who work.

Sinaitic legislation established the norms guiding Yahweh's historical
judgment, as the Bible would interpret it. Any violation of these commandments would bring judgment on Israel as a consequence, carried out by this
God, defender of the poor:

> You shall not ill-treat any widow or fatherless child. If you do, be sure
> that I will listen if they appeal to me; my anger will be roused and I will
> kill you with the sword; your own wives shall become widows and your
> children fatherless [Exod. 22:22–24].

> But if you do not obey the Lord your God by diligently observing all
> his commandments and statutes which I lay upon you this day, then all
> these maledictions shall come to you and light upon you: a curse upon
> you in the city; a curse upon you in the country. A curse upon your
> basket and your kneading-trough. A curse upon the fruit of your body,
> the fruit of your land, the offspring of your herds and of your lambing
> flocks . . . [Deut. 28:15–18].

In synthesis, in a society built on the commandments of the liberator God
of the exodus, violence against the weak is a sign of abandoning God.
Yahweh is the just judge and defender of the weak:

> . . . for Yahweh your God is God of gods and Lord of lords, the great,
> mighty, and terrible God. He is no respecter of persons and is not to be

bribed; he secures justice for widows and orphans, and loves the alien who lives among you, giving him food and clothing [Deut. 10:17–18].

As the just judge, Yahweh would then intervene in judgment in favor of the oppressed: he never lets himself be bribed or impressed by power and riches. Jesus, who presented himself in Galilee as the herald of the kingdom of this same God, made pronouncements continuing along the same lines as this legislation, for a new society based on justice:

How blessed are you who are in need; the kingdom of God is yours. . . . But alas for you who are rich; you have had your time of happiness [Luke 6:20, 24].

If the God who will be king in the kingdom announced by Jesus is the Yahweh of the exodus, it is natural that the intervention of the divine judge brings good fortune to the oppressed, and mourning and misfortune to their oppressors.

In the Preaching of the Prophets

The prophets are presented in the biblical texts primarily as the bearers of the judgments of Yahweh. A few noteworthy cases illustrate the motives for divine judgment as perceived by these religious men of Israel: the judgments on Solomon, on Ahab, and on Jerusalem.

Solomon is condemned by word of the prophet Ahijah of Shiloh:

This is the word of the Lord: "I am going to tear the kingdom from the hand of Solomon. . . . I have done this because Solomon has forsaken me; he has prostrated himself before Ashtoreth goddess of the Sidonians, Kemosh god of Moab, and Milcom god of the Ammonites, and has not conformed to my ways" [1 Kings 11:31–34].

God brings down Solomon's kingdom as much for erecting altars to other gods that cannot save the people as for forgetting Yahweh's commandments; it is a fair judgment. The description of Solomon's reign tells how he made the people submit to forced labor (1 Kings 5:13–18) and how he built temples to other gods (1 Kings 11:1–8), his idolatry being closely connected to his injustices. Therefore, the just intervention of Yahweh is a defense of Yahweh's honor and simultaneously a defense of the poor among the people.

King Ahab's case is similar. As part of his politics of alliances, Ahab had permitted the worship of Baal of Tyre and made it official. Elijah denounced this official policy, for which he incurred persecution by the royal state. But the prophet's condemnation of Ahab was due not only to his persecution of the prophets of Yahweh, but also to his murder of Naboth in order to rob him of his vineyard. For both sins Elijah announced Ahab's ignominious death (1 Kings 21:17–24).

The best documented case is God's judgment on the city of Jerusalem, as foretold by several prophets. Isaiah denounced the officials of the city for being murderers, for loving bribery, and for disregarding widows and orphans, for which God would take revenge on them as his enemies (Isa. 1:21–26). Micah declared that Yahweh would turn the city into a heap of rubble because the officials sought to protect themselves through worship of Yahweh while murdering and accepting bribes (Mic. 3:9–12). Jeremiah elaborated further on the same theme:

> You steal, you murder, you commit adultery and perjury, you burn sacrifices to Baal, you run after other gods whom you have not known; then you come and stand before me in this house, which bears my name, and say, "We are safe"; safe, you think, to indulge in all these abominations [Jer. 7:8–10].

Injustice combines with idolatry as a motive for intervention by the divine judge. The inhabitants of Jerusalem had converted the house of Yahweh into a den of thieves, believing that there they would be safe from the consequences of their wrongdoing. However, Yahweh does not accept worship divorced from justice, and he judged them for their actions.

The same theme appears once again in the preachings of Jesus who, in this way, as in so many others, is the successor of the great prophets of Israel:

> O Jerusalem, Jerusalem, the city that murders the prophets and stones the messengers sent to her! How often have I longed to gather your children, as a hen gathers her brood under her wings; but you would not let me [Luke 13:34].
> Then he went to the temple and began driving out the traders, with these words: "Scripture says, 'My house shall be a house of prayer'; but you have made it a robber's cave" [Luke 19:45–46].
> When you see Jerusalem encircled by armies, then you may be sure that her destruction is near [Luke 21:20].

When Jesus proclaims the gospel of the imminent coming of the kingdom of God, he also announces the destruction of Jerusalem. In doing so, he quotes the remarkable words of Jeremiah describing how the temple had been turned into a den of thieves. Criminals who murdered the prophets and exploited the people through their businesses shrewdly used the temple as a refuge.

The Instruments of Divine Judgment

It should not be necessary to point out that historical judgments are normally carried out by human instruments. To any reader of the Bible, it soon becomes evident that most instances of divine judgment occur this way. Recent experience confirms this observation. However, there are always those who draw a line between divine judgment and human judgments. Appealing at times to the biblical passage, "Justice is mine, says the Lord, I will repay" (Rom. 12:19; Deut. 32:35; Heb. 10:30), this position states that judgment is not the province of humans, who should accept injustice with resignation while waiting for God to vindicate them.[11]

It is true that the ancient traditions of Israel exalt the power of Yahweh as a warrior (Exod. 15:3). These traditions also recognize that Yahweh is God the savior, as differentiated from the other supposed gods who are no more than sticks and stones (Isa. 45:20–21). When the Israelites tell of his feats in remote antiquity, and when they look ahead to the terrifying last judgment, they tend to exalt God's role as the warrior judge who carries out judgments unaided (as emphasized in Isa. 63:5). According to ancient Israelite history, Yahweh descended on Sodom and Gomorrah to see whether or not they were committing the crime they had been accused of. Once the veracity of the accusations was established, his judgment on those cities was a rain of fire and sulfur (Gen. 19:24–25). Likewise in the story of the plagues, when Yahweh confronted the pharaoh with a show of strength, the Hebrew slaves turned out to be no more than spectators to the miracles of God (Exod. 7–10). The same occurred in the apocalyptic visions of Yahweh's judgment of the nations in the books of Ezekiel, Daniel, and Revelation.

If divine judgment were a matter pertaining solely to God, discussion would be limited to the remote past or to the distant future. In *our* world, and in *these* times, there are no rains of fire and sulfur falling on sinful cities; nor does water turn into blood to persuade oppressors to liberate their victims. Talk of the absolute and terrifying divine judgment, uniquely in terms of distant times and places, becomes demagogic. The biblical texts are more honest.

The People of God

The principal characteristic of the founding revolution of Israel was its rejection of the state, as represented by the pharaoh in the story of the exodus. Israel began its national existence as a coalition of peasant groups who rejected the apparatus of a political state.[12] They did not need a human king, because Yahweh was their king (1 Sam. 8; Judg. 8:22–23). Nor did they have a professional army.[13] They trusted in the abilities of a free people gathered together under Yahweh's leadership:

> There is none like the God of Jeshurun
> he rides the heavens to your help,
> riding the clouds in his glory,
> who humbled the gods of old
> and subdued the ancient powers;
> who drove out the enemy before you
> and gave the word to destroy.

Israel rests in security,
the tribes of Jacob by themselves,
in a land of corn and wine
where the skies drip with dew.
Happy are you, people of Israel,
   peerless, set free;
the Lord is the shield that guards you,
the Blessed One is your glorious sword.
Your enemies come cringing to you,
and you shall trample their bodies under foot
[Deut. 33:26–29].

This song praising Yahweh for his military leadership of the Israelites in their crossing of the desert and entrance into the land of Canaan is one of the oldest poems in the Bible. It is a vivid expression of the idea of Israel and Yahweh's partnership in warfare.[14]

In this first phase of their existence, the Israelites as a people depended on their king Yahweh to fight for them ("for Yahweh fought for Israel"—Josh. 10:14). On the other hand, Israel fought "Yahweh's battles" (1 Sam. 18:17).[15] When it was necessary to fight, the free men of Israel left their plows and their wives to come to the call of the man whom Yahweh had imbued with his spirit. Following him, they went into combat, confident that they were fighting the wars of Yahweh (e.g., the battle against Midian in Judg. 6–8, and the battle against the Ammonites in 1 Sam. 11). A very ancient poem even implies that the Israelites came to Yahweh's aid (Judg. 5:23). Through the victories of its militias, Israel felt that it was an instrument of Yahweh's judgment, the just divine judge.

In addition to these wars in which the militias of Israel acted as instruments of divine judgment, there are instances when groups fulfilled the same function against sinners among the people of Israel itself. This is the case of the Levites, in the story of Exodus 32:25–29, who consecrate themselves to Yahweh by killing all the Israelites who had worshiped the golden calf built by Aaron. A similar case is that of Phinehas, who consecrated himself to Yahweh by killing with his spear an Israelite who had worshiped Baal of Peor with a Midianite woman (Num. 25:6–13).

Inspired Individuals

Among the stories of Israel, there are many in which God mandates particular individuals to carry out his judgment. Ehud of Benjamin killed the king of Moab to set off the uprising that would give Israel its freedom (Judg. 3:12–30). Samuel was commanded by Yahweh to kill Agag, king of the Amalekites, with his sword, to avenge the evil that the Amalekites had committed (1 Sam. 15:32–33). The prophet Elisha appointed Jehu to carry out Yahweh's sentence on the house of Ahab for the many crimes and acts of idolatry he had committed; Jehu's orders were to exterminate the royal family and take the place of the king of Israel (2 Kings 9:1–10). The book of Judith is a fictional work about a woman who, with God's help, kills the blasphemous and murderous general Holophernes.

In summary, although in the biblical narratives God's judgment is carried out mainly by the armed people fighting Yahweh's wars, there are many cases of individuals whom Yahweh uses as instruments of his judgment against the powerful who have oppressed the weak and committed idolatry.

Pagan Armies

There is a temptation for any religious people to simply identify its own interests with those of God. Based on the Bible, my thesis has been that the true God is the one who sees that justice is done. Perhaps the best evidence that the prophets of Israel did not view Yahweh simply as a national God is that in their prophecies Yahweh can use the armies of the enemies of Israel to carry out his just judgment:

> The Assyrian! He is the rod that I wield in my anger,
> and the staff of my wrath is in his hand.
> I send him against a godless nation,
>   I bid him march against a people who rouse my wrath,
>   to spoil and plunder at will
>   and trample them down like mud in the streets [Isa. 10:5–6].

The prophet announced that the Assyrian empire's conquest of Judah is a just judgment for the crimes that the people of Jerusalem had been committing.

One century later, the prophet Jeremiah sent this message to a meeting of ambassadors in the city of Jerusalem: "I now give all these lands to my servant Nebuchadrezzar king of Babylon" (Jer. 27:6). Several years later, when King Zedekiah was surrounded by Babylonian troops in Jerusalem, Jeremiah announced to him that Yahweh was fighting with Babylonia against the people of the city (Jer. 21:1–10).

Half a century later, Deutero-Isaiah spoke to the Jewish community in exile and announced that Yahweh would deliver all the people into the hands of the Persian armies so that Israel would be saved (Isa. 41:1–5, 45:1–7).

Jesus proclaimed that the coming of the kingdom of God would be accompanied by Roman troops marching to besiege and take possession of the city of Jerusalem (Luke 21:20–23).

UNAVOIDABLE HISTORICAL CHOICES
AND DIVINE JUDGMENT

Given the long history of religious wars, it would be easy for Christians to think that God's historical judgments recorded in the Bible were a matter of defending the true religion—that the wars of Yahweh were religious wars.

Nothing could be further from the truth. The God of the exodus is God the liberator, and his judgment on idolatry is a judgment against those who use religion to camouflage domination. The wars of Yahweh are not waged to defend religion; they almost always are waged against those who purport to be the official representatives of religion.

The pharaoh pretended to be God, and as such to have the right to over-work "his" subjects. Against this supposed god, Yahweh presented himself as the God of the enslaved: "Let my people go." To which the official god replies, "Who is Yahweh that I should obey him and let Israel go? I care nothing for Yahweh: and I tell you I will not let Israel go" (Exod. 5:2). The struggles that ensued, starting with this confrontation, surpassed by far the confines of a religious war. Soon it involved the whole population of Egypt, and in the end it demanded that all take a stand with regard to the fundamental antagonism. The plagues sent by Yahweh affected the whole population of Egypt, and soon the Egyptians saw that they would be forced to make some decisions, even if solely for their own convenience: "Those of Pharaoh's subjects who feared the word of Yahweh hurried their slaves and cattle into their houses. But those who did not take to heart the word of Yahweh left their slaves and cattle in the open" (Exod. 9:20–21). When the moment arrived when the enslaved finally left the country of their oppression, the whole population had to make a class option: either they left to follow Yahweh, the God of the Hebrews, or they stayed with the pharaoh, the god of the Egyptian system. "The Israelites set out from Rameses on the way to Succoth. . . . And with them too went a large company of every kind" (Exod. 12:37–38).

John the evangelist made a generalization about the choices that divine judgment demands of persons: "Here lies the test: the light has come into the world, but men have preferred darkness to light because their deeds were evil" (John 3:19). When faced with the struggle between Yahweh and the pharaoh, the men and women of Egypt had to choose between uniting with the now liberated slaves, or continuing under slavery and serving the pharaoh, the god who legitimized injustice.

The confrontation between Yahweh and Solomon presents an even more dramatic instance of class-based options, for Solomon imposed forced labor on the people of Israel . . . to construct a sumptuous temple for Yahweh! The official representative of the worship of Yahweh used religion to hide the reality of the oppression that he imposed on the people. In this situation, the prophet Ahijah appointed Jeroboam to lead an uprising against the king in Yahweh's name (1 Kings 11:29–39). In his oracle, Ahijah mentions Solomon's idolatry in serving the gods of his wives as the principal motive for the judgment against him. But a reading of the description of the uprising shows that it was not the ideological trappings that mobilized the people, but rather the stark reality of their oppression: "Your father laid a cruel yoke upon us; but if you will now lighten the cruel slavery he imposed on us and the heavy yoke he laid on us, we will serve you" (1 Kings 12:4). What worse slavery could there be than having to work without pay to construct a palace to

Yahweh, God the liberator? In this class confrontation, there was an option between the real Yahweh of the people and the false Yahweh of Solomon and his son.

A similar situation presented itself in the following century during the dynasty of Omri, when the monarch made an alliance with Tyre to consolidate his power against the Aramaean threat. This alliance was legitimized by the god Baal. Internally, the alliance meant an increased exploitation, because in Asian social formations of that time the state, to all intents and purposes, was the ruling class.[16]

The prophet Elijah dramatized the unavoidable choice for the king and the people: "How long will you sit on the fence? If Yahweh is God, follow him; but if Baal, then follow him" (1 Kings 18:21). The choice between Yahweh and Baal was the ideological expression of the class antagonism in which the state was pitted against the masses of Israel.

Two centuries later, in the kingdom of Judah, Jeremiah presented the unavoidable historical option once again. The reform movement carried out by Josiah had just ended, a reform praised highly by the deuteronomist editors of the books of Kings. Josiah commanded that the places of worship other than the temple in Jerusalem be destroyed, and that the feast days become occasions for massive pilgrimages to the capital. By these measures he purified the religion, and the state gained greater control over it. The reform thus entailed perfecting the mechanisms of domination.

As far as Jeremiah was concerned, the temple had turned into a den where thieves hid and took refuge. For this reason, God the liberator called on Babylon to destroy the capital and deport its leaders, thereby liberating the people. Jeremiah's advice to the masses was to lay down their arms and surrender to the invading army. Thus they saved their lives (Jer. 21:8-10). To Jeremiah, the war was a war between rulers; it was neither a war of Yahweh nor a war of the people of Yahweh. It is against this background of the historical class options involved in God's judgments that one should interpret Jesus' decisive words on the option of being with him or against him:

> Whoever then will acknowledge me before men, I will acknowledge him before my Father in heaven; and whoever disowns me before men, I will disown him before my Father in heaven. You must not think that I have come to bring peace to the earth; I have not come to bring peace, but a sword. I have come to set a man against his father, a daughter against her mother, a son's wife against her mother-in-law; and a man will find his enemies under his own roof [Matt. 10:32-36].
>
> It is easier for a camel to pass through the eye of a needle than for a rich man to enter the kingdom of God [Mark 10:25].

Jesus identified himself with the poor of Galilee. This identification brought him into confrontations with the Pharisees, whose interpretations of the law imposed heavy burdens on the poor. Later it also brought him face to face with the priests in the temple in Jerusalem. Finally, it caused him to suffer all the weight of the repressive power of the Roman state, in collusion with the Jewish authorities. The apostles testified that God was condemning the "justice" of the powerful through his resurrection. God who is the just judge, the only true God, could not take both sides. Either he was on the side of the rulers, or he was with the oppressed masses. The God of the exodus had no choice but to confront the false god of the temple. History repeats itself.

NOTES

1. Here, and in other biblical quotations in this chapter, the original Hebrew text has undergone Elohist revisions; it reads "God" [NEB: "The LORD"] where I have restored the original term "Yahweh." The early Israelite mythology held that Yahweh was the supreme God who presided over the assembly of the other gods.

2. See Martin Lange and Reinhold Iblacker, eds., *Witnesses of Hope,* William E. Jerman, trans. (Maryknoll, N.Y.: Orbis, 1981).

3. The problem of the origins of this name has been widely debated. Among other works, see William F. Albright, *From the Stone Age to Christianity* (Baltimore: Johns Hopkins University Press, 1959); H. H. Rowley, *From Joseph to Joshua: Biblical Traditions in the Light of Archaeology* (London: Oxford University Press, 1950), pp. 149–63; and Frank Moore Cross, *Canaanite Myth and Hebrew Epic* (Cambridge: Harvard University Press, 1973), pp. 3–75.

4. For a broad discussion of the concept of the ancient Near East, see H. H. Schmid, *Gerechtigkeit als Weltordnung* (Tübingen: Mohr, 1968) pp. 13–77.

5. An excellent analysis of the Israelite profession of faith is that by Gerhard von Rad, in *Gesammelte Studien zum Alten Testament* (Munich: Kaiser, 1958) Engl. trans., *The Problem of the Hexateuch and Other Essays*, E. W. Trueman Dicken, trans. (New York: McGraw-Hill, 1966), pp. 13–78.

6. The Hebrew text speaks of the oppression by Aram Naharaim, but here I accept the correction made by many other historians—to substitute Edom for Aram.

7. In recent years, studies of the apocalyptic works have proliferated. Prominent among them are those of Otto Ploger, *Theokratie und Eschatologie* (2nd ed., Neukirchen: Neukirchener Verlag, 1962), and Paul D. Hanson, *The Dawn of Apocalyptic: The Historical and Sociological Roots of Jewish Apocalyptic Eschatology* (Philadelphia: Fortress, 1975). See Jorge Pixley, "Lo apocalíptico en el Antiguo Testamento," *Revista Biblica*, 38 (1976): 297–309.

8. The most important study of this tradition is that of Duane L. Christensen, *Transformation of the War Oracle in Old Testament Prophecy* (Missoula, Mont.: Scholars Press, 1975). For topics related to Yahweh the warrior, see G. Ernest Wright, *The Old Testament and Theology* (New York: Harper, 1969), pp. 121–50, and Patrick D. Miller, Jr., *The Divine Warrior in Early Israel* (Cambridge: Harvard University Press, 1973).

9. This passage has a complicated editorial history, which is discussed competently in Christensen, *Transformation of the War Oracle,* pp. 193–207.

10. The political significance of Israel's alliance with Yahweh has given rise to many studies since the appearance of the study of George E. Mendenhall, "Covenant Forms in Israelite Tradition," *Biblical Archaeologist,* 17/3 (Sept. 1954): 50–76. The

same researcher recently reformulated his thinking on this matter in his book *The Tenth Generation: The Origins of the Biblical Traditions* (Baltimore: Johns Hopkins University Press, 1973). See also Jorge Pixley, *Reino de Dios* (Buenos Aires: La Aurora, 1977), Engl. trans., *God's Kingdom,* Donald E. Walsh, trans. (Maryknoll, N.Y.: Orbis, 1981).

11. Of the three times that this saying is found in the Bible, only in Romans is it a call to desist from vengeance—not as an eternal principle, but as prudent advice. The other two passages are threats in which the saying assures that this judgment will stand because it depends not on humans but on God.

12. See Pixley, *God's Kingdom.*

13. Jorge Pixley, "Fuerzas militares y Pueblo de Dios en la Biblia," *Christus,* 514 (1978): 12–20.

14. For an analysis of this canticle, see Frank Moore Cross, Jr., and David Noel Freedman, *Studies in Ancient Yahwistic Poetry* (Missoula, Mont.: Scholars Press, 1975), pp. 97–122, and Miller, *The Divine Warrior in Early Israel,* pp. 75–87.

15. There is an extensive bibliography on the holy war in Israel. Prominent works are those of Gerhard von Rad, *Der Heilige Krieg im alten Israel* (4th ed., Göttingen: Vandenhoeck & Ruprecht, 1965); Rudolf Smend, *Jahwekrieg und Stämmebund* (Göttingen: Vandenhoeck & Ruprecht, 1966); Fritz Stolz, *Jahwes und Israels Kriege* (Zürich: Theologischer Verlag, 1972). See also the chapters on military affairs in Roland de Vaux, *Ancient Israel: Its Life and Institutions* (New York: McGraw-Hill, 1961).

16. On the Asian mode of production, which dominated in monarchic Israel, see the studies collected by Roger Bartra, ed., *El modo de producción asiático* (México City: Era, 1969).

IV

JON SOBRINO

The Epiphany of the God of Life in Jesus of Nazareth

Theology in Latin America has rightfully stressed that the Christian should follow a liberator Jesus and should invoke a liberator God. But, unlike other geographical areas where liberation bears a direct relationship to "freedom,"[1] in Latin America it bears a relationship to something even more fundamental and original: it bears a relationship to "life," which, in its complexity, includes freedom, but is a more basic datum.

That is what I wish to analyze in this study on Jesus of Nazareth. I wish to recall attention to the most fundamental of theological realities: that God is a living God, and that God gives life. However, to do justice to the study of this fundamental truth, this Christian tautology, we must analyze its implications, concretize what is said in it in a general way, and point out the historical options and their consequences for our position. Otherwise, there would be a serious danger of mouthing a routine avowal of a God of life, but actually ignoring, manipulating, or even denying its truth.

If, as believers, we assert that the true divinity has manifested itself in Jesus, then we must distinguish that divinity from false divinities. But raising this issue—ostensibly such a simple matter—is of extreme importance owing to its theoretical and practical consequences. This is because the true concept of divinity can be arrived at on the basis of the internal coherence of the qualities that are attributed to divinity, and from the explanational capacity of a given conceptualization of God to better comprehend nature, history, or—in a word—everything.[2]

However, in pursuing this undertaking, we do not have to search for what might be the most profound coherence within God per se, because, according to the biblical tradition that was inherited and shared by Jesus, it consists in the coherence between "the true God" and "the living God," between being a living being and engendering life in history. We must not forget that the Jews did not swear by the "true" God, but rather by the "living" God.[3]

If this is so, distinctions among the various divinities who are invoked and, moreover, the distinction between true and false divinities, are not drawn in all their radicality by recourse to the principle that there is one true divinity and the others are false, but by recourse to the principle that there is a living God who gives life, and there are other divinities that are not living and do not give life. But the second part of this principle is still rather mild and exploratory; it grants too much and is not definitive. In theory, it might be claimed that false divinities neither have life nor give it; in other words, they do not have any influence on the real lives of human beings, because they themselves lack life. The conviction that false gods are *nothing* is clearly present in biblical tradition (see Ps. 10, 81; 1 Chron. 16:26).

However, the deepest aspect of the distinction between true and false divinities is found in the genesis of the false divinities. According to the Scriptures, if false divinities are nothing, then they do not exist of themselves but have been created by humans. And the creation of divinity by humans—in other words, idolatry—leads historically not just to the absence of life, but to death. This historicization of idolatry appears in two of the classic passages dealing with it (Wisd. 13–14; Rom. 1:18–32): humans become dehumanized and dehumanize others; they themselves go to their death, and give death to others. Thus the final option wherein the problem of true divinity is posed is that between the living God who gives life and the gods who are not such, and whose invocation leads to death. Hence, idolatry is not just an intellectual mistake but the choice of death and the fruits of death.

The early Christians stated the reality of the true God very well, from the positive standpoint: *gloria Dei, vivens homo* ("the glory of God—a living human being"). However, there must be added to this the tragic reality of the other side of the coin: *vanitas Dei, moriens homo* ("the denial of God—a dying human being"). The deep correlation between "God" and "life" is what makes it possible to progress in the knowledge of the true God and in the unmasking of false divinities. The God in whose name life is engendered will be the true divinity; and the worship of the true God will progress in the process of engendering life. Conversely, the gods in whose name death is produced will be false divinities; and there will be an increasing lapse into idolatry as death proliferates.

To raise the issue of true divinity in this manner is not an idle or merely academic undertaking in Latin America. What lies behind a theology of "liberation" and a theology of "captivity" is the fundamental perception that no theo-logy can be elaborated realistically apart from this basic point. In Latin America, life and death are not merely fruitful concepts for progress in the speculative understanding of God; they are brute realities. And, because ours is a continent that has not yet been exposed on a massive scale to secularizing influences, they are realities that come about through the invocation of various divinities. These divinities have been made quite explicit in a religious, and particularly in a Christian, framework, and have become implicit in secular substitutes, such as various social, economic, and political ideologies.

Hence it is not academic to question whether or not the true God in Jesus is addressed by various invocations, even when they are explicitly Christian; to determine whether the *vivens homo* or the *moriens homo* proceeds historically from various invocations. It is a matter of recovering the luminous simplicity of the profound correlation between God and life, and of understanding what is religious not as something extra added to life, but rather life as the essence of what is religious.

We are basing this analysis on Jesus of Nazareth. Associating Jesus with God is "automatic" for a Christian, by virtue of the faith and dogma of the church and, more generally, by virtue of an institutionalized Christian culture. But associating Jesus of Nazareth with the God of life deserves special attention. It is a matter of reaffirming the simplicity of something that is obvious but often distorted in the complexity of manipulations.

One need only open the gospels at the beginning and reflect on the very name "Jesus" (Luke 1:31; Matt. 1:21). The scenes in which the angel conveys the name of the child to be born are, of course, the product of theological reflection by believers, but hence all the more important in their significance: they are theological summaries of the entire background reality of Jesus of Nazareth. They are not a prologue, but an epilogue.[4]

The child's name is "Jesus," *Yeshua*, an abbreviation of *Yehoshua*, which means "Yahweh is salvation." To be sure, one would have to read the entire gospel, and even the subsequent history of the gospel—namely, the life of the church—in order to fathom the depths of what is said here. But what is fundamental has been said: since the coming of Jesus, the first and last thing that can be said about God is that God saves—to the full.

The essence of that salvation has also been well expressed in the canticles of Luke's Gospel: mercy, alliance, friendship, peace, salvation of enemies, enlightenment, and justice. If we move from a christological consideration—that is, the consideration of Jesus as a mediator of salvation—to a theo-logical consideration, we discover that the fundamental mediations of the reality of God are nothing other than life and everything that fosters it. And we also find ourselves, concretely, in the presence of the threatened poor. Here, "Yahweh is salvation" does not have any ethereal, spiritualistic, and unverifiable meaning, or a religious meaning that would apply to only this or that part of the world. It has, rather, the significance of giving real life in the presence of threats to life and the oppression of life, in the presence of the machinations of other divinities.

What we are now attempting, in analyzing the reality of God in Jesus, is only to fathom the meaning of "Jesus" and "Yahweh is salvation." It is an attempt to comprehend the mediator, Jesus of Nazareth, so as to comprehend the mediations of God's reality. They are what lend a final meaning to the person of Jesus and, for the believer, they are the final criterion for distinguishing the true God and for recovering that God from the idolatry of death.

Hence, analyzing the reality of God in Jesus deals with two meanings, both of which must be stressed: the historical meaning and the faith meaning. In the first meaning, Jesus should be considered a historical figure, parallel, for example, to the figures of Moses or Jeremiah. The attempt is to understand who God is to Jesus, and to make a historical analysis of how that God appears in the mediator and his mediations. This analysis of the historical Jesus must take into account Jesus' notions of God and, more particularly, his praxis and final destiny, which demonstrate the concrete reality of those notions.[5]

In the second meaning, Jesus should be considered a participant in the very reality of God, as his Son. This is the analysis carried out by faith. In it one grasps and accepts the basic norms set for the mediator and his mediation. In this way, the Father of Jesus, through the path of the Son and in the history begun by the Spirit, becomes God *for us*. This is not merely a matter of learning who God was to Jesus, just as one might learn who God was to Moses or Jeremiah, but rather of grasping Jesus' fundamental relationship with the Father, wherein one will learn who God is, in what sense he is a God of life, how life is given, the relationship that exists between giving life and giving one's own life, and so forth.

In this study, I shall be emphasizing the historical aspect, although in accepting in faith the fundamental normativeness of that history, we are also asserting its faith meaning. In other words, by associating ourselves today with the fundamental structure of the role of the mediator and of his mediations, the Father of Jesus will also be a reality to us as a God of life. We shall consider two points from the historical aspect: Jesus' struggle against the divinities of oppression, on which we shall expand further, and the positive significance of God to Jesus.

Because this topic, by its very nature, is quite extensive, we shall attempt to summarize the fundamental points in a series of theses. We shall describe Jesus' path in a systematic manner, illustrating it with major passages from the synoptic gospels. This is a systematic, not an exegetical, study, but based on the fundamentally historical features of the life of Jesus and what is revealed in them concerning the reality of God to him.

JESUS' STRUGGLE AGAINST THE DIVINITIES OF DEATH

The fact that Jesus was a nonconformist with respect to the religious situation of his time and his people is something both obvious and generally accepted.[6] What is important is to ascertain the extent and, in particular, the origin of that nonconformity, not only in the realm of Jesus' possible psychological or even ethical attitudes, but also in the theo-logical realm—that is, the realm of his vision of God.

To summarize briefly in advance what we mean, Jesus struggled resolutely against any type of social force which, in one way or another, mediately or immediately, dehumanized human beings, causing their death. In this respect, the human being, living and living fully, was a clear-cut criterion of Jesus' course of action.

In that struggle, Jesus discovered that the forces of death had come to be justified by explicit religious concepts of life, or those that implicitly assumed some type of divinity as absolute. Hence much of his public ministry was aimed at unmasking false divinities.

In this process, Jesus set his activity more and more within a context of position-taking, as attested to by the many controversies. His controversial involvement brought upon him many attacks and persecution and, in the end, death. The gods of oppression, against whom he had struggled, dealt him death.

Thesis 1: *To Jesus, God's archetypal plan is for human beings to have life. Life, in all its fullness, including its materiality, is God's first mediation. This insight explains Jesus' attitude toward the Jewish law (as a manifestation of God's will), his interpretation, criticism, heightening, and deepening of it. There must be "bread," as a symbol of life, for everyone.*

In order to understand Jesus' perception of the reality of God, and the subsequent struggles that it caused him, we must begin with something very fundamental: Jesus proclaimed life as the archetypal plan of God for humans; and therefore the fulfillment of life is the first mediation of the reality of God. To be sure, we shall have to observe in Jesus *how* life is engendered; but what is important now is to stress *that* God's first mediation is the engendering of life.

Even though this is so simple, it must be stressed. First, because automatically relating God's plan to the spiritual redemption of the soul is still very common. And there are two other reasons, which have their own validity, but should be brought up, at least logically, only after, not before, stating the more fundamental truth. There is every reason to stress in Latin America that a creation-oriented theology is inadequate and "ideologized," because the inertia of creation does not lead from historical sin to the engendering of life.[7] It is also very important to keep in mind, in the elaboration of the concept of true life, that it must be according to God's plan, and in alignment with the historical circumstances that govern it and make it possible.[8] But both these considerations must be integrated into God's archetypal plan for life.

We shall consider, from two vantage points, how Jesus viewed God's archetypal plan with regard to life. To Jesus, the fundamental thing about the divine law was that it was an expression of God's plan. It contains something very profound concerning God's will—profound, not because it is a law, but because it is an expression of the divine will.

We have already noted that Jesus was a nonconformist with respect to the Old Testament law, but we must probe why, and in what way. In order to understand Jesus' attitude toward the law, we must remember that in his time there was both the written Torah—that is, the Pentateuch—and the oral Torah, called Halakah, the scribes' interpretation of the written Torah.

In the gospels, Jesus talks about the written Torah as if it were something recent—because it contained the abiding laws of the will of God.[9] The passages in question relate to the observance of the second part of the decalogue (Mark 10:19 and elsewhere)—in other words, respect for human life in its various manifestations, assistance to parents in need (Mark 7:10; Matt. 15:4), and the equating of love for God with love for one's neighbor (Mark 12:28–34 and elsewhere). This archetypal will of God must be respected, because it governs the communal life—and hence *life*—of human beings.

In addition, Jesus probes deeply into at least two specific areas of the law concerned with its preservation. Insofar as marriage is concerned, there must be a return to the original decree of the true will of God (Mark 10:6; cf. Gen. 1:27), whereby man and woman become one, and whereby the man leaves his own family (Mark 10:7; cf. Gen. 2:24). And Jesus defends married life in his radicalization of adultery (Matt. 5:27 ff.), relating it to the ancient law (Exod. 20:14).

But radicalization of the law to the advantage of life can be observed when Jesus talks about life itself. The "thou shalt not kill" (Exod. 20:13) applies to anger and abuse of one's fellow human being (Matt. 5:21 ff.). Not only must life be protected, but its origins must be insured as well. The law of retaliation, which even went so far as to exact a life for a life (Exod. 21:23), is abolished (Matt. 5:38–42). In other passages, not directly concerned with the law, but rather with life, the synoptic gospels make major omissions, all aimed at demonstrating the God of life. When Jesus responds to the Baptist's emissaries (Matt. 11:2–6; Luke 7:18–28), he points out positive signs of life— the blind see, the lame walk—but he omits the continuation of Isaiah's text, on the extermination of the ruthless (Isa. 29:20). And the same type of omission occurs in the quotation from Isaiah 61:2 made by Luke when he recounts Jesus' words in the Galilean synagogue. Luke concludes with the mission of "proclaim[ing] the year of the Lord's favor" (Luke 4:19; cf. Isa. 61:2a); but he omits "a day of the vengeance of our God" (Isa. 61:2b).

From the Old Testament quotations, Jesus' reinforcement of them, and the omissions, we see how Jesus interprets the archetypal will of God as life, and how he probes deeply in that direction. In these considerations there is no attempt to extract, primarily, consequences for a Christian ethic (which must take into account a series of current historical mediations), but rather for theology, for the concept of the God of Jesus as the God of life.

That intention is more clearly evident in the criticism that Jesus makes of the Halakah—that is, of the interpretation of the law. In Mark 7:8–13 (cf.

Matt. 15:3–9), it becomes very evident that the human traditions presumably created in the name of God run counter to God's original intention. This logion involves casuistic traditions entailing disregard for the obligation to assist one's parents, even when "the support that had to be given to them was fictitiously given to the temple."[10]

And there is the more general criticism of the human traditions contrary to God's original will in the famous passage about the human being and the Sabbath (Mark 2:23–28 and parallels). Jesus tried to argue in various ways to a position contrary to that of the Halakah, citing the case of David (Mark 2:25 ff.; cf. 1 Sam. 21:2–7), who, in need, took the bread of the presence, and the action of the priests in the temple on the Sabbath (Matt. 12:5); he also argued *ad hominem*, using the same method as those who criticized him (Matt. 12:11). But the fundamental argument, based on principle, lies in the will of God itself: "The Sabbath was made for the sake of man" (Mark 2:27); the Sabbath is God's creation, not for its own sake, but for the life of the human being, in the form of rest (Deut. 5:14). As Jeremias comments, the fact that the creation of humankind took place on the sixth day, whereas the ordinance for rest was given on the seventh day, informs us that it was God's creative will that the day of rest be in the service of human beings, and for their benefit.[11]

Jesus' criticism of the Halakah and his radicalization of the Torah have ultimately, therefore, a final theo-logical motivation: lying at their source is God's archetypal will that the human being should live. The fact that the concrete details concerning what "living" means are of course devised in accordance with the various mentalities in different periods does not detract any importance from this fundamental assertion. "The will of God is not a mystery, at least insofar as it relates to brothers and sisters, and deals with love. The creator who can be placed in opposition to the creature is a false God."[12]

This fundamental understanding of God, whose archetypal will is for the life of human beings on the most elementary level, and hence on the level of making life possible, can be found throughout the gospels. We shall focus on only one element of life, but it is the symbol of all life: bread, food.

Jesus spoke more than once about bread and food. In the Lord's Prayer the petition for bread occupies an important place. Although Matthew and Luke do not coincide on all the petitions, both include this one, and as the first petition made in the plural, aimed at expressing the best desires of and for human beings. We are already familiar with the discussion about the meaning of *epiousion* ([bread] sufficient for the day—Matt. 6:11; Luke 11:3), which can mean "what is necessary for daily existence," or "for the future, for tomorrow."[13] On the basis of this latter meaning, one could spiritualize the petition for bread in the sense of an expectation of the bread of life. But even Jeremias who, for linguistic reasons, upholds the latter meaning, warns that "it would be a crass misunderstanding were we to think that this amounted to a spiritualization of the petition for bread."[14] The bread of life and earthly bread are not opposed. It is right for us to ask that the bread of life come now, in the midst of our poverty-stricken existence.

We must recall again the passage concerning the grain plucked on the Sabbath.[15] In the final versions, the incident occurred on the Sabbath, which Jesus' disciples apparently broke by plucking the ears of grain. This was followed by Jesus' argument with the Pharisees. It is the intention of these later versions to show that Jesus was the master of the Sabbath and (as we have observed) that the Sabbath is for the sake of humankind, and therefore religious laws must be humanized.

But underlying this controversy there is something even more fundamental than the proper use of what is religious. In the earliest account, the discussion is not about the Sabbath and its observance. When Jesus argued about what David did—eating the bread of the covenant—he did not mention the matter of the Sabbath at all. The question about David was not that he had taken bread on the Sabbath, but rather merely that he had taken and eaten it. What the Pharisees objected to was the fact that the disciples had picked and eaten grain from someone else's field; not the fact that they had done so on the Sabbath. It is a matter of a strictly human, not a religious, problem: the disciples' hunger and their taking another's food to satisfy it. And what Jesus is asserting, in defending them, is that, "in the case of need (here, the disciples' hunger), every law must give way to a vital need."[16]

What is at stake in this controversy is not primarily a religious problem, but rather a human problem: the disciples' hunger. And what Jesus taught was that there cannot be a law that prohibits the satisfaction of basic needs of life, whether it be on the Sabbath or not. Such a law could not be a mediation of the will of a God of life. Hunger could not be assuaged in the name of a god that would decree such laws. The logion of the Sabbath would become generalized later, for the human being cannot be dehumanized in the name of religious laws. But it is important to stress the primarily material aspect of this controversy, because it explains more clearly the primary relationship between God and life.

Bread and food are, thus, primary mediations of the reality of God. This is why Jesus favors and defends them; this is why he eats with publicans (Mark 2:15–17 and parallels). This is why he pays little heed to the ritual ablutions before eating (Mark 7:2–5; Matt. 15:2), the former being human institutions and the latter a divine institution. This is why the miracle of the multiplication of loaves (apart from the christological and liturgical intention of the evangelists) emphasizes that those who are hungry must be fed, and stresses that they ate and had their fill (Mark 6:30–44 and parallels; Mark 8:1–10; Matt. 15:32–39). This is why the one who feeds the hungry has encountered both man and the Son of man (Matt. 25:35–40).

For Jesus the first mediation of the reality of God is life. God is the God of life, and is manifested through life. This is why we must ask for bread and why we may pluck grain from another's field in order to satisfy hunger. From the foundational horizon of the archetypal will of God, Jesus observes that

God is a God of life, and fosters the life of human beings. This is certainly a primary and generic horizon, which was to become historicized and concrete in the life of Jesus himself. Life would appear as a reconquest of life in the presence of oppression and death; giving life would be salvation, redemption, liberation; life would have to be rescued from death, death itself yielding life. But, logically and in principle, one can understand the God of Jesus only from the positive horizon of life. God is a fathomless mystery, but our attempts to conceptualize him dare not allow this basic truth to be lost sight of.

However, what is paradoxical (paradoxical in principle, though of frequent occurrence in history) is the fact that, when Jesus announced this God of life and historicized the announcement, then controversy, persecution, and death itself emerged. The divinities of death did not allow the one making this proclamation to go unpunished—a proclamation that was a response to the innermost essence and deepest desire of every human being.

Thesis 2: *The eschatological horizon of Jesus' mission is the kingdom of God, a kingdom of life for everyone. But, in order to make it a reality, there must be participation in it by those who for centuries have been deprived of life in its various forms: the poor and the oppressed. Hence Jesus' proclamation is partial, and the God of life appears only partially to those deprived of life.*

Jesus began his public ministry by announcing the good news of the kingdom of God. In its ultimate essence, that kingdom is nothing but full life in which everyone can participate. However, the overall content of the preaching of the kingdom of God does not sufficiently explain what is meant by the God of life, or why Jesus, who announced "good" news, came to such a dire end in his mission.

The reason lies in the fact that then, as now, "kingdom of God" was a symbol of fullness, but open to different interpretations. If that fullness referred only to the universal scope of the intended hearers of the message, then dire consequences would not have resulted for Jesus—but the essence of the revelation of the kingdom would have been misunderstood.

And it is not that the universality of the hearers is an incorrect notion per se. There are in the gospels sufficient symbols of that universality in Jesus' contacts with Martha, Mary, Lazarus, Zaccheus, the Roman centurion, Nicodemus, and others. This does not mean that the universality of the hearers should be ignored on the basis of the gospel. What it means is that such a view is not the primary or the most correct one for understanding the fullness of life of the God of Jesus.

The most correct view is gained rather from a different standpoint. Jesus announced the kingdom of God to the poor; he announced life to those who had it least. That God is God must undergo a historical verification, which is nothing but the giving of life to those deprived of it for centuries: the poor and oppressed majorities.[17] And therefore, together with the announcement of the coming of the kingdom of God (Mark 1:15; Matt. 4:17), the poor appear as its privileged recipients (Matt. 5:3; Luke 6:20).

In order to highlight the true locus of the relationship between God and life, Jesus, like the prophets before him, deliberately pointed out a partial locus, that of the poor deprived of life. We shall illustrate this, which can be found in many places throughout the gospels, with the passage from the first preaching, in the Nazareth synagogue (Luke 4:16-44).[18] This passage is of unique importance, because it introduces the program of Jesus' public ministry according to Luke. The fact that Luke puts it at the beginning of Jesus' public activity, changing the sequence of Mark (where it follows later, 8:22-9:9), and the fundamental content of that passage in particular, attest to its vital significance. In it, there appear Jesus' prophetic anointing (v. 18a), the determination of his mission as an evangelizer (vv. 18 and 43), the content of that mission as the good news of the kingdom (v. 43), the urgent need for carrying it out (v. 43), and its fulfillment in the present (v. 21).

This scene introduces Jesus the mediator, the mediation that must be performed, and the recipients of that mediation. The central point of the scene is Luke 4:18: "He has sent me to announce good news to the poor." Let us observe just two important aspects of it. The content of that good news is, as has already been noted, the kingdom of God (4:18 and 4:43). The special significance of his evangelizing is, through the parallelism with Isaiah 61: 1ff., "not only the proclamation, but also the fulfillment of the message that was proclaimed. . . ."[19] "That news will be good only insofar as it achieves the liberation of the oppressed."[20]

Who the poor and oppressed are can be inferred from the meaning of poor in Isaiah 61:1-2a and 58:6, quoted in Luke 4:18 ff. In Isaiah the poor are all those who are bent under any type of yoke. The mission of the anointed one of Yahweh is that of total liberation, which includes, and very specifically, liberation from material poverty. When Luke quotes Isaiah in those passages, he makes some changes that help to better understand his own text. On the one hand, he omits the expression "to bind up the broken-hearted," and replaces it with "set free those who have been crushed," from Isaiah 58:6. He thereby precludes the legitimation of a spiritualizing interpretation, and underscores the material aspect that is an essential factor in total liberation. On the other hand, as has been commented on before, he omits the second part of Isaiah 61:2, "a day of the vengeance of our God," and concludes with the proclamation of the year of God's favor, "thus presenting salvation in Jesus as the jubilee year in which the liberation of the enslaved takes place."[21]

In the parallel passages from Luke 7:22-23 and Matthew 11:4-6, where John the Baptist's emissaries are given the same signs, there is also an indication, and in the same manner, of who the poor are and what happens to them when the God of the kingdom approaches them. What happens is that they recover life, because, among the ancients, even verbally, these persons—the blind, lame, lepers, and others—are compared with the dead. "The status of such persons, according to the thinking of that time, could no longer be called life. They are virtually dead. . . . Now those who resembled the dead are brought to life."[22]

According to Jeremias, therein lies the innovation of Jesus' announcement of the good news, in which the poor return to life. And therefore, whatever else the fullness of life may include, "the material liberation from any type of oppression, resulting from injustice, is associated with the biblical message as an essential religious value."[23]

Jesus' vision of God obliged him to preach and to act on behalf of life, and its fullness. In these passages the fullness of life is not measured in view of a life already well established, and then noticing what is lacking to its fullness, but rather starting with the conviction that there can be life in an absolute form—that is, the awareness of fullness comes first. To make this consideration realistic, Jesus, like the prophets, concentrated on those areas where the life of individuals is most precarious, most threatened, or even nonexistent. And for that reason the program for his mission is partial, and announces a God of partial life to those who lack it on the most elementary levels.[24] Hence, apart from that locus, any announcement of a God of life cannot but be idealistic.

And that partiality is what caused scandal (Matt. 11:6; Luke 7:23).[25] The fact that life is offered to the poor, and that God's salvation is directed to them, and furthermore "only to the poor,"[26] is what caused scandal among powerful minorities, and what brought about the persecution of Jesus. But on the other hand, it is only in God's partiality toward those without life that there is a guarantee that God is a God of life for everyone.

Thesis 3: *Lack of life is not caused only by the limitations of what has been created, but rather by the free will of minority groups, who use their power for their own interests, and against others. That is why Jesus anathematizes the rich, the Pharisees, the scribes, the priests, and the rulers: because they deprive the majorities of life, in its various forms.*

Jesus points out that the absence of life and its annihilation, in addition to its obvious natural limitations, are the result of human sin. Hence his reproaches and anathemas. These are abundant in the synoptic gospels, and may be regarded from different standpoints: either as an unmasking of false values and hypocritical attitudes among those who are anathematized, or as an unmasking of deprivations in others' lives. The second viewpoint is of direct concern to us, although we do not question the reality of the first. It is not merely a matter of observing how Jesus anathematizes individuals for their direct relationship with wealth, power, knowledge, and the like, but furthermore the type of oppressive relationship that is established with other persons in that way. Let us note a few clear-cut examples of anathemas and reproaches from this twofold standpoint.

"Alas for you who are rich" is the comment in the first denunciation (Luke 6:24). There is here an absolute condemnation of wealth, primarily because of its results for the rich person per se: "You have had your time of happiness" (Luke 6:24), and it will do that person no good on the day of judgment (Luke 12:13–21). But, in particular, there is condemnation of the intrinsic root of the evil of wealth, which is relative: wealth is unjust. The moderate Jerusalem Bible comments: "It is called 'unjust,' not only because those who possess it have acquired it by evil means, but also, in a more general way, because there is some injustice in the origin of nearly all fortunes."[27] Hence wealth is not merely the possession of goods, which makes it extremely difficult to open one's heart to God (Matt. 19:13–26; Mark 10:23–27), but rather an accumulation of goods, which deprives others of the goods to which they are entitled. For that reason, the rich are the oppressors of the poor, according to Luke. Thus the conversion of Zaccheus is not praised only because of the giving away of riches, but also because of the proper distribution of them to others (Luke 19:8). Therefore, the rich are "oppressors of the poor,"[28] and states of poverty are "caused by the oppressor."[29] The rich deprive others of what is necessary for life, and that is why Jesus anathematized them.

Chapters 23 of Matthew and 11 of Luke contain the famous anathemas against the scribes and Pharisees. In the current literary format, these anathemas are preceded by some comments that are also shared by Mark (10:43b and 16:37b–40) on religious hypocrisy and the vanity of the scribes and Pharisees. The latter bear the external signs of compliance with God's will, keep their phylacteries wide and their cloak fringes long, seek the first seats at banquets and in the synagogues (Matt. 23:5–7; Luke 20:46, 11:43; Mark 12:38–39). They seek thereby to remind others of God's will, and to appear as the ones best complying with it.

In view of this, Jesus wants to caution his disciples against the casuistry of the law and against the hypocrisy of the scribes and Pharisees. But, in doing so, he condemns not only their false subjective attitude, but also the objective oppressive consequences for others. "Beware of . . . [those] who eat up the property of widows, while they say long prayers for appearance' sake" (Mark 12:38–40). And, more generally, Jesus condemns them because they "load men with intolerable burdens, and will not put a single finger to the load" (Luke 11:46).

What is particularly emphasized in these passages is the conceit and hypocrisy of the scribes and Pharisees. That hypocrisy evokes severe judgment from Jesus: "They will receive the severest sentence" (Mark 12:40; Luke 20:47). But the fundamental flaw was not the overweening malice of their hypocritical subjective attitude, but rather the fact of oppressing others, imposing heavy burdens on them and taking over the property of widows. That is the fundamental sin, and the fundamental negation of the will of God, subjecting it to hypocritical pride.

The anathemas pronounced against the scribes and Pharisees (Matt. 23:13–36; Luke 11:37–54) concur fittingly with these rebukes. Both lists have much in common. Therefore, we shall arrange them as Boismard has done,[30] starting with a list of the anathemas in Luke. The first three anathemas are against the Pharisees, whose hypocrisy is thrown directly in their faces:

> You clean the outside of cup and plate; but inside you there is nothing but greed and wickedness [Luke 11:39].
> You pay tithes of mint and rue and every garden-herb, but have no care for justice [11:42].
> You are like unmarked graves [11:44, explaining the contrast with Matt. 23:27: "covered with whitewash; . . . but inside they are full of dead men's bones and all kinds of filth"].

The internal/external contradiction—that is, the hypocrisy—of the Pharisees is clearly present in these implications. But, once again, what at bottom makes these attitudes hypocritical are the objective consequences to others stemming from the Pharisees' internal wickedness. Their hearts are filled with greed and wickedness (Luke 11:39; Matt. 23:35); they have no care for justice and the love of God, and that is precisely what must be "practiced" (Luke 11:42; Matt. 23:23). The solution to the hypocritical inconsistency between the external and the internal lies not only in internal change, but in external objectivity: "Let what is in the cup be given in charity, and all is clean" (Luke 11:41).

The anathemas against the scribes do not explain their false internal attitude so much as they demonstrate directly their objective and oppressive wickedness, based on the consequences of their actions:

> You load men with intolerable burdens, and will not put a single finger to the load [Luke 11:46].
> You build the tombs of the prophets whom your fathers murdered, and so testify that you approve of the deeds your fathers did [11:47–48].
> You have taken away the key of knowledge. You did not go in yourselves, and those who were on their way in, you stopped [11:52].

There appears clearly here not only the hypocrisy, but the direct oppression of the people by the scribes. Their malice is disclosed clearly, whether or not hypocrisy is present. Others suffer and are deprived of their rights by what the scribes do.

In the final additions made to Matthew's text there is also repeated a phrase addressed to the scribes and Pharisees: "Blind fools" (Matt. 23:17; cf. 23:29, 26).[31]

They travel over sea and land to win one convert; and when they have gained one, they make that person fit for hell (Matt. 23:15). This is the stress placed on the intrinsic wickedness of the scribes and Pharisees: not only are they headed in the wrong direction, but they also misguide others and lead them into danger.

Hence, whatever the pride and hypocrisy of the scribes and Pharisees may be, the anathemas focus on the objective reality of the deprivation of others of something important, and of oppression. They commit injustice against them, they rob them, they impose intolerable burdens on them, they deprive them of knowledge and of entry into the kingdom, they lead them along a dangerous path, and they kill the prophets. Jesus condemns conceit and hypocrisy because of the evil that they entail; but he also condemns the objective basis that makes such hypocrisy possible: depriving human beings of life in the various spheres of their existence.

Jesus' castigation of the priests reaches a peak in the expulsion from the temple (Mark 11:15-59 and parallels). These narratives, plus those that follow, on Jesus' authority (Mark 11:27-33 and parallels), have been highly theologized in christology and in Jewish eschatology—that is, the future of the Jewish people as the chosen people. But the original core of the narrative appears to be in Mark 11:15-16.[32] The priests have committed the horrendous crime of defiling the essence of the temple. But, once again, their crime does not entail a religious wickedness alone, but a human one as well. "The priests have converted the temple into a den of thieves, a den from which evildoers continually emerge to commit their evil deeds. The priests misuse their vocation, which is to conduct worship for the glory of God. Instead, they engage in business, and accrue profits."[33] Although not in the form of anathemas, these harsh rebukes by Jesus have the same logical structure: fellow human beings are being oppressed in areas of their human existence, and with the overbearing wickedness that makes it possible in the name of an institution willed by God.

Finally, Jesus rebukes "those with political power," saying that "the recognized rulers lord it over their subjects, and their great men make them feel the weight of authority" (Mark 10:42 and elsewhere). This is certainly a general rebuke, unlike the other, detailed ones, although it is confirmed by Jesus' harsh words about the ruler Herod (Luke 13:32). Once again, the point lies in the relational aspect of political power. Regardless of the fact that, in a given era, power may have grandeur and honor, and even God's blessing, Jesus condemns a power whose historical consequences are oppression and deprivation of life—here, in the realm of political rights.

When we scan Jesus' anathemas and rebukes, we see that they contain very sharp attacks on the individuals at whom they are directed, either because they have upset the scale of values, in the case of possessions and power, or because, overturning the values of religion and knowledge, they hypocritically boast of it. But there is something more profound underlying these anathemas. Jesus made it clear that the anathematized were dehumanized themselves—something that cannot take place without dehumanizing others. So, in his anathemas, he does not use merely formal logic, analyzing how certain attitudes dehumanize the human being, but a material logic as well, observing how human beings become dehumanized by dehumanizing others.

The understanding that Jesus had of the God of life lies at the root of this logic. What makes the attitude and actions of the anathematized intolerable is the fact that they deprive others of life, whether of life itself, or of the possessions, freedoms, knowledge, and the like, necessary for life. It is important to stress this, so as not to confuse two areas. As we shall see later, Jesus will anathematize the dehumanization of others in the name of God, under the invocation of God. That is the sin against religion. But at the root of this sin is the fact that it is a human being who is dehumanized; it is a sin against humanity. To deprive the human being of life in the name of God is a double evil, because God is the God of life. This observation is important, so as not to resolve the issue of religious hypocrisy on the basis of its internal aspect alone. Because it would be of little use not to be hypocritical internally, if one were to continue oppressing others externally. The greatest disharmony with the God of life lies precisely here.

Thesis 4: *Jesus' understanding of a God of life comes into conflict with the private interests of those who do not want to give life to others. This explains the controversies that Jesus entered into. Underlying the more explicit issue of the law and its casuistry are problems relating to the lives of human beings.*

Jesus' controversies also touch on the issue of the God of life, which, by that very reason (ironically but tragically), is seen to be controversial. Because of their value as exemplars, we shall concentrate on the five famous controversies that Mark puts almost at the beginning of Jesus' public activity (Mark 2:1-3; cf. Luke 5:17 and 6:11), and Matthew divides into two sections (Matt. 9:1-17 and 12:1-4). The five controversies have to do with: (1) the cure and pardon of the paralytic; (2) Jesus' dining with public sinners; (3) the question about fasting; (4) the grain picked on the Sabbath; and (5) the cure of the man with the withered hand.[34]

In their final version, these five accounts have the same literary structure of a controversy. But it is fitting to divide them into two groups, so as to observe just what the controversy and its theo-logical dimension are. Controversies 2, 3, and 4 have several features in common. Incidents are recorded that, by their very nature and in the society of that time, had controversy inherent in them: eating with sinners, not fasting when others do so, taking what belongs to another. This is the main core of the controversy. What is involved here is the breaking of accepted social norms: fasting, respecting private property, and avoiding the company of sinners. To break such norms was unacceptable, and this is why Jesus and his disciples were accused of wrongdoing.

The other two accounts (1 and 5), at their core, relate a miracle—something that, of itself, should not have triggered a controversy. In their final written form, however, they are made controversial by additional circumstances. In the first account, Jesus declares that he has the power not only to heal, but also to forgive sins. In the fifth account, Jesus works a cure on the Sabbath. Therefore, in these accounts the controversy is not based on the social event described—unlike the other three—but rather a social event is given a religious dimension. The account of the grain-plucking takes on a controversial significance when the change is made from the original incident of simply taking another's property in a case of need to a consideration that the incident took place on a Sabbath.

The importance of this analysis, as regards Jesus' understanding of God, is twofold. In the first place, Jesus defends the human and historical mediations of whatever is according to the will of the God of life. To the society of his time, these mediations could be of two types: the socially accepted type, such as cures, or the socially unaccepted type, such as friendly relations with publicans, not fasting, and taking what is necessary for life even though it belongs to someone else. The latter type is what caused controversy, even before it was formulated in religious terms. And, in defending his "antisocial" attitude, Jesus not only provoked controversy, but also declared that God is, before all else, the God of life.

In the second place, when a controversy is interpreted from a religious standpoint, it becomes clear in the synoptic gospels that Jesus is giving a religious explanation of his understanding of the God of life, defending it against those who attack him and condemning their understanding of God. This appears in various ways in the five accounts, depending on the nature of the attacks and on the theological perspectives of the authors.

Confining ourselves to a few key points, we can say that Jesus makes use of a controversy in order to present a new image of the proper relationship between the human being and the religious realm. Religion is not worship alone, but a worship that is at least compatible with, and positively contributive to, giving life to human beings. And therefore religion that prevents the furtherance of life is false. This is proven by the reference in Matthew to Hosea 6:6 in connection with a meal shared with publicans (Matt. 9:13) and the plucked grain (Matt. 12:7). And it is consistent with Matthew's view of Christian worship (Matt. 5:23).

This appears more clearly in Jesus' famous statement about the Sabbath. Jesus does good works on the Sabbath; he cures the crippled (Luke 13: 10–17). In defending himself, he sometimes argues *ad hominem* (Luke 14:1–6); but he argues mainly on principle: the Sabbath is for the human being, not the human being for the Sabbath (Mark 2:27). The same formula can be framed in terms of what we might call the rights of God and the rights of humans. In the Jewish mentality of the time, the Sabbath served as the day of God's celebration with the angels in heaven, and the Jewish people, by reason of its divine election, was allowed to participate in that celebration. Hence it appeared to them that nothing could be allowed to impede or threaten the divine celebration.[35] However, Jesus claims that the rights of God cannot be in contradiction to the rights of humans, when these rights are what foster human life.

In the narratives of the synoptic gospels, the immediate justification for Jesus' stand is *christo*logical: "The Son of Man is sovereign over the Sabbath'' (Matt. 12:8 and elsewhere). But the ultimate justification is *theo*logical, as stated in the quotation from Hosea, and in what we have noted previously. Any alleged manifestation of God's will that runs counter to the real life of human beings is an outright denial of the most profound reality of God.

This is how the two levels of the controversy—the human and the religious—are combined; and hence it is possible to make a human controversy the substratum of a religious controversy. The controversies do not essentially involve different religious explanations of the reality of God, which would also entail different legal requirements. They involve different understandings of the reality of God, which will naturally come out in religious explanations. And, because what one understands as the reality of God can differ, from person to person, discussion therefore emerges. And, because the realities compared are not only different but conflicting, controversy emerges.

> **Thesis 5:** *Jesus knows that human beings have not only different, but conflicting, notions of God, and that their invocation causes life and death; humans invoke divinities even when death is the result. Thus, Jesus not only explains the true concept of divinity, but also exposes the use made of false concepts of divinity to oppress human beings and deprive them of life.*

Jesus realizes that there are different, and even opposing, concepts of God; but he also realizes that actions contrary to the reality and the will of God are justified in the name of God. Therefore, his controversies not only affirm and clarify the true reality of God, but also expose the religious justification of human oppression.

The passage in Mark 7:1–23 (cf. Matt. 15:1–20) is the classic example in the synoptic gospels. The occasion is an undramatic incident: his disciples ate without washing their hands—in other words, they ate with impure hands (Mark 7:2)—thereby breaking the ancient tradition on which the Pharisees insisted. Such traditions abounded, particularly regulations for legal purity. And according to the synoptic gospels, Jesus and his disciples broke them unabashedly (Mark 1:41, 5:41; Luke 7:14, 11:38).

When attacked by the Pharisees, Jesus gives two types of response. The first relates to the value of human traditions (Mark 7:6–13), and the second to true purity (Mark 7:14–23). In both responses, not only is the true doctrine pointed out, but opposed traditions are also exposed as being a means of ignoring the true will of God, and thus of oppressing one's neighbor in their name.

In the first case, Jesus exposes how humans make their own traditions, and their legislation "is in contradiction with God's commandment."[36] The contradiction can be seen clearly in its content: parents do not receive the assistance they need from their children—in the name of religious legislation exacted by humans (Mark 7:12). The word of God is thereby abrogated (Mark

THE EPIPHANY OF THE GOD OF LIFE

7:13) and the "rights of one's neighbor are violated."[37] What Jesus repudiates in these remarks is not that humans explain and interpret the word of God, or the methods that they use for this purpose. What he repudiates is the "explanation itself,"[38] for the word of God is abrogated by it.

As regards legal purity, Jesus explicitly responds to the issue of what is pure and impure. The fundamental assertion is that what comes from outside does not make persons impure (Mark 7:15). Therefore, religious traditions that arbitrarily assign a criterion of the will of God to what is external (eating without washing one's hands, touching a corpse or a leper) are false. And this is a thundering assertion, because it meant "putting in doubt the suppositions of the entire ancient liturgical ritual, including everything involved in its practice of sacrifice and expiation."[39] "There is invalidated here the entire Old Testament legislation, with its distinctions between animals and meals that are pure or impure."[40]

The positive aspect of Jesus' teaching is clear. The criterion of wickedness is not found in regulations external to the human being, but in what originates from within the human being. And evil deeds are evil because they run counter to the will of God: "acts of fornication, of theft, murder, adultery, ruthless greed, and malice; fraud, indecency, envy, slander, arrogance, and folly" (Mark 7:22).

What the entire passage from Mark shows is that the Pharisees dealt wrongly with the issue of the true will of God, locating it in laws and traditions merely because they had been declared obligatory. And, in particular, they used—misused—that issue in order to conceal evil acts against a neighbor (Mark 7:22) and to positively oppress a neighbor (Mark 7:12). Hence Jesus' exposé of the spurious use made of legislation as a presumed mediation of God's will, in order to act counter to the true will of God.

The law, as a human mechanism, cannot survive in independence of the originative will of God. "In the exposition that Jesus makes of this for us, God's will is crystal clear: there is nothing incomprehensible about it."[41] What human beings had done was to make it artificially complex and artificially difficult. In this way the law seemed to mirror the incomprehensibility of God. But human beings, out of self-interest, used the law's contrived difficulty and complexity in order not to do what God truly wanted. And that is what Jesus exposed. In the name of that spurious use of the law, it is possible, and may even be thought "obligatory" in practice, to fail to take care of one's parents in need, and it is possible to conceal internal impurity with external purity.

In the matter of what the chief commandment is, Jesus made another illuminating clarification (Matt. 22:34–40 and elsewhere), although not in such an explicit manner. In his time it was not an idle question; it was discussed assiduously.[42] Moreover, at that time also "there was no lack of declarations explicitly forbidding the making of a distinction between what is primary [in the law] and what is secondary."[43] Inasmuch as the entire law came from God, no human discriminations were allowable.

The danger of manipulation contained in this idea is obvious. Hence,

Jesus' response is all the more important. In the first place, Jesus prioritizes the commandments, and hence the will of God. Not everything is equal: some things are more urgent than others. But, secondly and more importantly, Jesus sets forth the first commandment (love of God) in such a way that humans cannot have recourse to it in order to disregard clear-cut obligations to fellow humans, which is an innate tendency amply documented in history.

The synoptic gospels present this aspect of Jesus' teaching in various ways.[44] In Mark, Jesus answers the scribe's question about the first commandment by adding to it the second commandment, regarding love for one's neighbor, and concluding: "There is no other commandment greater than these" (Mark 12:31). By using the plural, "these," he therefore includes love for one's neighbor in "the great commandment." In Matthew, Jesus responds in the same way, adding that the second commandment is "like" the first (Matt. 22:39). In Luke, the correct response is given by the lawyer himself who questioned Jesus in order to test him, and he puts the two commandments together (Luke 10:27). But, immediately thereafter, Luke puts in Jesus' mouth the parable of the good Samaritan, so that there would be no doubt about who one's neighbor is, and in order to expose those who passed for experts with respect to the first commandment—the priests and Levites (Luke 10:31 ff.)—but who did not keep the second commandment.

In his teaching on the love for God, Jesus touches on the human tendency to manipulate not only certain provisions of the law, but even the greatest and most sacred of commandments—love for God—precisely to disregard the express will of the God whom one must love: love for one's neighbor. Hence, Jesus exposes the use of religious law because in its name disregard is shown for what God, in fact, wills for human life.

Thesis 6: *The defense that Jesus makes of human life as a fundamental mediation of the reality of God causes others—generally the leaders of the Jewish people, who, objectively, invoke other divinities—to reproach and persecute him, the mediator. Alternative divinities, reflected in the plurality of mediations, are also clearly reflected in the wish for alternative mediators.*

As we have observed, Jesus' anathemas, controversies, and exposés have an objective purpose. It is, essentially, to elucidate the true reality of God and God's defense of human life. However, it is both natural and understandable that the objective controversy also becomes a subjective controversy—in other words, that personal attacks and, in this instance, the persecution of Jesus ensue. And the attack on him increasingly assumes the features of an exclusionary alternative. The persecution of Jesus aims at eliminating him.

The Synoptic Gospels. The dimension of basic alternatives runs through the synoptic gospels in various forms. We cannot analyze it in full here, but only enumerate some of its formulations as prototypes. On the anthropological level, it is affirmed in the Beatitudes and the denunciations (Luke

6:20–26), and in saving and losing life (Mark 8:35 and parallels). On the christological level, it is asserted that one must be with Jesus or against him (Matt. 12:30). And on the level of divinity—the most important one for our purposes—the alternative is expressed clearly: "No servant can be slave to two masters; for either he will hate the first and love the second, or he will be devoted to the first and think nothing of the second. You cannot serve God and Money" (Matt. 6:24; Luke 16:13).

Jesus probably did not present that alternative in all its radical essence at the outset, although in the programed announcement of the kingdom belief in the good news is linked with repentance (Mark 1:15; Matt. 4:17). But the depth and radical essence of the alternative at stake—the fact that human beings simply do not accept God, and manipulate him in order to serve another god—is disclosed gradually.

Jesus' determination to present God as an alternative, and an exclusive alternative, becomes intensified concurrently with the fate that he himself experiences upon announcing the true God who cherishes human life. It has been rightly claimed that *temptation* was the atmosphere in which all of Jesus' life took place, and that it related to true messianism—that is, to the true will of God concerning him.[45] But it is also a fact that *persecution* was the atmosphere in which his mission took place, at least as of a certain date. Although it is difficult to determine the various periods of Jesus' life exactly,[46] "the gospels are faithful to history when they state that successes and failures, sympathy and hostility, were the fabric of Jesus' life from the beginning."[47]

From his preaching and healing ministry, Jesus embarked on controversies, something that he did not seek out in the first stage of his mission.[48] His interpretation of the will of God, his closeness to those officially rejected by society, and his forgiveness of sins made him suspect. His extraordinary healing powers evoked a clear expression of that suspicion, and explicitly on the theological level: "If his critics were not willing to admit that the 'finger of God' was evident here, then there was only one alternative remaining for them. . . . Hence the conclusion: 'He casts out devils by Beelzebub, prince of devils'; in other words, he was a sorcerer."[49] This is the fundamental issue: whether or not the finger of God is present in the divinity mediation represented by Jesus. Because the leaders of the people did not believe in the mediation, they therefore persecuted the mediator.

A brief summary of the provocation and persecution of Jesus, to the time of Judas's betrayal, will be helpful to our purposes. Luke puts the first serious attack against Jesus nearly at the beginning of his mission in Nazareth, where he refused to repeat the wonders that he had worked in Capernaum. The conclusion of the passage is that his infuriated fellow townsmen threw him out of the town and tried to hurl him over a cliff (Luke 4:28 ff.).

This rather local controversy was compounded, from nearly the beginning of the gospel, by persecution, not because of village issues, but because of his interpretation of the will of God. After the fifth controversy in Mark, when

Jesus cured the man with the withered hand on the Sabbath, the Pharisees conspired with the Herodians to find a way to eliminate him (Mark 3:6 and parallels). And they were already lying in wait to see whether he would work cures on the Sabbath, so that they could bring charges against him (Mark 3:2 and parallels).

During the period preceding his entry into Jerusalem, it is evident that many of the questions directed at him by the scribes and Pharisees were designed to tempt him, to put him to the test. They hoped to seize upon some remark out of which they could make an accusation against him (Matt. 19:3; Luke 10:25, 11:16, 53–54, 14:1). In Luke 13:31, the Pharisees themselves warn Jesus that Herod wants to kill him—although their intention was perhaps just to have Jesus leave the place where he was.

Once he was in Jerusalem, and even before Judas's betrayal, it is obvious that the malicious plots against Jesus were mounting, and that the leaders wanted to put an end to him. All three synoptic gospels present five scenes in which Jesus is in danger. In the passage concerning the tribute to Caesar (Mark 12:13–17, and parallels), the Pharisees and Herodians are sent to "trap him with a question." In the passage on the discussion about the resurrection of the dead (Mark 12:19–23 and elsewhere), the Sadducees try to discredit him. The passage on the expulsion of the moneylenders from the temple (Mark 11:15–19 and parallels) concludes with the deliberations of the high priests and scribes to kill him, although they feared the people. The passage from the parable on the murderous vintners (Mark 12:1–12 and parallels) also concludes with the intention to arrest him, because the chief priests and others realized that the parable was aimed against them; but they were afraid of the people. Finally, Matthew and Mark, who introduce into this scene (Mark 12:28–34; Matt. 22:34–35) the discussion of the first commandment, also present the incident as an insidious temptation of Jesus by the Pharisees. All these passages conclude with a summary, preceding Judas's betrayal: "The chief priests and the doctors of the law were trying to devise some cunning plan to seize him and put him to death" (Mark 14:1 and parallels).

St. John's Gospel. We shall now summarize what St. John's Gospel contributes to the understanding of the persecution of Jesus throughout his public life, noting that, for theological reasons, John makes the Jewish people as a whole more responsible for it, and not merely their leaders, as the synoptic gospels do.

From the very beginning of his first stay in Jerusalem, Jesus distrusted "the Jews" (2:24). During his second stay in Jerusalem, "it was works of this kind done on the Sabbath that stirred the Jews to persecute Jesus. . . . This made the Jews still more determined to kill him, because he was not only breaking the Sabbath, but, by calling God his own Father, he claimed equality with God" (5:16, 18). When the Feast of Tabernacles was approaching, "Jesus went about in Galilee. He wished to avoid Judea because the Jews were looking for a chance to kill him" (7:1). They were asking, "Where is he?'' (7:11). And, in the temple, Jesus asked them, "Why are you trying to kill me?'' (7:19). Some Jerusalemites remarked, "Is not this the man they want to put to death?'' (7:25). "At this they tried to seize him, but no one laid a hand on him because his appointed hour had not yet come" (7:30). "The Pharisees overheard these mutterings of the people about him, so [they] sent temple police to arrest him" (7:44).

In another discussion with the Pharisees, Jesus was teaching in the temple, "Yet no one arrested him, because his hour had not yet come" (8:20). At the end of this discourse, "They picked up stones to throw at him, but Jesus was not to be seen; and he left the temple" (8:59). The parents of the blind man cured by Jesus were afraid to speak, "because they were afraid of the Jews; for the Jewish authorities had already agreed that anyone who acknowledged Jesus as Messiah should be banned from the synagogue" (9:22). At the end of his discourse at the Festival of the Dedication, "Once again the Jews picked up stones to stone him" (10:31), and his reasoning "provoked them to make one more attempt to seize him. But he escaped from their clutches" (10:39). On the way to Bethany, to visit Lazarus's family, his disciples said, "Rabbi, it is not long since the Jews there were wanting to stone you. Are you going there again?'' (11:8). After the resurrection of Lazarus, many Jews believed in him; the Pharisees met with the Council and Caiaphas and, "from that day on they plotted his death" (11:53). At the last Passover feast, "the chief priests and the Pharisees had given orders that anyone who knew where he was should give information, so that they might arrest him" (11:57).

This brief review of the synoptic gospels and St. John as a whole demonstrates, although not in every detail, that, historically, persecution followed Jesus throughout his life and mission. It certainly serves to prove that his final persecution and death were not fortuitous.

But, more important still, it highlights the objective theological background of the persecution, although the reasoning has been theologized by the evangelists in the light of subsequent reflection. He was persecuted for reasons that have been made theologically explicit in the strict sense: for his position regarding the Sabbath, and for the relationship he claimed with the Father (particularly in John). And there is in the persecution itself a deeply theological symbolism. In Luke, the first attack occurs in the synagogue. In John, the heaviest attacks occur in the temple. The fact that they drive Jesus out of the synagogue and out of the temple is a symbolic expression of excommunication, and of Jesus' nonacceptance by the prevailing religion. Persecution leads to exclusion from the places most closely associated with God's presence.

The essential datum is that divinities are battling; their different mediations are battling; and hence their mediators, too, are battling. Whereas Jesus' controversies point out the fact of alternative divinities, the persecution of Jesus seeks the exclusionary alternative. The false divinities and their mediators want to exclude, and eliminate, the mediator of the true divinity.

Thesis 7: *The politico-religious trial of Jesus clearly demarcates alternative divinities: either the kingdom of God, on the one hand, or the Jewish theocracy, or Pax Romana, on the other. The divinities that are not the Father of Jesus are not only false, but lethal. The mediator of the true God is killed in the name of the false divinities.*

Jesus was violently deprived of life, as is seen in the formulations of the original kerygma, both in their more historical versions (see Thesis 9) and in their more theologized versions (Acts 2:23, 3:13–15, 4:10, 5:30, 10:39, in Peter's discourses, and Acts 13:28, in a discourse of Paul). The fact that in these texts the Jews are held responsible for Jesus' death, and their blame is emphasized—because the initial Christian polemic took place in Jerusalem, does not detract anything from the underlying truth. Jesus was a victim of the oppression he had preached against, and a victim of the most acute form of oppression—death.

Granted the historical fact of his death, an analysis must be made of the theological context of that death. We are not dealing here with the soteriological significance that believers subsequently ascribed to that death, after the resurrection, but rather with what is discovered about God from the fact that Jesus was executed. And the first thing that is discovered is that he was killed "in the name of God," he was killed by those who invoked God in what they were doing. This appears indirectly in the trial before Pilate, and explicitly in the trial before the Sanhedrin.

There is a tendency in the synoptic gospels, especially Luke, to transfer the ultimate blame for Jesus' death to the Jews and their leaders, not to Pilate.[50] Nevertheless, Jesus died on the cross as a political criminal, and by the type of death that only the Romans, the political authority, could enjoin. Passing over details that are not pertinent here, the important thing is to consider the type of charge that made conviction by Pilate likely. What is historically most probable is the account in Luke 23:2 and John 19:12–15.[51] Jesus was accused of inciting to rebellion and of not paying tribute to Caesar. The historical aspect of these charges may be related to the uprising mentioned in Mark 15:7, in which the Jews may have wanted to implicate Jesus.[52] Or, more generally, the Jews "might have stressed how politically dangerous the apocalyptic impulses in Jesus' preaching were."[53]

Although the first charge—that of subversion—lacks historical grounds, the insinuation that Jesus' action ran counter to the political interests of Rome is coherent, even though Jesus himself may not have sought it directly. In fact, as is noted in the gospel accounts, Pilate did not decide to convict him on the basis of participation in the uprising, as a concrete, isolated event, because he found no evidence for that. What prompted him to convict Jesus was the alternative presented in John 19:12: either Jesus or Caesar. It is not isolated matters, but symbolic totalities, that are involved here. "It may be said that Jesus was crucified by the Romans, not only for tactical reasons and reasons based on the standard policy of calm and order in Jerusalem, but essentially in the name of the gods of the Roman state, that guaranteed the Pax Romana."[54]

In the trial before Pilate, the alternative of two persons, two mediators—Jesus and Pilate—appears directly. In the realm of "persons" there is very little logic in the trial, and Pilate wants to release Jesus. But if one moves from mediators to mediations, then one understands the conclusion of the trial: Jesus' condemnation to death. For the alternative was between the kingdom of God and the Roman empire, and each of these two socio-political totalities invoked different gods: the Father of Jesus, and the Roman gods. So Jesus died, not because of a mistake by Pilate, but because of the logic of the divinities of death and oppression. The ultimate reason for which he could be sent to his death, without denying his personal innocence, is the invocation of the divinity of Caesar. Death could be imposed in the name of that divinity.

The fact that Jesus died in the name of a divinity appears more explicitly in the religious trial, owing to the very nature of the matter at issue. It lends itself to a more theological formulation of Jesus' conflict. There has been a great deal of discussion about historical aspects of the trial.[55] For our purposes, it will suffice to note that at the Festival of the Dedication, as described in John 10:22-39, a clear-cut religious conflict appears between Jesus and the Jews. The interrogation before the chief priest (John 18:19-24) may have been a private interrogation. And the meeting of the Sanhedrin may have taken place the morning after the arrest of Jesus, for the purpose of preparing the charges before Pilate, who could have him executed. Hence, the synoptic traditions may have wanted to historicize what was the cause of Jesus' death: "the increasing hostility of the Jewish leaders (especially the chief priests), which, in John, reaches its high point at the Festival of the Dedication."[56]

This historicizing is done in such a way that the death alternative was posed between the chief priests and Jesus. It is stressed that they wanted an "allegation . . . on which a death-sentence could be based" (Matt. 26:59; Mark 14:55), and the conclusion was that "he should die" (Matt. 26:66; Mark 14:64). Important for our purposes are the accusations that created a logic calling for his death. According to John, the interrogation before Annas related to the teachings of Jesus and his disciples (John 18:19). But in the accusation before the Sanhedrin it related to two key points concerning Jesus as a mediator and the mediation of the God of Jesus. The cause of the conviction appears in the charge that Jesus has blasphemed by declaring himself the Christ (Matt. 26:64; Mark 14:62; Luke 22:67; John 10:24). But, in addition to this cause, which probably comes from redactional sources, we must consider the other cause, which relates not so much to Jesus' claims about himself, as to the claims of a new mediation of God, and not only new, but different and contrary: the temple (Matt. 26:61; Mark 14:58; John 2:19). Only by understanding what the temple meant in the religious, political, and economic spheres[57] can one understand the totality that Jesus offers as an alternative to the temple. Jesus offers not a change in, but an alternative to, the temple. The destruction of the temple implies the surpassing of the law, as the leaders of the people interpreted it, and even as it appeared in some of the prophetic and apocalyptic traditions; and it implies no longer making the temple the center of a political, social, and economic theocracy.[58]

Therefore, Jesus—and here we are not treating more strictly christological considerations of his own person—is the mediator of a mediation of God that is in opposition to the concrete mediations included in the practical understanding of the religion of his time. And the divinity on whose name the temple is based is what brings Jesus to death. The editorial adjunct in Matthew 26:63 serves to demonstrate this symbolically. The chief priest "charges him by the living God," in order to be able to send Jesus to his death—even though that decision had already been made. Jesus dies at the hands of false divinities, and they are explicitly invoked for his death, even though, ironically, it is the living God who is named.

Hence, the deepest significance of both trials will not be discovered by considering them as a confrontation between persons, between Pilate and Jesus, between the chief priest and Jesus—in other words, between what we have termed *mediators*. The deeper significance lies in the *mediations* of the true divinity—mediations that are in conflict. And these mediations are associated with the life and death of human beings, as we have observed earlier. What appears in the trials is the *total* character of the alternative mediations. It involves the Pax Romana and a theocracy based on the temple, on the one hand, and the kingdom of God on the other. Hence it involves totalities of life and history, ultimately based on and justified by a certain understanding of God. And as a result of the invocation of the divinities, Jesus was killed. This is the underlying fact that reveals Jesus' historical destiny: the divinities are at odds, and from them life or death results.

What appears in the trials at the end of his life is only the logical conclusion of what his life had been. "His death cannot be understood without his life, and his life cannot be understood without the one for whom he lived—that is, his God and Father—and without what he lived for—that is, the gospel of the kingdom of the poor."[59]

What we have said about Jesus' death, therefore, harks back to his life and its theo-logical dimension, which is expressed in the interaction of an "invocation of God" and "service to the kingdom of God." What is typical of Jesus' invocation of God is not something that can be formulated and handed down over the centuries. Rather, he adopts an action pattern in which decisions are made on concrete and real-life matters, in a way that is distinct and viable in the given milieu. The newness of the God of Jesus does not lie in the formulation of Jesus' invocations, or even in the invocation "Father," but rather, "it is in action that Jesus wills that the invocation of the Father is to achieve a new form."[60]

When the image of God is studied in the activity of Jesus, his doctrine on God can be outlined in terms of the divine mediations that Jesus came to serve. And it is from within that service that he invoked God. This is why God appeared so conflictual to him, demanding the choice of an alternative. "Jesus does not say that God is the Father, which would not have been original; but he says that God is the destroyer of all oppression, including that inflicted by religion, and that I invoke God as the Father in his leveling of concrete instances of oppression."[61] And this is why the different concepts of God symbolically present in the death-sentence scenes appear in their concrete reality in his confrontation with the most diverse of parties and factions.

If Jesus' death had its causes in his concrete life, then conflict and adherence to an alternative must also be sought there. Hence, putting aside all pietistic or merely symbolic qualities, his life cannot be understood apart from "the battle between God and the gods—that is, between the God whom Jesus preached as his Father and the god of the law, as interpreted by the guardians of the law, and the political gods of the Roman occupation forces."[62]

THE MEANING OF GOD TO JESUS

The paschal mystery throws light on the divinity alternative. The gods of oppression kill Jesus and the true God resurrects him, restores him to life—to life in abundance. But this, of course, is grasped only by those who, after the life of Jesus, believe in him. Jesus' historical life ended with the paradox that the one who defends the God of life dies, and yet Jesus was faithful to that God to the end.

What we should like to consider briefly now is the importance to Jesus during his own life of the reality of God, not only the conviction that God is a God of life, but also the importance of the fact that Jesus invoked God, explaining his life in relationship to God—to put it briefly, Jesus' understanding of God, and what experiences he converted into mediations of the experience of God.

In order to clarify this point, we must retrieve a concept that has understandably been neglected because of its frequent manipulation, but is necessary to penetrate to the ultimate origin of Jesus' life: "mystery."[63] From what has been said earlier, the reader will readily understand that to turn to mystery now does not mean to abandon history, or to search out a place parallel to the historical process, or much less to turn away from the historical process. To refer to mystery means to refer to the ultimate quality of life and, in its ultimacy, to refer to God as the one who makes life something ultimate, not something temporary.[64]

The fact that life is something ultimate is evident to Jesus when it is seen as the mediation of God, something that is holy and dare not be manipulated, something that must be served and not be used for one's own service, something that is the gift most radically given and something that is most authentically one's own, something that is most concrete and real, and, to be properly understood, can be conceived only as open and limitless.

Life appears to Jesus as something that is given and is to be given: as a gift and a task. In this way, Jesus elaborates a notion of God in association with life, and an experience of God in association with the giving of life and, in the end, with the giving of one's own life.[65]

In what follows, we can only summarize very briefly and in a more systematic fashion than we have thus far, what appears to be the core of Jesus' vision and experience of God—that is, what is really a mystery to Jesus, and how that mystery affected his life.[66]

Thesis 8: *To Jesus, the ultimate mystery of life transcends concrete life. God is always greater, because the reality of God is—precisely— love. And God is at the same time lesser, because he is hidden in smallness and poverty. God's yes to the poor and his no to poverty, the result of sin, is what makes it intrinsically possible for Jesus' understanding of God to carry transcendence within itself.*

When Jesus inherited the various traditions concerning God from the Old Testament, he also inherited the various notions of the transcendence of God, explained in different ways in the exodist, prophetic, sapiential, and apocalyptic traditions. God is greater than nature and history, although Jesus does not use the systematic terms employed here. God is the creator (Mark 10:6, 13:19) and sovereign (Matt. 19:23–25, 10:28). The human being is God's servant (Luke 17:7–10; Matt. 6:24; Luke 16:13). God is incomprehensible (Matt. 11:25), and to God all things are possible (Matt. 19:26).

These are only examples of how Jesus formulated the transcendence of God. But the most typical aspect of Jesus' understanding of God is that God is greater because he is love, and that this greater love of God is also partial— that is, it takes sides. Although it has been reiterated so often, we must remember that, unlike other religious teachers of his time, Jesus announced the coming of God's kingdom in grace, not in vengeful justice. God comes to save and to give life, not to take it away. The fact of God's being greater appears especially when the impossibility of life ceases to be impossible. And in this regard, although it was not typical of Jesus to call God "Father,"[67] the fact that Jesus does so does not betoken only his special relationship with God, but also the love-charged essence of Jesus' understanding of God. And hence, although it may not be new from a historical standpoint, Jesus' concentration on love as a form of relating to God is, indeed, of paramount importance.[68]

The fact of God's being greater is shown to Jesus in God's loving intentions for the world, but the historical and credible reality of that love appears to him in God's partiality toward the lowly. To Jesus, God is love because God loves those whom no one else loves, because God is concerned about those for whom no one else has any concern. The previously quoted passages from the prophetic traditions—where God comes to the defense of the weak—the declaration of the poor as the privileged members of the kingdom to come, and

Luke's moving parables on the forgiveness of sinners show how Jesus understood that God is love.

What we are trying to say in these few pages is, therefore, that Jesus had the inner conviction that love exists in the ultimate depths of reality, that it is in relation to that love that human beings truly live, and that their life is truly life when they give life to others, when they love them. In this core of love, Jesus sees the reality of God, and from this core he judges the concrete events of history and views his own future. It is the concrete way that Jesus had (certainly not a conceptual way) of asserting that the reality of God is transcendent.

But, in addition, because the reality of God is seen to be partial toward the poor, love is not greater only on the basis of its own reality, but also in its historical materialization as love for the poor. In fact, if God's preferential love for the poor and the denunciation made by God of the poverty inflicted on the poor are considered together, love appears in the historical tension between yes and no, a tension that, by its own objective nature, generates history. And the history that is generated when one attempts to live according to God's love transcends itself, and is therefore a mediation of God's transcendence. Love, therefore, is greater not only on the basis of its own reality, apart from anything else, but also on the basis of the history that it necessarily gives birth to, and the history that emerges from it dialectically. Thus, one cannot establish the notion of God as love in an idealistic or scientific manner, but as a notion that, in order to endure as such, must repeatedly arise from the new history of love.[69]

The absolute yes that Jesus gives to love for human beings, and the maintenance of that yes throughout history, even in the presence of the negation of love, is the mediation of the understanding of God as love—a God who becomes manifest as lesser in his hiddenness among the lowly and the poor, and who becomes manifest as greater and transcendent in the condemnation of poverty.

Thesis 9: *To that understanding of God there corresponds in Jesus a series of historical experiences that are mediations to him of the God who is greater. Those experiences are of two types: the celebration of what already exists of true life, and the constant search for what is the will of God.*

The understanding of God as a God who is love, and therefore greater, and who is partial to the lowly, is neither idealistic nor merely conceptual or noetic. That understanding is reflected in Jesus' own experience, as we can infer from his words and his deeds.

When a systematic reconstruction is made of that experience, what appears very clearly is that Jesus was utterly convinced that living is living for others and serving others. Thus, it corresponds to the reality of his vision of God.

His historical service to others appears throughout the gospels, and is sum-marized in the phrase, "he went about doing good"; or in the famous saying of Bonhoeffer that Jesus is "the man for others." His orientation to the mystery of God certainly makes his life an ex-istence—a life not centered upon itself, but directed to someone else who gives it meaning. But, precisely because his orientation is to a particular God, and not to just any divinity, his ex-istence is pro-existence. Existing for others and the conviction that one is thereby related to God is Jesus' fundamental experience.

That pro-existence is what Jesus celebrates and what Jesus seeks, and in it there are mediations of the experience of God. Jesus' meals with the poor and with sinners, and the prayer of thanksgiving because the kingdom has been revealed to the lowly, show the historical meaning that emerges in living for others. And when that "living for" is converted into "being with" others, then love becomes clear, not only as an ethical requirement of praxis, but also as a reality with meaning and fulfillment, as a mediation of the fact that love is really the ultimate thing and, as such, fulfilling, and hence God's media-tion.

There are obscure periods in history, beyond which one cannot go at this or that specific time.[70] But, throughout history, one can and should go beyond any particular moment, because one must always search out the true forms of pro-existence. This is a profound experience that Jesus had throughout his life. Jesus' temptations, his ignorance of God's plans, and his prayer seeking God's will are manifestations not only of what is truly human, and hence limited, in his serving experience, but also of the conditions that make possi-ble the experience of God as God.[71]

The fact that Jesus' life is marked not only by the decision to serve others, and thus relate to God, but is also marked by *how* to serve, is the manifesta-tion of a radical orientation toward what is absolute, a radical attitude of respect for, and nonmanipulation of, what is ultimate. Although it still sounds rather shocking to some christologies, the fact of not possessing God is what causes Jesus to really possess God, to the extent to which this can be done in history. The fact that Jesus went through different theo-logical phases during his life; the fact that he went through a "conversion" process, not as a choice between good and evil, but as a choice between the good that must be done and the manner in which it must be done; the fact that Jesus did not know everything and that, not knowing, he sought how to know so as to serve better, and sought to serve so as to know better—all this shows that Jesus' experience of God was not one of definitive possession, but one of a search for God, whereby he allowed God to be God far more effectively than through mere verbal declarations of God's transcendence.

Thesis 10: *To Jesus, accepting the mystery of God meant treasuring it throughout his life, never manipulating it. His experience of God is radically historical. His faith grows into fidelity.*

Jesus, like many others, has the fundamental experience of the truth that one relates to the God of life by giving life to others, and this happens historically when he gives his own life. And, like many others, he also has the fundamental experience of the truth that, often, life does not seem to flourish for the one who fosters it, and even goes badly for that person. In other words, Jesus experiences the truth that sin appears to have more force than does love.

From a strictly theo-logical standpoint, this appears in all its harshness in the death on the cross. From that God whom he called Father, whose closeness was so real to him, and whose coming he expected soon, he heard only silence.[72] The God of life abandoned him to the death of his physical person, certainly, and apparently abandoned his cause as well.

The vacuous atmosphere in which the final phase of his life took place is unmistakable, although his last entry into Jerusalem may have revived his hopes. The important thing to note is that Jesus did not succumb to the temptation that might seem inevitable to us in such a situation, nor did he seek a logic for his experience of God that would preclude or soften the tragedy. Jesus did not succumb to resignation, skepticism, or cynicism, which would have been understandable attitudes toward the historical failure of the praxis of love. Nor did he assume the attitude of "eat, drink, and be merry, for tomorrow we die," or its Epicurean version, or the more subtle one of finding meaning for one's own life (including the suffering in it and death) dissociated from the meaning of life for others. The problem for Jesus did not consist in the fact that his death might not have the meaning of a martyr's death, but rather in the noninauguration of the kingdom of God.[73]

In this situation, it would be quite understandable to abandon the concept of the God of life. But Jesus kept it to the end. His faith in the mystery of God became fidelity to that mystery. Described in human terms, and from a negative point of view, Jesus gave signs that he could not be or act any other way. Despite the fact that injustice triumphed, he was faithful to the practice of love; despite the fact that the kingdom of God did not arrive, he retained his hope.

To be sure, it is very difficult, if not impossible, for us to know for certain what Jesus' concrete experience was, especially at the end of his life. However, the first Christian theologians were successful in working out the fundamental structure of his theological experience. The author of the Letter to the Hebrews is perhaps the one who best reproduced it.

Jesus' entire life is described in terms of dedication to the life of human beings. Jesus "stands for us all" (Heb. 2:9), giving us deliverance (2:10). He carries out that program of life historically, by "learning obedience" (5:8), experiencing contradiction (12:3), with prayers and supplication, and with a great outcry and tears to the one who could save him from death (5:7). And Jesus remains faithful to that task, despite the contradictions. Hence, he is

described as one who lived the faith originally and fully (12:2), and as the
faithful witness to the one who appointed him (3:2).

Hebrews admirably summarizes how Jesus exercised historical fidelity,
from within history, to the praxis of love for human beings and fidelity to the
mystery of God. His fidelity to history makes his fidelity to God credible; and
his fidelity to God, to the one who appointed him, engenders his fidelity to
history, to living "on behalf of others." Jesus is faithful to the deep conviction that the mystery of and for human life is really what is ultimate, and what
cannot be brought into question, despite all contrary appearances. He knows
that herein lies the mediation of God, and that God can be invoked from
within its course. And he also knows that when that invocation really is to
God, it is so radical that one must remain faithful to life even in the presence
of death and against death.

Divine Radicalization of the Historical. In the New Testament, of
course, Jesus' experience of God is not expressed against the background of
atheism, taken literally; it is expressed objectively against the background of
idolatry. Hence, what we have said about the meaning of God to Jesus does
not demonstrate the existence of God to secularized milieux. We have merely
sought to point out that the radical life and praxis of Jesus are based on his
radical conviction that, in the heart of created reality, there is something
ultimate, which is for the sake of human beings, and that it must be maintained at any cost. In this sense, God, for Jesus, is not something *added* to
historical life, much less something opposed to historical life. Jesus invokes
God to radicalize what is historical, and to maintain what the realm of history
discloses about an inexhaustible mystery that cannot be manipulated.

In essence, Jesus, in his reality as a human being, does not define or demar-
cate God, nor does he make God comprehensible either to himself or to us.
But neither does he allow history to be incomprehensible, and life a total
mystery. To Jesus, "allowing God to be God" is something that, essentially,
lacks a verifiable meaning. But, to Jesus, not allowing God to be God, in the
most crass or in the most subtle way, is the fundamental failure, because it
entails manipulation, impoverishment, ignorance, and the suppression of
life. The ultimate mystery is the guarantee of the integrity of the penultimate.
Even though daily life and history, bereft of ultimate mystery, may *conceptually* (in an atheistic ideology) attain a more radical quality, they lose it from
a practical, historical standpoint. When human beings set themselves up as
absolute judges of the ultimate, they dehumanize other human beings.

At the beginning of this essay it was quite clear that, for Jesus, there could
be no *gloria Dei* without *vivens homo*. We now wish to point out that no
vivens homo can exist without *gloria Dei*. According to Jesus, the human
being is humanized more and better with God than without God; although
there is always the temptation to create divinities in order to dehumanize the
human being. With a God who, in the beginning, established the criteria of
being human, who offers a future to all humankind, who holds human beings
responsible for history, who keeps silence on the cross so that we humans will

not manipulate what is absurd, tragic, and failed in existence, and who denounces any type of oppression of humans by their fellow humans—with this God, Jesus believes that the humanization of human beings and of history is not only better explained but better assured than without this God.[74] And, although these comments may seem banal, I cannot find a better way of asserting the importance of seeking the glory of God so that humans may truly live.

This is, very briefly and systematically described, the meaning of God to Jesus. What Jesus offers us are not formulations of the reality of God, or even the formulation of "Father," but rather the structure for relating to the ultimate mystery, a relationship formulated as "affiliation."

The Letter to the Hebrews also asserts this clearly. Jesus remained faithful to the one who appointed him (3:2); and he did so "as a son, set over his household" (3:6). The letter goes on to say that "we are that household of his" (3:6), not once and for all, or in a merely declaratory manner, but rather with the clearly understood condition that our history enter into the complexity that we have previously described, and with fidelity to the history that is lived in accordance with the mystery of God: "if only we are fearless and keep our hope high" (3:6).

NOTES

1. See, for example, Wolfhart Pannenberg, *Was ist der Mensch?* (Göttingen: Vanderhoek & Ruprecht, 1962, rev. 1964), pp. 5-31; Engl. trans., *What Is Man? Contemporary Anthropology in Theological Perspective,* Duan A. Priebe, trans. (Philadelphia: Fortress, 1970), pp. 1-27. Freedom is conceived as "openness to the world" (p. 3). "The human being is completely directed into the 'open' " (p. 8). And "the word [God] can be used in a meaningful way only if it means the entity toward which the human being's boundless independence is directed" (p. 10). It is not that Pannenberg disregards the complexity of the human being's historical life, as is evident throughout the work cited, but in relating the human being to God methodologically, he does so by concentrating on the freedom of the human being. See also, on this topic, his work *Gottesgedanke und menschliche Freiheit* (Göttingen, 1972).

2. "Affirmations concerning the divine reality or divine action lend themselves to an examination of their implications for the understanding of finite reality," Wolfhart Pannenberg, "Wie wahr ist das Reden von Gott?" in *Evangelische Kommentare* 4 (1971): 631. Or, stated christologically, "As long as the whole of reality can be understood more deeply and more convincingly through Jesus than without him, it proves true in our everyday experience and personal knowledge that in Jesus the creative origin of all reality stands revealed" ("The Revelation of God in Jesus of Nazareth," *Theology as History,* New Frontiers in Theology, Vol. 3, J. M. Robinson and J. B. Cobb, eds. [New York: Harper & Row, 1976], p. 133).

3. See A. Deissler, "El Dios del Antiguo Testamento," in *Dios como problema,* J. Ratzinger, ed. (Madrid, 1973), pp. 65-69.

4. See Carlos Escudero Freire, *Devolver el Evangelio a los pobres* (Salamanca, 1978), p. 9.

5. "One must be very careful when speaking of the 'notions of God' that Jesus had, for Jesus does not expound on notions of God that may be formulated and taught to others. Rather, he acts in such a way that the concrete decisions and practices that he adopts are different from those of his environment. He uses a parable or an image in such a way that one may sense from his manner of acting, together with his proclamation (which tells about an event), and from their mutual interaction, that God is such, or, more aptly, that God acts in such and such a way" (H. Kessler, *Erlösung als Befreiung* [Düsseldorf, 1972], pp. 77 ff.). I have also used this way of approaching Jesus' understanding of God in "Jesús y el Reino de Dios," *Sal Terrae* (May 1978), pp. 345–64.

6. See J. Ernst, *Anfänge der Christologie* (Stuttgart, 1972); Ernst Käsemann, *Der Ruf der Freiheit,* 3rd ed. rev. (Tübingen: Mohr, 1968), Engl. trans., *Jesus Means Freedom* (Philadelphia: Fortress, 1970), pp. 16–41; Christian Duquoc, *Christologie: Essai dogmatique sur l'homme Jésus* (Paris: Cerf, 1968), Span. trans., *Cristología* (Salamanca, 1972), pp. 109 ff.; Jürgen Moltmann, *Der gekreuzigte Gott,* 2nd ed. (Munich: Kaiser, 1973), Engl. trans., *The Crucified God: The Cross of Christ as the Foundation and Criticism of Christian Theology,* R. A. Wilson and John Bowden, trans. (New York: Harper & Row, 1974), pp. 136–45: Joachim Jeremias, *Neutestament-liche Theologie,* I: *Die Verkündigung Jesu* (Gütersloh: Mohn, 1971), Engl. trans., *New Testament Theology: The Proclamation of Jesus,* John Bowden, trans. (New York: Scribner's, 1971), pp. 250–56; Günther Bornkamm, *Jesus von Nazaret,* 3rd ed. (Stuttgart: Kohlhammer, 1959), Engl. trans., *Jesus of Nazareth* (New York: Harper; London: Hodder & Stoughton, 1960), pp. 96–100; Herbert Braun, *Jesus: Der Mann aus Nazaret und seine Zeit* (Stuttgart: Kreuz, 1969), pp. 72 ff.; Leonardo Boff, *Jesucristo el Libertador: Ensaio de Cristología critica para o nosso tempo* (Petrópolis: Vozes, 1972), Engl. trans., *Jesus Christ Liberator: A Critical Christology for Our Time,* Patrick Hughes, trans. (Maryknoll, N.Y.: Orbis, 1978), pp. 101–4; José Miranda, *Marx y la Biblia* (Salamanca: Sígueme, 1971), Engl. trans., *Marx and the Bible: A Critique of the Philosophy of Oppression,* John Eagleson, trans. (Maryknoll, N.Y.: Orbis, 1974). If I emphasize the fact that Jesus was a nonconformist, it is for the purpose of showing that European and Latin American theologians are in agreement with it. The problem will be to ascertain exactly in what respect and for what reason he was a nonconformist.

7. See I. Ellacuría, "El pueblo crucificado. Ensayo de soterología histórica," in *Cruz y Resurrección* (Mexico City, 1978).

8. This idea is repeated often, sometimes to insist, rightfully, that theology should not reduce human life to its purely socio-political dimensions; but sometimes to keep the notion of supernatural life apart from historical life, as noted in some official documents—for example, the Declaration on Human Advancement and Christian Salvation (International Theological Commission) or the Consultation Document (Puebla).

9. Here we are analyzing the confirmation and instensification that Jesus makes of the Decalogue. Later on, we shall see how he criticizes certain scriptural passages dealing with ritual regulations. In the latter sense, it may be said that "the scriptures themselves . . . had to submit to Jesus' criticism" (Bornkamm, *Jesus of Nazareth,* pp. 97–98).

10. Jeremias, *New Testament Theology,* p. 210.

11. Ibid., p. 208.

12. Käsemann, *Jesus Means Freedom,* p. 26.

13. See Leonardo Boff, *The Lord's Prayer* (Maryknoll, N.Y.: Orbis, 1983).

14. Jeremias, *New Testament Theology,* p. 200.

15. For the reconstruction of the most original traditions in this passage we are following P. Benoit and M. E. Boismard, *Sinopse des quatre Evangiles* (Paris, 1972), pp. 105 ff. and 115-17.

16. Ibid., p. 116.

17. On the disputed historical and theological meaning of "the poor," see I. Ellacuría, "Las Bienaventuras como Carta Fundacional de la Iglesia de los Pobres," in *Reino de Dios, Iglesia de los pobres y organizaciones populares,* Centro de Reflexión Teológica (San Salvador: UCA Ed., 1978).

18. See Carlos Escudero Freire, *Devolver el Evangelio,* pp. 259-77.

19. Ibid., p. 271.

20. Ibid., p. 270.

21. Ibid., p. 266.

22. Jeremias, *New Testament Theology,* p. 104.

23. Escudero Freire, *Devolver el Evangelio,* p. 273.

24. See Sobrino, "Jesús y el Reino de Dios," pp. 356 ff.

25. See Jeremias, *New Testament Theology,* p. 109.

26. Ibid., p. 116.

27. St. Jerome is more categorical when he asserts: "Hence all riches derive from injustice, and unless one loses, the other cannot gain. Therefore it is clear to me that the familiar proverb is eminently true: 'The rich person is either unjust or an heir of an unjust person' " (*Letters, PL,* 22, 984).

28. Escudero Freire, *Devolver el Evangelio,* p. 273.

29. Ibid., p. 315.

30. *Synopse,* pp. 354-56.

31. Ibid., pp. 357 ff.

32. Ibid., p. 335.

33. Jeremias, *New Testament Theology,* p. 145.

34. See Boismard, *Synopse,* pp. 105 ff.

35. See H. Braun, *Jesus,* pp. 161 ff.

36. Jeremias, *New Testament Theology,* p. 210.

37. Duquoc, *Cristología,* p. 110.

38. Bornkamm, *Jesus of Nazareth,* p. 97.

39. Käsemann, *Exegetische Versuche und Besinnungen,* Vol. 1 (Göttingen, 1969), p. 207.

40. Braun, *Jesus,* p. 73.

41. Bornkamm, *Jesus of Nazareth,* p. 106.

42. See I. Ellacuría, "Fe y Justicia," *Christus* (October 1977): 23 ff.

43. Bornkamm, *Jesus of Nazareth,* p. 100.

44. See Boismard, *Synopse,* pp. 349-52.

45. See C. Schutz, "Los misterios de la vida y actividad pública de Jesús," in *Mysterium salutis: Manual de teología como historia de la salvación* (Madrid: Ed. Cristianidad, 1969), III/II, p. 92. Internally, Jesus lives with the dilemma of true and false messianism, and that dilemma "existed as a real problem throughout his life" (Igna-

cio Ellacuría, *Teología política* [San Salvador: Secretariado Social Interdiocesano, 1973), Eng. trans., *Freedom Made Flesh: The Mission of Christ and His Church,* John Drury, trans. (Maryknoll, N.Y.: Orbis, 1976), p. 56.

46. See Bornkamm, *Jesus of Nazareth,* p. 157; C. H. Dodd, *The Founder of Christianity* (London: Macmillan, 1970), p. 137.

47. Bornkamm, *Jesus of Nazareth,* p. 153.

48. See Dodd, *Founder,* p. 127.

49. Ibid., pp. 128–29.

50. See Boismard, *Synopse,* p. 417; Bornkamm, *Jesus of Nazareth,* p. 164.

51. Bornkamm, *Jesus of Nazareth,* p. 164.

52. See Boismard, *Synopse,* p. 417.

53. Braun, *Jesus,* p. 51.

54. Moltmann, *The Crucified God,* p. 136.

55. See Braun, *Jesus,* pp. 49 ff.; Bornkamm, *Jesus of Nazareth,* pp. 163–67.

56. Boismard, *Synopse,* p. 408.

57. See Joachim Jeremias, *Jerusalem zur Zeit Jesu* (Göttingen: Vandenhoek & Ruprecht, 1962, rev. 1967), Engl. trans., *Jerusalem in the Time of Jesus: An Investigation into Economic and Social Conditions during the New Testament Period,* F. H. Cave and C. H. Cave, trans. (Philadelphia: Fortress, 1969); Fernando Belo, *Lecture matérialiste de l'évangile de Marc: Récit-Pratique-Idéologie,* 2nd ed. rev. (Paris: Du Cerf, 1975), Engl. trans., *A Materialist Reading of the Gospel of Mark,* Matthew J. O'Connell, trans. (Maryknoll, N.Y.: Orbis, 1981).

58. See Moltmann, *The Crucified God,* pp. 128–30. Historically, those responsible for Jesus' death were those who were protecting the interests of the temple: "It may be reasonably thought that the architects of this death were primarily the members of the priestly caste, exasperated upon seeing Jesus appear as a religious reformer of the cultural practices that were in effect in his time" (Boismard, *Synopse,* p. 408).

59. Moltmann, *The Crucified God,* p. 127.

60. Christian Duquoc, "El Dios de Jesús y la crisis de Dios en nuestro tiempo," in *Jesucristo en la historia y en la fe,* A. Vargas-Machuca, ed. (Salamanca, 1977), p. 49.

61. Ibid.

62. Moltmann, *The Crucified God,* p. 127.

63. See K. Rahner's analysis, in both its positive and expositive aspects, as a polemic of what "mystery" means theo-logically, *Theological Investigations,* Vol. 4, Kevin Smyth, trans. (Baltimore: Helicon, 1966), pp. 36–73.

64. In essence, this is the ultimate problem of theodicy. It involves "justifying God," but on the basis of the supremacy of life. If death has the last word, then life is vain as a mediation of God, and the reality of God is vain; and reality itself and what takes place in it will be vain as well. M. Horkheimer, in *Die Sehnsucht nach dem ganz Anderen* (Hamburg, 1970), although he himself does not claim to be a believer in the conventional sense, has put it admirably: "[God] is important, because theology is present in any authentic human action. . . . A policy that does not preserve a theology within itself, even if only in a very unreflective way, will in the long run be nothing more than some form of 'business,' regardless of how well it is conducted" (p. 60). And although the author does not know how to identify the positive content of theology, and does not wish to do so, he defines it as the ultimate justification of life: "An expression of a desire, of a desire that the murderer may not be able to emerge victorious over the innocent victim" (p. 62).

65. The relationship of the mystery and its qualification as a mystery in experience itself is a transcendental relationship. "The whither of the experience of transcendence is always there in the nameless, the indefinable, the unattainable. For a name distinguishes and demarcates, pins down something by giving it a name chosen among many other names. But the infinite horizon, the whither of transcendence, cannot be so defined. We may reflect upon it, objectivate it, conceive of it so to speak as one object among others, and define it conceptually: but this set of concepts is only true, and a correct and intelligible expression of the content when this expression and description is once more conditioned by a transcendent act directed to the whither of this transcendence" (Rahner, *Theological Investigations,* Vol. 4, p. 50).

66. Here we are of course referring to Jesus' experience as a human being, without treating of the eternal trinitarian relationship between the Son and the Father. Because we cannot go into greater detail here, I shall give a bibliography on the subject. Its size will also show that this consideration of Jesus' theo-logical experience is of great current interest, and is not an invention of Latin American theology. Jeremias, *New Testament Theology,* pp. 61–68, 250–56; Bornkamm, *Jesus of Nazareth,* pp. 103–52; Braun, *Jesus,* pp. 159–70; Norman Perrin, *Rediscovering the Teaching of Jesus* (New York: Harper & Row, 1967), pp. 148–53; K. Niederwimmer, *Jesus* (Göttingen: Vandenhoek, 1968), pp. 53–70; Wolfhart Pannenberg, *Grundzüge der Christologie* (Gütersloh: Mohn, 1964), Engl. trans., *Jesus, God and Man,* Lewis T. Wilkins and Duane A. Priebe, trans. (Philadelphia: Westminster, 1968), pp. 223–35; Moltmann, *The Crucified God,* pp. 112–53; Karl Rahner and Wilhelm Thüsing, *Christologie, systematisch und exegetisch* (Freiberg: Herder, 1972), Engl. trans., *A New Christology,* David Smith and Verdant Green, trans. (New York: Crossroads, 1980), pp. 8–15, 161, 191–94; Leonardo Boff, *La experiencia de Dios* (Bogotá, 1975), pp. 54–68; idem, *Jesus Christ Liberator,* p. 145; W. Wiederkehr, "Esbozo de cristología sistemática," in *Mysterium salutis* III/I, pp. 649–52; Piet Schoonenberg, *Hij is ein God van Mensen* (The Hague: Momberg, 1969), Engl. trans., *The Christ: A Study of the God-Man Relationship in the Whole of Creation and in Jesus Christ,* Della Coulton, trans. (New York: Herder and Herder, 1971), pp. 130–40; Duquoc, *Christología,* pp. 226–44; idem, "The Hope of Jesus," *Concilium* 59, *The Dimensions of Spirituality* (New York: Herder and Herder, 1970), pp. 21–30; G. I. Gonzalez Faus, *La humanidad nueva* (Madrid, 1974), pp. 114–22; Urs von Balthasar, "Fides Christi," *Verbum Caro: Skizzen zur Theologie,* 2 vols. (Einsiedeln: Johannes), Span. trans., *Ensayos teológicos* II (Madrid: Sponsa Verbi, 1964), pp. 51–96; E. Fuchs, "Jesus und der Glaube," *Zur Frage nach dem historischen Jesus* (Tübingen: Mohr, 1960), pp. 238–57; Christian Duquoc et al., "El Dios de Jesús y la crisis de Dios en nuestro tiempo," in *Jesucristo en la historia y en la fe* (Salamanca, 1977), pp. 21–85.

67. Jeremias has stressed the historical quality and originality of this invocation (*New Testament Theology,* pp. 63–68). Duquoc also accepts its genuineness, though he does not see its originality in the invocation itself, but in its inclusion within liberating action ("El Dios de Jesús y la crisis de Dios en nuestro tiempo," p. 49).

68. It is still important to remember that the first Christian theologians defined God as "love" (1 John 4:8, 16), and declared love for one's neighbor to be the fundamental commandment (1 John 4:11; John 13:34, 15:12, 17; Gal. 5:14; Rom. 13:8 ff.).

69. Pannenberg has shown (in *Theology and the Kingdom of God,* Richard J. Neuhaus, ed. [Philadelphia: Westminster, 1969], pp. 64–71) that, from a conceptual standpoint, the notions of God as creator, as power over everything, and as absolute

future are reconcilable only if God's ultimate reality is love. But this analysis is conceptual, based on the coherence of these concepts. What we are attempting is, rather, to show that history indicates that it *must* be so.

70. Jon Sobrino, *Cristología desde América Latina* (Mexico City: Centro de Reflexión Teológica, 1976), Engl. trans., *Christology at the Crossroads,* John Drury, trans. (Maryknoll, N.Y.: Orbis, 1978), p. 126.

71. Ibid., pp. 96–99.

72. "Not until we understand his abandonment by the God and Father whose imminence and closeness he had proclaimed in a unique, gracious, and festive way, can we understand what was distinct about his death" (Moltman, *The Crucified God,* p. 149).

73. Ernst Bloch (in *Das Prinzip Hoffnung,* 3 vols. [Frankfurt: Suhrkamp, 1959]) makes a very keen analysis of the meaning of the martyr's death, in this instance that of the "red hero": "As soon as he confesses his cause leading to martyrdom, the cause for which he has lived, he goes clearly, dispassionately, and consciously toward the nothingness in which he has been taught to believe as a free spirit" (p. 1378). It is different for Jesus, not on the psychological level, but on the theo-logical one; because to Jesus, what was at stake was not only the meaning of "his" life, but the reality of the kingdom of God. Nevertheless, Bloch himself, when he passes from psychological to metaphysical considerations, poses the problem of the survival of what is real as such, in the end—the supremacy of life: "Because the central moment in our existence has not yet occurred absolutely in the process of its objectivization, and, finally, in its fulfillment; and hence the hero cannot really succumb to what is perishable" (p. 1387). When it actually happens, death will be extraterritorial to him (p. 1391).

74. "As Bonhoeffer rightly said, the only credible God is the God of the mystics. But this is not a God unrelated to human history. On the contrary, if it is true, as we recalled above, that one must go through man to reach God, it is equally certain that the 'passing through' to that gratuitous God strips me, leaves me naked, universalizes my love for others, and makes it gratuitous. Both movements need each other dialectically and move toward a synthesis" (Gustavo Gutiérrez, *A Theology of Liberation* [Maryknoll, N.Y.: Orbis, 1973], p. 206).

V

VICTORIO ARAYA G.

The God of the Strategic Covenant

The mystery of a God who cannot be reduced to our point of view judges us on the basis of concrete, historical action toward the poor (Matt. 25), and rejects deceitful love, which forgets brother and sister and seeks to direct itself toward God spiritually, more to domesticate God than to be challenged by the divine word (1 John 4:20). Hence, in order to know and love God, one must be cognizant of the concrete living conditions of the poor today, and make a radical change in the society that has fabricated them.   —*Gustavo Gutiérrez[1]*

The following reflections are intended to serve as a contribution to the effort to intensify and clarify the search for an answer to the question of God in our oppressed world. How is it possible to affirm, confess, and celebrate faith in God in a context such as Latin America, typified by centuries of hunger, exploitation, and poverty for the vast majority of our people? "Recognizing ourselves as the people of God entails re-posing the question: Who is our God?"[2]

While certain Western theologians of the rich world, in an acritical, apolitical adaptation to the pragmatism of the masses in consumer societies, were

103

taking up Nietzsche's cry "God is dead!," the weekly *Literárni Noviny* ("Literary Gazette") of the Union of Czechoslovak Writers was publishing a series of articles by the Czech Marxist philosopher V. Gardavsky entitled "God Is Not Entirely Dead."

Whereas, to the nonbelieving, "enlightened" bourgeois of the rich world, the "God hypothesis" is increasingly less pertinent, because it "explains" to an increasingly lesser extent a world and a history governed by autonomous rationality—"adulthood," as Kant put it—the key question in the world of the exploited, who combine their status of exploitation with a deep experience of faith, is increasingly less "Does God exist?" and more "Is God really on the side of those who are struggling for justice against oppression?" God, the God of the covenant, is experienced as a strategic ally in their struggle. What is at stake is not an ontological issue—does God exist—but rather a concrete, historical issue: the death of the poor. "The creed of the poor does not consist so much in stating that God exists, as in proclaiming vivaciously that God walks along the path of the people, that God fights in the daily battles of the downtrodden."[3] This creed of the poor who carry on the struggle has found telling expressions in songs such as the hymn from the Nicaraguan Mass:

> You are the God of the poor,
> the human, unassuming God,
> the God who sweats in the street,
> the God with a weathered countenance;
> that is why I speak to you,
> as my people speak,
> because you are God the laborer,
> Christ the worker.

Affirming, confessing, and celebrating faith in God from within our context of oppression is possible only if, as in the biblical exodus, belief in God entails taking a stand for liberation and against exploitation.[4] Faith in God finds its meaning in the struggle to transform history. Celebration finds its main altar in action taken in solidarity with the aspirations and historical march forward of the oppressed, in their daily, systematic struggle to experience freedom, justice, and fellowship; in their daily struggle for bread, work, health, housing: in other words, the struggle for the right to life.

To many activists, the question "Who is our God?" may seem an idle question. "It would be better for us to be silent about what God is and can do." "I don't believe in God, because I believe in human nature." "I don't believe in God, because I believe in justice." "I don't believe in God, because God is a tool for the exploitation and subjugation practiced by the ruling class." To the custodians of the churches' official orthodoxies, the question about God in our context of oppression and the struggle against it is highly suspect, especially if it is not couched in the traditional language of dogmatic theology, wherein the "proper, biblical" manner is to speak of the eternal, wise, and infinite God, rather than the God who sweats in the street, the God with a weathered countenance, God the laborer.

We think the question is very timely. There is nothing trite about it, nor does it indicate a lack of faith. On the contrary, it is a question prompted by faith; it is a faith-ful and vibrant question! It stems from the life of many believers who, without renouncing their faith, and without the cowardice of wanting to conceal it, assume a genuine, effective, comradely, class commitment to the interests and struggles of the exploited peoples of our continent to liberate themselves from the violent, antilife structures that are crushing them and turning their world into a graveyard of capitalism.

Although the question is still valid, the classic manner of asking it has become invalid. The question can no longer be asked in the atmosphere germane to the theology of the rich world. For example, the German theologian Dietrich Bonhoeffer asked about the conditions for the possible announcement of God to a world (such as the European) that thought it had reached "adulthood."

Our question is, rather, how does one tell the nonperson, the nonhuman, that God is love, that God is justice and liberation, that Christ identifies himself with the lowest of the low?[5]

Progressive European theology, by reason of its privileged interlocutor—the nonbeliever, atheist, or skeptic—has had to act in the abstract, speculative realm. Its interlocutor questions faith, and puts its questions—about God, for example—in the realm of the religious and its philosophical assumptions. Theological reflection that assumes the perspective of the poor, and that seeks to express itself from the "reverse image of history"—from the "other history," which is the history of "the other"—must, by reason of *its* privileged interlocutor, act in the realm of the economic and the political. The oppressed, the exploited class, "the wretched of the earth," do not primarily question the religious world, or ask about its philosophical assumptions. They question, first and foremost, the economic, social, and political "order" that is oppressing and alienating them, and the ideology that attempts to justify that domination.[6] They do not have, basically, an atheistic or skeptical bias. The issue is not the existence of God, but that of the oppressed, with their most fundamental rights denied: work, health, housing, food. It is not the existence of God, but the death of the poor, confronted with a system that systematically exploits, alienates, and exterminates the poor, and corrodes the right to life of the teeming majorities doomed to "death before their time."

From the oppressed world, and for any reflection that wants to assume the perspective of the poor, the question about God is inseparably linked with the political realm and the historical struggle against oppression.

The great challenge to our theological reflection will not be, as it is for the progressive theology of the rich world, atheism linked with secularism and with crises in the Western world, but rather the harsh fact of exploitation.

The problem to be reflected upon is *idolatry,* the negation of idols as an affirmation of faith, the necessary illegitimizing (conscious apostasy) of gods with a feigned "Christian" countenance, in whose name the oppression that some humans impose on others is legitimized. Here we come to grips with the fundamental and fundamentalizing view of this whole book. The question and answer about God are presented in a drastically different atmosphere:

1) It is the perception of the battle of the gods in the historical context of oppression/liberation. Every system of oppression produces its idols.

2) It is the taming of the gods in view of the exploited majorities who are deprived of the right to life, and doomed to "die before their time."

3) It is the anti-idolatrous perception of false gods, of fetishes that kill, and of the ideologico-theological weapons of death. In the Bible, which refers again and again to the battle of the gods, faith is possible only through the abandonment of false gods. Faith illegitimizes the idols of oppression.

In the context of oppression/liberation, and of the people's struggle for life and the means for life, as in the case of the early Christians who were accused of being "atheists" because they rejected the official worship of the gods of the imperialist power, some form of "atheism" must take shape— that is to say, "the renunciation of the idols of oppression has become once again essential to the Christian faith of the oppressed."[7]

The comment by Ernst Bloch that "only an atheist can be a good Christian" is supplemented by that of Jürgen Moltmann that "only a Christian can be a good atheist," precisely because of the iconoclastic quality that faith must have. Only one who denies the idols of oppression can encounter the liberating God.

Neutrality and Non-Self-Fulfillment: Idolatry

With the foregoing comments on the question concerning God, its new context, and the starting point for its answer behind us, I should like to analyze two of the most common blockages of a religious nature. These obstructive barriers confine the practice of faith to an idolatrous practice; in other words, faith remains a captive in the service and worship of a false god, and a captive of a false practice of liberation. These obstructions are an example of what has been termed the "Baalicization of the church"—that is, the acceptance of false gods and their demands.

"Smile, God Loves You." One of the most deeply entrenched platitudes of traditional religious experience is the affirmation that "God is love." But is this not a teaching of the New Testament? To be sure, the love of God is a basic element in biblical tradition. What is not biblical is the abstract, universal plane to which the understanding and preaching of the love of God has been relegated. In an obvious distortion of the biblical message, the affirmation that "God is love" has come to mean that "God is neutral." Opening oneself to the suggestion of the mystery of God's love means embarking on a type of relationship, and a faith experience, whose specific quality is determined apart from, and over and above, the historical and political strife in which the ordinary human being moves. It is the neutrality of a love that is shared by all alike, which loves everyone alike, the "good and the bad," the "just and the unjust."

The love of God, so conceived, is so broad and universal that it can include in the category of "children of God" and "brothers and sisters" both the exploited and their exploiters, hostile social classes that, because they are engaged in a dynamic, historical battle, constitute a clear negation of true fellowship among humans, children of the same God, and of the historical design of a just, free society of equals, which is so clearly expressed in biblical tradition. Examining the revelation and announcement of God in history, we discover that the God of the Scriptures is a God who takes sides with the poor. It is precisely in the relationship between God and the poor that the heart of biblical faith lies. It is in the liberation of the poor that the true theophany—revelation of God—occurs.[8]

God is not neutral. God battles against the idols of oppression; God takes sides with the poor and oppressed.

> God has a *cause* in history, and therefore has *enemies*. God's action in history is not ethereally all-embracing; it is specific and precise. It is action on and with the oppressed, in the midst of history, on behalf of their liberation.[9]

If God is not neutral, if God has taken an option, then it cannot be maintained in a general, universal, and abstract way that God loves us, that we can "smile" because God is on the side of all of us alike. Failure to recognize this truth puts us off the track in the search for the liberating God. Faith is reduced to idolatry, especially because "everyone," in the theology of oppression (which also has its gods), really means "a few": the few who attempt to monopolize Christianity (a specific idea of God) as an ideology to legitimize their power to oppress others. It is important not to forget the age-old symbiosis between the "Christian" language of the rich world and the language of bourgeois law. Inasmuch as the subject of bourgeois law—its "everyone": all citizens have a right to . . .—is not really the human being as such, but only owners, the divine providence expounded in bourgeois theologies as extending to "everyone," is in fact a divine providence extended to only "a few."[10]

I do not mean that anyone is excluded from the love of God. God's love *is* for everyone. We might also say that God is *with* everyone, but not in everything that they do; he is in their search for justice and the demands of his kingdom.

"I Believe in an All-Powerful God." Confronted with the need to transform history, confronted with the need to construct a new social order where new relationships of freedom and justice will be created among human beings, we find a type of false religious practice that stems from a false conceptualization of the human being vis-à-vis God. God and the human being are thought to be so incomparable that God ends up substituting for human initiative and action. Human initiative is viewed as a challenge to God. When faced with a God who can do everything, who knows everything, in contrast to the human being who knows nothing and can do nothing, the contest always ends in God's favor. God must be saved, even if the human being is lost. This emphasis may be noted in many religious traditions of Protestant origin, which have come to our Latin American countries from the Anglo-Saxon religious world, where there is evidence of a radical anthropological pessimism, with connotations that are, clearly, more ideological than biblical.

It is argued that "history is a failure," that "God, not the human being, is the lord of history," that history has taught us that every human design for liberation is distorted and produces new forms of oppression, that all emphasis on what is historical—because it is temporal and material—leads to a new form of "idolatry," and that human beings cannot carry out any historical design except insofar as they renounce initiatives and confess their impotence, depending totally on God. Many other similar emphases of this type of religious logic could readily be cited—a logic that, to some extent, is a modified version of the apologetic dilemma represented by the "God of science": a God of explanation was exalted as a substitute for science, a substitute for human knowledge. A "God of the gaps" often appears to rescue human impotence; the "God of alibis" makes up for the flaws in human action by dint of supernatural interventions.[11]

False gods come to light with their oppressive demands. Faith becomes idolatry. There is nurtured on this experience of faith, as a false practice of liberation, a religious ethic marked by conservatism and historical evasion, reinforced with an anti-biblical worldview. The role of the Christian is reduced to that of passive resignation, simply waiting for "new heavens" and "new earths." The dimension of protest, struggle, and historical initiative—to assume the risks entailed in the construction of a new earth—disappears.

The biblical perspective is quite different. The true God does not substitute for the human being in the task of re-creating and transforming the world. When God created the world, he also associated the human being with its preservation and ongoing transformation. This is precisely "the space for living as a human being," as the theologian José Míguez Bonino calls it; in other words, the space in which God has invited human beings "to act for themselves." God will not invade that space, or convert it into a controlled zone. The incarnation of the Word does not mean that God has come to substitute for the human being, but rather to pave the way so that we may perform our human task. The human task is to ponder the meaning of history, to take the option on behalf of the lowly (Matt. 25:40), to ensure that justice and love will be restored and shown to be victorious. Our task is to make history, and to seek in the realm of human intelligence the instruments for struggle and transformation.[12]

God is revealed as the imperative of justice and love that we must fulfill. In response to the need for justice and love, faith becomes authentic, and the human being discovers the ability for self-fulfillment and for being a subject—not an object—of history. God is not a substitute for the human being, a blind destiny without an open horizon for human creativity and historical initiative. The responsibility for transforming the cosmos and the commitment to one's fellow humans are the mainstays, the lifeblood of the experience of faith according to biblical revelation. In contrast to the other religions of its time—we are told by Raúl Vidales—the Israelite religion conceived of the human being as one meant for the task of "re-creating" the cosmos. The human being is a created creator.

This is the very basis of biblical religion, as Vidales has well pointed out:

The biblical people is not "religious" because of its dedication to worship, but rather because it proved capable of transforming the world through its work, and because it was collectively fulfilled insofar as it constructed a community of free persons.[13]

The task of transforming and dominating the cosmos in a lasting freedom that is struggled for and shared with others is an essential component of the practice of religion, according to the Bible. Far from allowing them to evade their task and vocation to transform nature and construct an increasingly more just world, it consists precisely in that endeavor. Creation is not merely an act of liberation on the part of God, but also an act of self-liberation on the part of the people.

But this task, as it appears in the Bible, is social and socializing; hence the design to transform nature is necessarily carried out as a task of collective production, from which stem social relationships based on mutual solidarity and responsibility: humans are primarily responsible for humans. When resistance to that design appears, and moreover, when the lives and rights of fellow humans are directly attacked, fratricide appears (Gen. 4:9). This dual historical relationship of solidarity/fidelity (with nature and with fellow humans) is the basis of the covenant that gave origination and significance to the people of Israel. Its history began precisely with an experience of political liberation: the exodus.[14]

From this biblical perspective, God, far from being a rival and a substitute for the historical liberating initiative of the human being, is revealed, on the contrary, as the guarantor of the possibility of carrying out the human historical design beyond the limits of human ability. This point is central to the theological reflection devoted to "the reverse image of history." Franz Hinkelammert brings out this aspect very well, when, in treating of the ideological weapons of death and the need to detect fetishes, he writes on utopia and the biblical God:

> The orientation of theology toward life—the essence of liberation theology—is the affirmation of human hope in all its forms, and of utopia as the *anima naturaliter christiana* [naturally Christian spirit]. The god of anti-utopian theology (and hence anti-human theology) is the destroyer of human utopias, the "messiah" who destroys messianic movements, the rival of humans, the Zeus of the Prometheus legend. The theology of life affirms God as the guarantor of the possibility of reaching a human utopia beyond the limits of human ability. Every utopia goes beyond human ability, and implies a hope beyond human hope. In the theology of life, its possibility is affirmed, and hence its legitimacy beyond demonstrable human possibility. It affirms a God who has the power to guarantee the final success of human hope, and who is committed to his covenant with humankind, and therefore has guaranteed the success of human enterprise.[15]

God is not perceived as a substitute for the human being. God dare not be conceived as a rival of the human being. Quite the contrary: any image of God that puts him in rivalry with humans must be denounced as an idol.[16]

The First Step on the Pathway to God: Atheism

The possibility and legitimacy of giving a name to the mystery of a God who cannot be reduced to our point of view, who is revealed to us as the God of the poor, of whom we sing as the "human and unassuming God, the God with a weathered countenance, and the laborer God," make sense only if we do not dissociate it from the historical struggle for life, for the social production of real life.

From this perspective the confession and affirmation of faith in God do not place emphasis so much on the fact of God's existence as on the fact of God's presence along the pathway of the poor who walk onward, seeking the implementation of freedom, justice, and fellowship in their daily, organized struggle for bread, work, and health. More than a provident God, the God of the Bible is revealed to us as the God of the poor, the one who has "cast his lot with the poor of the earth." As a result, God's love is not neutrality; it is a demand for justice. And therefore God has enemies. God is *with* everyone, but not in the same way; God is to be found in the demands he has laid down for his kingdom.

The experience of struggle for material, corporal life represents the starting point for a new way of living, confessing, and celebrating faith in God. Thanks to faith, the human being is discovered to be a created creator, responsible for brothers and sisters, capable of transforming and using the cosmos in a freedom that is again and again struggled for and shared. God does not appear as an enemy, or as a replacement for humans, or as blind destiny. On the contrary, God is the ever open horizon leading to creativity and historical initiative, he is the demand for justice and love, the one who beckons to us to go forward, reminding us of our vocation to transform nature and create a more just world.

Faith lived in the struggle for material, corporal life is compelled to seek the illegitimization of the gods that produce and inhabit systems of oppression. Faith assumes an iconoclastic, anti-idolatrous dimension, negating false, fetishizing gods that are so alive and indispensable in the faith of dominators. Only by turning away from the idols of oppression can we take the path toward the encounter with the liberating God.

The Bible often returns to the theme that humans invent gods, fabricate them. To be sure, humans have long made *images* of gods. The prophet Isaiah mocks those who take a piece of wood and carve it to make themselves an idol. With the chips that are left over, Isaiah says, they make a fire and prepare a roast. And they place on a pedestal the carving that they have made, bow down before it, and pray: "My God, save me!" Isaiah thus scoffs at the worship of images.

But, at a deeper level, the Bible denounces all the mystification that we resort to in contriving ideas of God, according to our convenience and interests. We invent gods to protect our interests, to justify our blameworthy equanimity in the face of evil, to spare us the effort to strive for a better world, to justify our personal, family, class, or national selfishness. And then we worship them; but in reality we are worshiping ourselves. Jesus said, for example, that one "cannot worship God and Mammon" (the god of money or wealth). And Paul said that "greed is idolatry"—in other words, the worship of false gods. True, we do not always realize what we are doing—sometimes because we do not attach a religious significance to it. Some of us say that we are not religious, that we are not interested in religion; but we have made some creaturely thing (wealth, power, comfort) a god, and we sacrifice everything to it. Or, what is worse, we call ourselves Christians, we claim to worship the true God and to believe in Jesus Christ, but in reality we conceal under those names our own selfish group or class interests. We have kept the name of God, but we have emptied it of content. There can be no true faith if these false gods are not destroyed. This is the central problem: in order to believe in God we must first disbelieve in the gods that we have contrived; we must begin by being atheists.[17]

NOTES

1. *La fuerza histórica de los pobres* (Lima: CEP, 1978), p. xxxiii; in Eng. see *The Power of the Poor in History* (Maryknoll, N.Y.: Orbis Books, 1983).

2. Gustavo Gutiérrez, *Teología desde el reverso de la historia* (Lima: CEP, 1977), p. 52; included in Eng. in *The Power of the Poor in History*.

112 VICTORIO ARAYA G.

3. *El credo de los pobres* (Lima: CEP, 1978), p. 9.

4. See Pablo Richard and Esteban Torres, *Cristianismo, lucha ideológica y racionalidad socialista* (Salamanca: Sígueme, 1975), p. 72.

5. See Gutiérrez, *Teología desde el reverso*, p. 34.

6. Ibid., pp. 32, 58. See also Gutiérrez, *La fuerza histórica de los pobres*, pp. 30-31.

7. Hugo Assmann, "El tercer mundo evangeliza a las iglesias," in *Cuadernos de Cristianismo y Sociedad*, 19 (October 1975): 4.

8. See Gustavo Gutiérrez, "Revelación y anuncio de Dios en la historia," in MIEC/JECI *Servicio de Documentación* (Lima: October 21, 1977), pp. 8-9; included in Eng. in *The Power of the Poor in History*.

9. See Assmann, *El tercer mundo evangeliza*, p. 4. Italics added.

10. Ibid.

11. See José María González Ruiz, *Creer a pesar de todo* (Madrid: Marova, 1973), p. 212.

12. See José Miguéz Bonino, *Espacio para ser hombres* (Buenos Aires: Tierra Nueva, 1975), pp. 23-36; in Eng. see *Room to Be People* (Philadelphia: Fortress, 1979). See also, by the same author, *La fe en busca de eficacia* (Salamanca: Sígueme, 1977), p. 124; "Nuestra fe y nuestro tiempo," in *Cuadernos de Cristianismo y Sociedad* (July 1974): 8-9.

13. Raúl Vidales, "Caín, ¿qué has hecho de tu hermano?," in *Servir* (Mexico City), 71-72 (1977): 446-47.

14. Raúl Vidales, *Desde la tradición de los pobres* (Mexico City: Centro de Reflexión Teológica, 1978), pp. 169-70.

15. Franz Hinkelammert, *Las armas ideológicas de la muerte* (San José, Costa Rica: EDUCA/DEI, 1977), p. 195; English translation forthcoming from Orbis Books.

16. Ibid.

17. José Míguez Bonino, *Espacio para ser hombres*, pp. 17-18.

VI

JOAN CASAÑAS

The Task of
Making God Exist

ACTIVIST, WHAT DO YOU SEE IN THE NIGHT?

I was in a conversation with Christian activists of Unidad Popular ("Popular Unity") in Chile, shortly before the massacre of the people began, after the overthrow of Pres. Allende's government. We were discussing the importance of the religious language and expressions of Christian faith that Chileans, the majority of whom were believers, were incorporating into the struggle that was then underway in their homeland. We reached this conclusion: there is no need to tell the people that God is with them, that God will help them to overcome the right-wing plot; that God is their friend and will save them. For the more a people becomes organized and fights for socialism, the more it realizes that no one outside its world, not even God, is doing anything on behalf of the people's liberation other than what the people itself is doing. It would be better for us to be silent about what God is and what God can do. What do we know? It could happen, those activists agreed, that if a people struggles for a new society with enthusiasm, determination, dedication, and hope, the final result of the struggle may be a great surprise, a really new, unexpected society: a people of God. For the time being, it is a matter of

113

keeping on course without stopping, like Christ. What more there is to God
will be seen on the day of total victory.

I have used the expression "Christian activists." The meanings given to,
and the uses made of, the term "Christian" nowadays are so varied, diverse,
and even contradictory, that resorting to it, if unaccompanied by explanations, could lead more to confusion than to insights derived from dialogue
and reflection. The same thing holds true for the terms "faith," "God," and
many others. The adjective "Christian" befits (or befitted: some have now
died under the heel of the military) the activists of the group that I have
mentioned, for two reasons in general. They were deeply involved in the
struggle on behalf of socialism, with the conviction that it was what the "God
of the Bible" wanted. And the "God of the Bible" and his Christ so affected
them, motivated them, and stirred them, that they considered that God their
own.

It seems important to me to stress the fact that, in their studies and reflections related to the matter of God and faith, those Christian activists strove to
bring to light what was alive in the deepest, most serious, and most fundamental recesses of their dedicated praxis among the people. And they attempted to reflect upon and express their perceptions without feeling bound
by any kind of obligation of fidelity to the mental schemata and forms of
expression received from the Bible or from other sources in Christian tradition or religious tradition in general. It is not that they disdained the Bible or
tradition, but they made a dynamic interpretation of them, a dialectical interpretation between their praxis and the praxis reflected in the Bible, realiz-
ing that, even though it may have value as "revelation," the past can never
contain, limit, or subjugate the present—the liberation that is germinating in
contemporary history.

They wanted to know what we were living through and seeing, and what
had been given to us in the present; not what we had been "taught" as being
"good," and what we had "assented to" with "religious" fidelity. Comparison between the two could prove very fruitful and suggestive, but it is a second or third phase in the overall task, and we must attempt to avoid bypass-
ing the earlier phases.

Therefore, the conclusions drawn by those activists, specifically the one
that I have cited in the first paragraph above, were shared—not simply as a
tactical strategy, but also as something consistent with their experience in
struggle—by other militants who did not feel moved by "what is Christian,"
but who were not bound by the dogmatic inflexibility of a naive Marxism
either.

I believe that there are many such revolutionary activists, whether of Christian background or not, who are striving to bring to light those profound,
radically human, and deeply motivating and challenging dimensions of their
heroic daily work for the liberation of the oppressed, and who do not reject
the Bible as a great aid in educing and motivating the birth of a "revolutionary mystique" from within their praxis of liberation.

I consider it quite necessary and urgent, for the good and fullness of the proletarian revolution itself, that there be a methodical, consistent reflection based on and in the incipient perceptions and reflections of the popular activist rank and file. I do not think that even so-called progressive theology has taken this seriously. What it has done is to apply the Bible, perhaps read in a new light, to the events and vicissitudes of popular revolution scanned in its broad outlines. The new gospel that is being created in the consciousness of many vanguard members of the proletarian cause has, at least to date, remained very subordinate to the other one, the "untouchable, true one," perhaps the fetishized one.

The theological sparks that have so far burst from the revolutionary praxis that has taken place in the space and time of the history of the liberation of the oppressed in Latin America have not been spectacular. Judging by what many activists say at meetings of popular Christian communities, in an extemporaneous and faltering manner, as if fearing too great a break with the tradition of faith that they were taught, one notes that they find it difficult to adopt the language customarily used in regard to God by pastors and theologians of the church, including those who are favorable to a progressive theology open to the problems posed by a liberation praxis. Activists may have wanted to say something different about the matter of God, but they have not succeeded in formulating it very clearly. It may well be that many of them feel a certain sympathy with, or possibly nostalgia for, traditional formulas of faith and piety, although they do not really accept them, not even the less problematical among them.

A concrete example of this seems to me to be the "prayer of petition." Many individuals and groups of proven praxis in revolutionary faith, and with obvious practical love for the oppressed lived in openness to the transcendence proposed by the gospel, do not feel comfortable with a prayer that consists in asking for things from God, even though those things may be justice or the strength to fight for it. We even have to ask what has happened to the Lord's Prayer from the gospels. But who dares to question those elements of faith that a certain mentality has imposed upon believers as "essential" and "unchangeable" in Christianity? A little old woman from the Christian community in my neighborhood, a working woman who had been exploited all her life and who was very much aware of the nature of the conflict in our society, remarked at a community faith celebration, "Yes, we have asked God often to let justice come and let Somoza go, but God does not listen at all." I think this checks, or even checkmates, the most brilliant pages of theology, as far as talk about God and God's treatment of us is concerned. Hers was not the sarcasm of the rationalist spinning theories about God, but the disappointment of the poor exploited person who has nothing against God, but who senses that God should be something other than what has generally been thought and taught.

And I do not think that the more recent theories (with all their variations) about the crucified God, and the Father who refuses to act with force, and who suffers and sacrifices with the people until they are liberated from their oppressors, help to clarify the matter. I do not believe that the Omnipotent who, because he so chooses, shelves his omnipotence and allows himself to be oppressed and massacred with the people for the alleged reason that it is love that must conquer has been proven to be the type of God whom the most altruistic and heroic activists experience as an ultimate dimension and horizon in their struggle.

God Will Be

Sometimes, together with the activist who battles, shouts, prays, or blasphemes, there is the poet who captures in the most resounding and expressive way the deep voices that are heard just when the battle is the hardest and most heated. How did Ernesto Cardenal capture the activist perception (which was in the Bible, but which only present-day revolutionary activists have uncovered for us anew) that he left embodied in this remarkable passage from his "Oracle on Managua"?:

> Five years in the seminary.
> A seminarian, and then a Marxist.
> And God? Well, what about God?
> We must make distinctions.
> There are many Gods—the God of John D. Rockefeller. . . .
> You used to seek communion
> communion under the species of bread and wine.
> After all, to die for others
> was not an act of scientific analysis,
> but of faith, the praxis of Easter.
> And Yahweh said: I am not. I shall be.
> I am the one who shall be, so said Yahweh.
> I am Yahweh, a God who waits in the future
> (who cannot be just anywhere you please,
> a God who is not but who will be,
> a God who is love-among-humans, and who is not, but will be).
> We shall know God when there are no more Acahualincas.[1]

And together with the activist and the poet, there is sometimes the theologian, professionally trained or not, who pauses to reflect on and criticize the matter more in depth, and to compare it in detail with the trends of the praxis of faith, both within and outside "official belief," that have preceded us or surrounded us. Among many examples that I could mention, let me cite the Latin American R. Fernández Aldabalde:

> Just as a classless society cannot exist where mercantilism is in effect,
> the core of the faith experience—freedom experience—cannot be lived

there either. Emancipation related to religious—that is, ideological—forms of the Christian faith entails political and social emancipation and, in the final analysis, economic emancipation related to any type of production along mercantilistic lines.

It is this simple truth that must be understood by those of us who want to be faithful to the experience of Christian faith on our continent. It cannot be achieved with aggiornamento, in the sense of mere modernization. To modernize a fetish does not mean to do away with it. There is no way of experiencing faith in its radical form without struggling in a radical manner for the destruction of a system of domination.[2]

What Fernández Aldabalde says about faith can be applied equally to any certain, objective, and scientifically elaborated affirmation about God. (Or rather, about "the matter of God," because to speak simply of God, in our usual way, means to consider God already as a Someone, a You, and that is only a relative, human, historically framed, and surely nonexhaustive way of thinking and speaking of God.)

Along the same line as Fernández Aldabalde, but taking a direct stand on the study of what the Bible teaches about God, is Porfirio Miranda, in his book *Marx and the Bible.* Fernández quotes him in connection with the two paragraphs we have cited just above, a quotation that I shall repeat here, notwithstanding its length:

But Jeremiah's description of the "new covenant" (Jer. 31:31–34), *before* it asserts that all will know Yahweh, has Yahweh say, "And I will be (or I will become) their God and they will be (or they will become) my people" (Jer. 31:33), a likewise exceedingly pregnant expression that Ezek. 37:37 takes up again and Paul also adopts in 2 Cor. 6:16. The heart of the matter is that men will not have Yahweh as their God unless they love their neighbor and achieve justice completely on the earth. God will not be God until then. The God whom we claim to affirm when we prescind from the realization of justice is simply an idol, not the true God. The true God is not; he will be.

"I will be who I will be," Yahweh says to Moses when Moses asks him his name (Exod. 3:14). . . . In the very name "Yahweh" the essential futureness of the God of the Bible is unequivocally expressed. . . .

Contrary to everything we can include within our ontological categories, Yahweh is not, but rather will be. He will be when there is a people who fulfill certain conditions. . . .

According to Western ontology ("a philosophy of injustice," as Levinas says), first the object exists and then it is known, and it exists independently of whether it is known or not. Like a brick, like a thing, like an . . . object, precisely. Anyone would say that we cannot think of existence in any other way. And yet the biblical authors implacably insist that a god who is conceived as existing outside the interhuman summons to justice and love is not the God who revealed himself to them, but rather some idol. . . .

God will be only in a world of justice.[3]

The text from Jeremiah quoted and studied here by Miranda is:

The time is coming, says the Lord, when I will make a new covenant with Israel and Judah. It will not be like the covenant I made with their forefathers when I took them by the hand and led them out of Egypt. Although they broke my covenant, I was patient with them, says the Lord. But this is the covenant which I will make with Israel after those days, says the Lord; I will set my law within them and write it on their hearts; I will become their God and they shall be my people. No longer need they teach one another to know the Lord; all of them, high and low, shall know me, says the Lord, for I will forgive their wrongdoings and remember their sin no more [31:31–34].

We could provide more quotations (from activists, poets, and theologians) along this same line. The odd thing is that in reading these theologians— whom a possibly too quick classification assigns to the theology of hope or liberation—we find that many of them, on one page, hint at or clearly affirm the historical futurity of God's existence, and perhaps in the next paragraph or page again speak of God as someone known now, who is here, who is like this or that, who does and undoes, who speaks to us, and to whom we speak in return. And they offer no reason for the change from "not knowing" God, because God does not yet exist, to "knowing much," because we have faith. They speak with an aplomb and a forcefulness that do not even seem to take into account the well-known fact that "every time we say something about God, it is a human being who says it." They do not seem to be speaking in approximations, in symbolic, indirect language.

Perhaps the same thing was true for the prophet whom we have just quoted, and for other biblical authors: they assert that God will be God on the day when humans do justice; but they put this assertion in the mouth of the omnipotent God, as they do many other statements as well, the God whom, it is assumed, at least the prophet knows well, understands, and heeds. It is not a God so future as God himself claims.

When an attempt is made to probe this matter more deeply (something that the praxis of many activists is already pursuing and fostering), it becomes clear that the majority of theologians are still too bound (by a "fidelity" that I do not think can be categorized as "faith") to biblical language and thought patterns and to the guidelines that have been considered fundamental and untouchable in the traditional practice of the Christian faith, as well as to the authoritarian doctrinal attitude of ecclesiastical hierarchies, which still frame orthodoxy in certain specific affirmations about God and about Christ.

More often it is the activists of a people's struggle who, giving voice to an experience that deserves serious attention, because it is that of giving their lives for the oppressed, dare to bring up the issue, or hint at a new way of thinking and speaking about the matter of God today, and from the side of the people. (The other side, that of the oppressor, continues to firmly support the God who is known and praised before full justice arrives in the world; the already existent God who is justified and explained with a thousand subtle arguments that are, nonetheless, apparently compatible with the compendious affirmation that God is "totally different" and the "great unknown.")

One often sees in the introduction to a theology book the statement that in its pages an "inductive theology" will be elaborated, based on the praxis of liberating the people, one that will keep afloat what faith there is among the people's revolutionary activists and Christians. But, all of a sudden, perhaps before midway in the book, without prior notice or justification, there is a change of course. It begins to function as a "deductive theology," making the faith of activists fit into the schemata, affirmations, and language of the Bible or extrabiblical but officialized Christian tradition. And if what activists experience does not fit into those "revealed" categories, it is no longer considered "Christian faith."

It seems to me that the "inductive" way of reflecting on the matter of God—not depending on a "fidelity" to biblical and dogmatic thought patterns and expressions, but rather using them simply to evoke and provoke—is possible and effective (although, at the outset, it may seem to be heterodox to many). Pursuing it could make a contribution to the understanding of faith and, hence, to the anti-capitalist revolution that we want to wage. The cultural level and that of religious expression dare not be neglected in that revolution, as they have been until now. I am referring here to religious principles and expressions related to speaking about God, about faith as such, about prayer, and the like. With reference to the churches and the need for believers to take up a commitment to the oppressed, an effort has been made to open new paths. In fact, it has reached the point where these different aspects of the lived reality experienced by proponents of socialism have become inseparable, and yet they are kept in separate compartments (for example, justice as a future goal that the Christian must seek, and, on the other hand, a God already known, to whom praise must be given). The time will come when, in the conscientious praxis of many activists, a crisis will end, for some, in silence and a shrugging of shoulders, and for others with a return to "closeted interludes" of traditional spirituality, dissociated from the concrete political activity that they are carrying out. But interludes of this type will prove detrimental to such activity. And attempting to excuse such inconsistencies by arguing that revolutionary activity is not the whole of life, that there are other important areas beyond and outside it, is close to saying that there are segments of life and reality that are in no way touched by the political realm and the class struggle. The traditional Christianity chained to capitalism happily hovers over and settles down in those segments.

As we make this first activist perception (one that deserves detailed study not possible here), that "God is not, but will be," we shall fearlessly and with creative freedom relativize all the expressions and formulations that we have had to date for speaking about the matter of God. We shall accept and use them for what they are worth, and only that, as hypothetical thought patterns and functional expressions found while searching—when there is still much more searching to be done. This also applies to the matter of God's being a You and a Father. Some have already "dared" to relativize the matter of Father, thanks to a liberating dynamism toward the future. As to the You, nearly all believers seem to think that to renounce it would involve a very great "reduction," a complete or nearly complete loss of what we can now think or say about God. I do not believe this is so. There are changes in the objective designation of what we experience in life, which can be "reductions" from the standpoint of Greek ontology or a personalist or other philosophy, but which, from a different vital and creative standpoint, can lead to tremendous "expansions" of the area and horizon of our understanding, as to what we think and how we express it.

Let us, once and for all, allow the life and death of so many heroes of the people and of the revolution (long may it live!) speak out without being on the theological lookout to fit this speech, from its first stammers onward, into the categories, formulas, and patterns of the Bible or of subsequent Christian tradition. Let us compare experiences and expressions, yes (with the Bible, for example), so as to enhance them, unveil new meanings, broaden horizons, and evoke reactions, but not to fit into and subject to a "deposit of faith"—considered untouchable and definitive—what is open to reformulation. I believe that this fitting and subjecting is what is being done in the majority of theology books that appear nowadays.

Pursuit of Justice, Pursuit of God

Something quite similar to the matter of "God will be" seems to me evident also regarding another activist perception, which supplements and continues the first one. On the one hand, it is admitted in theological and pastoral books and articles that the only accurate knowledge that we can have of God lies in the pursuit of interpersonal justice; that it *is* the forging of this justice. Direct knowledge of God is impossible. Only by struggling for justice does one have a guarantee of being on the right path to the matter of God. Those who most sincerely dedicate their lives to that structural and personal justice in human history, and most tellingly hit upon effective paths toward attaining it, are the ones who can most fittingly know and say something about matters relating to God.

It is also maintained that this "knowledge" of God cannot be capitalized on, transferred, or sold; nor can it be taught. One who does not strive for justice, or who ceases to practice it, knows nothing at all about the matter of

God, and does not know that "God will be." This is a general consensus, and there are quotations to back it up, together with some excerpts from John's letters, or the famous text from Jeremiah:

> Shame on the man who builds his house by unjust means
>> And completes its roof-chambers by fraud,
>>> making his countrymen work without payment,
>>>> giving them no wage for their labor!
> Shame on the man who says, "I will build a spacious house
>> with airy roof-chambers,
>>> set windows in it, panel it with cedar
>>> and paint it with vermilion!"
>> If your cedar is more splendid,
>>> does that prove you a king?
> Think of your father: he ate and drank,
>> dealt justly and fairly; all went well with him.
>> He dispensed justice to the lowly and poor;
>> did this not show he knew me? says the Lord [22:13–15].

But, on the other hand, when those who fight and die today for real, concrete justice—the justice that capitalism impedes—do not speak of God and, for example, do not experience God as Father, it is thought and said, even in the most "advanced" theology or pastoral writing, that something is lacking in them. It is said that they must be "evangelized," that we have a "message" to give them, that we know something about God that they do not know. It seems to me that we are involving ourselves in a serious contradiction between knowledge acquired through conscious practice and knowledge acquired through learned and religiously accepted truths.

If many of those fighting and dying selflessly for the people's liberation (that is, placed in the practical life-situation acknowledged to be optimal for "knowing God") have not discovered that "God exists" and is "Father," is it not possible that this "message" that "God exists" and is "Father" may not be as profound, at least in its formulation, as it has generally seemed to us? Has what many activists have not discovered by giving their lives for the oppressed been discovered by a Videla, a Pinochet, a Somoza, or the bishops who honor them? Has some "apostle" told it to them, and they believed it with all their mind and heart? Is it so easy to know something about God in a world where injustice is so rampant?

Why is it that in many pastoral and theological books and articles the authentic quality of faith is located in the concrete praxis of liberation, but then suddenly it is put back where it was before: in the intellectual and volitional acceptance of some "revealed" formulations about God, about Christ, about the resurrection, and so forth? And in the long run the formulational criterion always prevails. The praxis of activists remains subject to the

standard of doctrinal content and its more or less updated verbal formulations, which always lie within untouchable and clearly demarcated limits,
which have been inherited.

I do not deny that there must be something positive in this kind of "safe
deposit" accumulation of thought patterns, concepts, images, and formulations. Perhaps it is an essential mediation for bringing up the matter of God
in liberating praxis. But it must be given the importance that it deserves, and
no more. And that importance must be rather slight, considering that any
criminal exploiter can know, accept, and meditate on those same concepts,
images, and formulations, experience them emotionally with great conviction, and profess them publicly. Can "professions of faith" that a Somoza
can adopt as well as an Ernesto Cardenal be anything very serious, anything
that actually touches the daily-life reality of the human person and of history? Must they not rather be something very superficial, something that
does not even get to be a popular slogan? But we observed virtually no official
of the church daring to say "no" to Somoza, or stating that what he "knew"
and "said" about God was not a "truth," or that neither he nor the nuncios
who preached in his palace knew anything at all about God. There is a craving
to preserve the cognitive value of those formulations and their content.

Perhaps no one dares to tell "Christian" oppressors that they know
nothing at all about God because it is only a short path from there to the
conclusion that the phrases "God exists," "God is Father," "Christ has
saved us," "the kingdom awaits us," and the like, say nothing objective and
serious about the matter of God. And if those phrases, of themselves, say
nothing valuable, what about most or nearly all of the churches' doctrine,
liturgy, preaching, and catechesis today? The institutional churches are
founded on this, not on historical liberating praxis. And although many
theologians and parish priests do use such phrases (Christ is the Son of God,
God is Father, the death of Christ has saved us, the world is filled with his
grace) when speaking or writing about faith and the matter of God, they fail
to explain them well; they seem to have forgotten something. They are no
longer "in the essence of Christianity" and they are not "evangelizing."
These and other similar expressions are held to be hallmarks of the "true
faith," although those who are crucified (and living!) today, the Christs of
today, may perhaps experience or say something different.

If Jesus of Nazareth addressed God as *Abba,* "Papa," in his personal
liberating practice of unbounded love for the oppressed, was it because someone told him that God was a Papa, and that he should believe it? Or was it
because that was the best expression he could find at the time to refer to the
ultimate and most profound aspect of his experience of love for the poor and
exploited? According to the generally accepted rule that only one whose practical life is governed by love can know anything about God, we would have to
say that the answer lies in the second alternative. Thus, the most "Christian"
approach to seeking ways of thinking and speaking about the matter of God
must be to heed what is experienced and said by those who live and die today,

loving as did Jesus of Nazareth. And, once having heard what they say, we must not try to capitalize on it, as if it were a path along which anyone could come to know God, or try to enshrine it as something that has been acquired once and for all, and that is certain forever. It is only a stimulus—to arouse new activists and redouble the efforts of those already at work—that can be ineffective the next day. For the activist experience is new each day, and the revolution takes new steps each day, and the most profound lesson of a revolutionary experience may be that it changes substantially when least expected. *Panta rhei*. God is not, but will be. In brief, we might say that God is gradually coming into existence as the proletarian revolution progresses.

Do the men and women who are fighting to the death against genocidal dictatorships, and against the capitalism that nurtures them, have to be told that "God is Father" (for example), as if they did not know it? Is it in this way that they may come to a more complete "faith"? Or should we remain silent and listen to what they say about the matter of God, even though it may seem faulty or odd to us? I would say that, according to the guidance that the Bible itself gives us—the guidance of the true value of praxis—we must simply heed the profound and serious things that they say in their lives and in their giving of their lives, whether the word "God" appears in it or not. And the substantial, concrete statements that they make, as the platform and horizon of their experience, will be the best and truest statements that can be made today about the matter of God.

Even though what they say may not have anything to do with what the Bible or tradition says, or with what others have said previously, or with what Jesus himself set forth in the gospel, it may be a good point of reference and comparison that can help us to probe to the greatest depths of the activist experience, and to retrieve what it entails. But it may also be a great obstacle, if it is taken as a basic, fixed, and unchangeable truth, a canon of "faith," or of the "essence of Christianity." All that has been lacking, from the time of Jesus of Nazareth to the present, is that the oppressed masses and their activist vindicators have not been able to grow as much as he in the experience of freedom, love, and the struggle for a renewed humankind, and in the dimensions of hope—in other words, in experience of the way toward the matter of God, and also in formulations of that experience.

No "reduction" is made of Jesus the Messiah when he is taken down as a fetish that "knew everything" and "said everything" about God, "did everything" so that we might come closer to God, and subjects everything to its predetermination. Anyone who makes an opening, as he did, wants others to enlarge on it, and does not want everyone to pass through the same opening that he left.

On that basis, "evangelizing" would mean motivating and aiding others to join the organized struggle of the oppressed. And it would mean motivating and aiding them to bring to light, express, and formulate the deepest levels of life, of love, of self-donation and generosity, of hope and creativity (of transcendence? . . . of divinity?) that they may encounter in the personal and communitarian activist experience; and not to tamper with anything that they encounter. It is fatal to try to live vicariously—on the experiences and formulations of others, in earlier times.

We should recall Bonhoeffer's well-known comment: "When the proletarian says that Jesus is a good man, he says more than the bourgeois says when he asserts that Jesus is God." Usually, when catechists or missionaries hear a worker or peasant say, "Jesus was a good man, one of us," they think that something is still missing in the proclamation of the "message," that "evangelization" has not reached its peak, and that this person must be made to understand that Jesus is "much more." I would call it, perhaps, "much more" in terms of Greek ontology (the ontology of oppression). But to a different (practical) way of observing and expressing things, statements such as "Son of God" and "unique liberator" may be intricate reductions of something that, in the proletarian's practice of liberation, could be very profound, substantive, transcendent, and illuminating: being a good man in the midst of proletarian life.

Some may perhaps, in order to recover and uphold certain safe, definitive assurances about the matter of God, point to the fact that "no one has seen God, but Jesus has revealed God to us." But when we analyze the essence of this "has revealed God to us," it turns out that, to many, it means something like this: Jesus loved greatly, therefore God is love; Jesus forgave, therefore God forgives; Jesus died on the cross, therefore God handed over his Son. And we think that we know much about God from this. But it may be too easy a path. It suggests that any landholding and fascist bishop in Latin America may know as much, or more, about God than does Bishop Pedro Casaldáliga.

I agree that, in Jesus, God has been manifested to us, in the sense that, by heeding the image of Jesus, we realize that one who loves the people and fights for the people as he did is on the right track for grasping and experiencing those profound, transcendent levels of reality that he termed God the Father. That person is on the path toward one day seeing that new world and new humankind that he termed the kingdom of God. But this is still not knowing anything about God, or having an understanding of God. This is only (but it is important!) discovering where to start on the path of historical human liberation, seeking and creating without inhibition, and with an equally uninhibited hope, open to any surprise. The important thing about Jesus of Nazareth is the practical path that he proposes and personally achieves with his life and the giving of his life, and not so much the theoretical conclusions or approaches regarding God, the "next life," and "providence" that are drawn from his life.

We might say that, with regard to the matter of God (and the kingdom proclaimed by Jesus of Nazareth), we are in the same situation as we are with regard to the communal society for which we are struggling, and the new human being who will be a member of it: we are underway, with the knowledge of what and how it will be. We are moved by the "hope principle." We embrace the possibility of attaining unexpected fulfillment, and we know that this fulfillment will be quite the opposite of the unjust society and human being, alienated and lifeless, that we have and are now. The one who can best picture and say something about all this is the one who has taken the most authentic, concrete steps in activism on behalf of change.

The churches, so concerned about dogmas, doctrines, liturgies, and assurances, do not appear to be guided by that rule, biblical though it is. They appear to be progressing only a temporal distance to something (Someone) that they already know rather well, if not very well. And the official or officialized theology is responsible for devising the arguments that explain and clarify the theoretical paradoxes that practical life discloses and poses regarding that already existing Someone—God.

It is difficult for us to live underway—always on the move—even when we have knowledge of the goal toward which we are heading, the name to be given it, and the manner of expressing it. But God is not; God will be. And if God does not exist yet, then ours is the task of making God exist (the task of intrahistorical justice), even without knowing what God is, or is like.

When things like this are said, we hear the cry of many Christians educated in the traditional understanding of the faith since childhood: "We have been left with nothing; you have taken away everything; there is no more liturgy, prayer, community. . . ." I think that this reaction results from a great myopia. Believers are emerging from an ideological enclosure and have not yet discerned the contours of the vast area that revolutionary praxis opens up to them. And a great lack of historical human sensitivity, inventiveness, and imagination helps them to believe that "we have been left with nothing, without prayer, without celebration."

As if instinctively, they reject the historical relativization of their faith and their most important options, because they have not been educated to be nomads, always on the move. Their ideas seem to them "clear and distinct," eternal, certain, almost subsistent, unlike those of "savages" or children. "That other person does not know, but I do." It is the same attitude as that of the first (and second) conquerors upon their arrival in the land that they called America: they "knew" a great deal about God and everything else, and they imposed their ideas on the "underprivileged."

I believe that the experience of struggle for and with the masses—a struggle imbued with the socialist philosophy—requires change that is resisted even by many theologians categorized as "progressive": a theology and a catechesis, for example, that will point out and offer practical guidelines, and help others to accept them as dialectically related theory and practice, without proffering "acquired truths," or those based on "revelation," concerning that nature and deeds of God, or, at most, offering them only as an evocative reference.

In the area of experience and language related to the matter of God, the path of life and struggle that one chooses to progress on is far more important than what may be clearly said about God's existence. This holds true for all the deeper aspects of human experience: the vantage point from which one chooses to learn (for example, to understand life, to experience love) is far more important than what may be said about what has been learned (for example, what may be asserted theoretically about life and love).

This is why many activists distrust the definitions of ultimate realities—life, love, freedom, hope, God—that they hear or read, or that occur to them. I mean the kind of definition that might lead any "devout" or "poetically inclined" member of the bourgeoisie to say, "Yes, I too see it that way. I believe it. I like it." An ominous sign. Can two viewpoints so utterly opposed really focus on the same object?

Usually, the "ultimate expressions" in our life, relating to our deepest, our most substantive and illuminating experiences, are cries of astonishment uttered at the conclusion of a series of perceptions and reflections. Some of them are direct and sudden, others are indirect, circuitous, but all are singular and unrepeatable, although multiple. They are cries of discovery along the way—a result of that way, an integral part of it. Hence, the value and meaning of the "ultimate expressions" of each individual depend mainly, and almost solely, on the concrete historical path (as part of the historical conflict of class struggle) that that individual has traversed, and is traversing. There are no "hermetic" discoveries in what is essential to life.

Hence, we must be careful in quoting the thoughts and expressions of others, and using them to back up our own opinions and attitudes. We may incorporate their thoughts and expressions in our own thinking, and even give them a meaning that we have originated. But perhaps if we studied the path traversed by that other person, we would find that it was very different from our own.

For example, there are many contemporary theologians who say that "God is futurity." But when we consider the praxis from which they speak, and the course of reflection that led them to it, it is easy for us to surmise that this is a different God and a different futurity from what, for example, we have been referring to since the first pages of this study. The phrase may be the same, but it involves a different "God" and a different "will be."

The ideal would be that the revolution always find words and phrases, with which to express its deepest dimensions, that could not in any way be confused with those used by a bourgeois culture—a vocabulary that that culture could not steal or disarrange, so as to assimilate it, take it into its possession or devaluate it. But this appears to be a difficult, if not impossible, task. It is like trying to prevent a factory-owner from considering as his own, and from stealing, the added value of a finished product—an added value that workers achieved by their labor on unfinished products.

Another example of a religious expression that, at first glance, appears to interpret well the faith of the Christian Marxist activist, but is quickly seen not to be so—because even a Jimmy Carter could accept it as his own—is this: faith is . . . "refusing to assess, by one's own efforts, the fruitfulness of one's own existence, and putting it instead in God's hands." This is an idea that has gained considerable currency in some spiritual circles, particularly in Europe. But, in order to ascertain what it really says, one would have to know what is meant by "one's own effort," what is meant by "fruitfulness," and what is known about that God in whose hands so many things are placed. Abstractions, generalizations, and universalisms, at least on that level of reflection on the faith, work in favor of oppressors. (It may be claimed that the very thing I am saying is a generalization. Yes, but it is based on an observation proven in reality, not on a view of the "essence" of things or a "revelation." If, in the future, reality begins showing us exceptions to that generalization, we shall have to temper the generalization.)

Pluralism in the Christian Churches

The famous problem of pluralism within Christian faith and within the churches is hovering very near, and we are touching it at every turn, even though it could go by unnoticed. It deserves lengthy treatment; but let us at least say something about it.

Many Christian activists of the popular cause, especially those who take part in meetings of Christians for Socialism, or similar movements, which are viewed with such disapproval by ecclesiastical officialdom, do not wish in any way to cease belonging to the official institutional church, or to be expelled from it. They demand full membership in the churches, with the same rights and obligations that everyone else has. And, for this purpose, they have to resort to the argument that, in the final analysis, says: "We all belong in the church, those on the right, the center, and the left. Christian faith does not exclude anyone; we Marxists can be believers, just as the others. There must be pluralism in the church."

Juan García Nieto, a leader of Christians for Socialism in Spain, has written:

> In upholding pluralism, we want to avoid the political option of Christians from being monopolized by the Christian Democratic or Social Democratic blocs, much less by conservative and right-wing groups. . . . The pluralism that we proclaim in our church must allow room for non-Marxist believers and believers who have opted for the socialist and Marxist path in their political option.
>
> The problem that concerns us lies in finding out whether general Christian understanding will serenely accept the fact that there will be Christians (as there are, in fact) on both sides of the median strip, that we shall not mutually condemn one another in the name of the same faith, and that this must remain, for believers, as a sign of a mysterious unity, and as a bond of a hope that is difficult but sure. . . .
>
> Based on a fundamental agreement concerning the word of Jesus as expressed in the gospel, there would be room for different theological structurings, even opposing ones, associated with analyses, strategies,

and social practices that are at odds with one another. The truth would emerge through a confrontation of these different theologies, not through formulations that are untouchable because of the mere fact that they belong to tradition and have been sanctioned by the official guardians of unity, the bishops.[4]

Posing and resolving the problem of pluralism in the church in this way seems to me to be an almost perfect way of making it impossible for any Marxist Christian to be excluded from it; but at the high cost of converting it into a world organization whose only purpose is to stay in existence, manipulated by the most clever, and also at the high cost of relegating faith to a very superficial area of our lives, as something that lends itself to all kinds of sarcasm, and does not interest or attract anyone who looks at it from the outside.

What kind of Christianity would it be that could survive unchanged on both sides of the median strip? What could there be in common between those who oppress and crush the people, and those who fight with the people to overthrow capitalism and create the classless society? They could have in common such things as the type of clothing they wear, the alphabet that they use, or the markings on the bullets that they fire. Is there nothing deeper than these things? Is the matter of God and of faith on such a superficial plane?

So that we may not "mutually condemn one another in the name of the same faith," it must remain distinct from our political options, and untouched by them. For it is in the name of those options that we are fighting and trying to defeat those on the other side of the divide. But then, what kind of faith is involved? The author quoted just above appears to be talking about the kind of faith that consists in accepting, with mind and heart, "revealed" formulations of a metaphysical nature about God, about Christ, and about creation. What other "sign of mysterious unity and of a difficult hope" could there be between positions that are so totally at odds as those entrenched in the class struggle?

Can there be a "fundamental agreement concerning the word of Jesus" that is not one of militancy on behalf of the liberation of the proletariat? If there is (apart from that stance), it would have to be an agreement in a faith that is superficial and alienating to the maximum degree. Can universally shared truth emerge from the confrontation of theological structurings that originate from strategies and socio-political practices that are at odds?

In the light of even these few considerations, it becomes apparent that the issue of pluralism within Christianity and within individual churches does not have such an easy theoretical solution. And the praxis of many activists for socialism confirms it.

It is not a matter of trying to decide who is good and who is evil "in the eyes of God," as if we were trying to keep accounts for God or tickets for admission to, or exclusion from, the "Lord of the church." It is simply a matter of ascertaining whether what can be validly thought and said about God is intrinsically related to the concrete struggles of the downtrodden, and not to the advantage of their oppressors. The God who is on the side of the one *and* the other—the "God who is" and the "God who will be"—is of little interest or attraction to the activist. No revolutionary is interested in more theories about pluralism than have already been contrived.

Perhaps the time has come to accept, with all its consequences, the fact that the "faiths" of those of us who sociologically make up the church are quite different, and some are irreconcilable. Trying to camouflage them, as if they were convergent (for the greater glory of the church, or so that we will not be expelled from it) is the best way of discrediting faith, Christ, and God, of causing them to be ridiculed, and of turning the church into a large but languid organization.

The Church: "Love It or Leave It"?

It may soon be necessary to choose between remaining in the church, with our ID cards up to date, confessing "the same faith" with all the capitalists and right wingers ensconced in it, or leaving this ecclesiastical circle in order to speak with revolutionary sincerity about the matter of God, of Jesus of Nazareth, of faith as a liberating option—in other words, in order to be able to contribute something substantial and needful to the revolution, on a concrete and perhaps unexpected level.

It would appear that in fact there are many intermediate positions between the extremes of the dilemma as I have just posed it. And this is understandable, because the first and last goal is neither to remain in the church nor to speak about the matter of God in a revolutionary way, but rather to carry on the revolution as soon as possible, and well. And the strategies and tactics required for carrying on the revolution as soon as possible, and well, might sometimes lead us to become very "ecclesiastical," despite everything, and at another time to maintain meticulously the liberating dignity of the matter of God and of Jesus of Nazareth. We must at all times pursue what is really most effective for the people's march forward—and it is not always easy to ascertain what would be most effective.

Others take the position of stating clearly that they are remaining in the official church so as not to become separated from a sector of the people that still trusts in it and has recourse to it, but does not find in it anything, or only very little, of value regarding God and Christian faith. They find that elsewhere.

Some will say that they are critical of the church and they know that it has become dissociated from the cause of Christ, but, on the other hand, they have received much from it and they love it, they feel linked with it, and they by no means want to leave it . . . and they begin comments of a sentimental nature. It is like the revolutionary who belongs to a "mixed" family: he has several fascist brothers, but an aunt who understands him, another brother who admires him, and so forth. In any event, he loves his family and will not abandon it. He would like the world to be different, but when he seeks an atmosphere in which to reflect on his inner struggle, to grow in activist commitment, and to fathom the depths of the revolution that he wants to take part in, he does not have recourse to his family, but rather turns away from it. And if one cannot reflect on one's inner struggle, grow in commitment, and sound the depths of revolution in the church, what shall one do in it? Drink coffee and smoke a cigarette once in a while, as one does at home, with the family? But revolutionaries will not confuse spheres of competence, for, by confusing them, they would deceive themselves, and deceive others.

I have asked some "progressive" theologians why, in many of their writings, generally at the most crucial point in the development of their reasoning, they use, when one would least expect it, horizons of understanding, symbols, and language that are solidly traditional, dogmatic, and fixed; the kind that activists of the socialist cause today do not understand, or that say nothing to them, and that they cannot adopt. More than one theologian has replied that he does so in order not to "provoke" the hierarchy, to avoid "admonitions" that would ban him from ecclesiastical institutions. He does not want to become too far removed from the structures, and thus be able, gradually, to bring them closer to the people in its struggle, and to encourage a "new" theology that would be an expression of the people.

This attitude has value. Sometimes it might be the best way of taking advantage, in a revolutionary way, of the scholarly reputation and influence, or the "spiritual prestige," of a theologian. But it must be recognized that this is at the cost (choosing one thing always means giving up something else) of becoming dissociated from activists, with respect to aiding them to probe deeply into the ultimate dimensions of their commitment; at the cost of not aiding them to build bridges of understanding and reflection so as to provide for the cultural and more infrastructural (life-and-death) levels of the revolution. Such a one ceases to aid them as a theologian, so as to aid them indirectly as an "appeaser" of bishops. If such persons believe that in this way their contribution will be more effective, then they are doing a good thing.

But I think that there are too many theological writings devised so as "not to provoke" the hierarchy, and too few that use thought categories and language that could aid activists on the revolutionary front to understand themselves better, and to dynamize their struggle more on all its levels. Could it not be that many theologians are unable to perform that second task, and take refuge in the first one, because they do not dare to take the steps that we have been advocating from the very first lines in this study?

Inasmuch as what I have been discussing is a question of strategy and tactics regarding the institutional church and proletarian revolution, it will sound wrong to some; it must be something sinister, some form of manipulation, treachery. But the issue is inevitable; no one can evade it. And we could prove that it is not something sinister or treacherous, but just the opposite, in a church that has so clearly distanced itself from the cause of the poor. To the revolutionary, the "game of utilization and manipulation" of the church begins precisely when it ceases to be a fellowship—a community of communities—whose language, gestures, commitments, and celebrations penetrate, in an effective, profound manner, the concrete history of the liberation of the oppressed. A church that is anything else is a dreadful ambiguity. And ambiguities lend themselves to manipulation.

I have witnessed very positive reactions on the faces of activists to such comments as this by Luís María Xirinachs:

> I am not leaving the institutional church; it is a home to many persons who cannot be abandoned. The church belongs at least as much to me as it does to those who claim to own it legally.[5]

The comment by Ernesto Cardenal, when asked why the church is nearly always lagging behind events in the world, was:

> Not the church, but the ecclesiastical institution; because we do not know what the church is. . . . I believe that the true church of Christ includes many who do not consider themselves to be inside the church, and even some who regard themselves as atheists. And there are many who do not belong to the church even though they may be members of the Roman Curia. It is up to us Christians to correct that; it is up to us to contend with a church that hobbles behind what is going on in the world. It is up to us to put our finger on the wound.[6]

The Question about God

Let us return to our initial question, now phrased this way: Activist, how do you answer the question about God?

If our understanding of reality has really convinced us that truth is an ongoing process and has no ideal, subsistent status of its own, but rather flows as a dialectical factor within liberating praxis, the response from the activists of liberation to the question about God will carry more weight than a thousand clear-cut, forcible affirmations taken from a doctrinal bank account comprising the words and deeds of Jesus of Nazareth and the statements made about him and his God by some of his first followers.

It is one thing for someone—such as Franz Hinkelammert, for example[7]— to show that a Marxism faithful to its profound logic and a Christianity such as reflected by the combined letters attributed to Paul in the New Testament are not at all incompatible. On the contrary, they are mutually supplementary and enriching. But it is something else for the men and women who are now consciously and resolutely staking their lives to bring in the kingdom of freedom (to make God be) to experience the same God as did St. Paul, and to be attuned to God's patterns and language.

Is it possible to conduct a survey of the experiences of "the ultimate" that we are seeking in the revolutionary activity of the proletariat and its allies?

Could we take a scientific sampling of activists, or compute a tally of their responses? Which activists should be considered sufficiently involved in the struggle to warrant having their responses being valued as indicative? At what time and how could they be asked about something so subtle and evasive? How could one evaluate the depth, the "ultimacy," or the absence thereof, in their experiences as expressed in words or other indices? Is it simply a matter of recording gestures and other self-expressions—certain looks, exclamations, laughter, or tears—which can never afterwards be replicated as they were, or kept on file somehow, or retrieved? There would be no end of methodological questions.

For the moment, it appears obvious that the task that I deem necessary and urgent must be performed completely, or almost completely, from within the revolutionary movement. (I say "or almost" because some assistance is provided by those who question, criticize, applaud, or reprove from outside.) Liberation theology, from its beginnings, has been stressing this basic, essential requirement of theological endeavors. We must stress it even more here. And we must keep in mind that all socio-political activism is always very limited in space and time, small in comparison with the proletarian struggle as a whole, fragmentary, and contingent on all kinds of unpredictable factors. As an unavoidable result, the orderly, coherent reflection that may be made on its basis—at levels that escape any measurement of a scientific type—will also, necessarily, be limited, partial, impermanent, and contingent. The path that we propose does not lead toward global, universal, finished theologies, to remain valid for many years. It is something ostensibly much more modest than those theologies.

It is very difficult today to express, for example, the poetic dimensions (the poetic added value) present in the people's anti-imperialist struggle, because the activist seldom has the charism to elucidate and express them, and the poet (the one who would have that charism) is seldom truly involved in the struggle (the "revolutionary poetry" that we have is often the revolution seen from outside, and nothing more). It is even more difficult to understand what it means to detect and illuminate elements that are presumably beyond the poetic realm—the ultimate, foundational, protogenic elements of the activist way of life.

Moreover, there have been no good results from anyone's setting out to "be active" in leftist political parties, trade unions, mass organizations, popular movements, and the like, so as to be able to "evangelize," so as to be able to engage in "liberation theology," so as to learn about activists' experiences regarding certain aspects of life, and so forth. That "so as" is fatal. And I know of many instances of it. No; participation must be taken seriously and entered into for its own merits as a liberating activity with flesh and bone of its own, because liberation is the imperative, whether or not there are certain secondary effects, which, no one denies, could prove very interesting. Any other motivation belies a merely intellectual or journalistic "approach" to the people and to activist groups, taking note of everything that they do and say, but without completely understanding it, because of their distance from the heart of liberative praxis. They gladly drink at the others' fountain, but do not themselves become a fountain. What is generally sought in such instances, perhaps unwittingly, is the opportunity to refer to "having been with them," quoting their words and deeds, so as to bolster theories worked out in a different atmosphere.

The attitude of "so as" could serve some purpose, but it in fact achieves very little along the line of what we are seeking here. It verges on becoming a theology and a pastoral ministry that turn away from what they theoretically seek.

We well know that the perfect militant, without the slightest selfishness, pride, or personal desire for power, and the unsullied saintly hero, do not exist; there are none, or else they are a rare exception, very difficult to find. But there are men and women who, close to that ideal, truly spend their lives in a sincerely combative, highly unselfish, truly loving, and humbly serving manner for the day-by-day, real, historical liberation of the proletarian masses. They were born and have always lived among the masses, or they have opted to live with them in view of the obvious reality of class struggle. It is in those individuals that we must seek the ever fleeting and theft-proof sign of "transcendence" today, of the "experience and language of faith" today, of "the matter of God" today, and of "the most sublime thing that the human being can find" today. They, of course, may perhaps not use, or understand, the terms "transcendence," "faith," "religion," "God," or "sublime"; they may use terms that are better.

When we delve into the task that I am proposing here, the first impression is that there is a bewildering variety of instances and examples of dedicated activism. It seems that the only thing we could do would be to make a compilation of narratives, which, sometimes of the same person, would lead us from the all to the nothing, from the most sublime to the most ridiculous. And that perhaps may not be the problem it seems, because we already know that the extremes, even though they may seem to be the maximum distance apart, are only a step away, and are touching. Confusion arises over the gamut of intermediates. It seems that there is no way of understanding and methodically arranging all the component data.

There is the Colombian guerrilla fighter who often prays the rosary with some of his comrades. And there is the guerrilla fighter who rejects all sentiments of a religious nature, or even an openness to transcendence, because of the great fear he has of succumbing to rapture that would curtail his involvement in the struggle. And there is the one who seems cold and insensitive to anything that might be a symbol, or poetry, or a mystique, but who readily and sincerely adapts to whatever the circumstances require for liberating efficacy. And there is the Montonero leader who, after years in jail and exile, attended a Mass on the fourth anniversary of the assassination of Miguel Enríquez[8] and stated publicly that the fact that he, the Montonero, was able to escape from jail and from Argentina was "a gift from God" (and no one

dared ask him what the death of Miguel Enríquez was, on the part of God).
There was another one, who did not attend that Mass, because for tactical
reasons, he feared his presence would be interpreted as a compromise with
the religious language and symbolism that, for him, mask a kind of magic.
And there was the one who attended for the sake of solidarity, observed,
listened, and departed, saying that all this was not so bad, that there was
something authentic about it, but that it had been expressed better by the
"unbelieving" relatives and political leaders who had spoken at the Mass
than by the priests with all their homilies and prayers.

I think that a more careful look at the thousands of instances that we could
mention, a long, sincere conversation with activist friends, and an analysis of
the various elements that comprise revolutionary experiences could give us a
major clarification of the panorama that we are viewing. And it could better
determine some points of reference that will guide our reflection on the matter of God in the people's revolution—that is, on the more deeply human and
liberating dimensions of this revolution.

I shall simply sketch thirteen points that, in my opinion, reality requires
that we take into account.

1. Living with a Discrepancy. What can be experienced and discovered
about life, love, and the matter of God from a real praxis of liberation is not
the same as what is known, said, and even practiced about life, love, and God
because traditional religious education teaches it and obliges one to practice
it. It is possible to live with a great discrepancy between the one level and the
other. Even many activists tend to consider the first level not serious, "religious," or valid in the sphere of "faith" if it does not coincide with the
second. That holds true in their own lives.

2. Activists in Search of Religious Coherence. Many activists who, in
the midst of the proletarian struggle, continue to accept and practice truths,
norms, and rituals associated with inherited religious education, admit that
such beliefs and practices are not closely related to their concrete praxis on
the socio-economic or politico-cultural level, are not dialectically related to
it, and are like empty spaces in it. Such beliefs and practices touch upon, but
are not attuned to aspects of the cultural revolution already in progress. But,
because they do not see an outright, palpable contradiction or a clear-cut,
categorical incompatibility between the two levels, they continue to maintain
the dualism.

They maintain the dualism for various reasons, which are at times superimposed. They do not want to lose something that has accompanied and
helped them for a long time. They do not want to be left without motivations
and stimuli that, for the moment, do not appear to be replaced by others.
They have the feeling that there is something constructive and valid in the
efforts of the religions, valid even for the best socialist society imaginable.
They feel, therefore, that they must remain in their religion somehow, even
though its present role is not at all clear. They want to remain with the people,
and the traditional practice of religion is an important part of the people's
life. And they have the feeling that the traditional forms of Christian faith,

relived in the praxis of liberation, could lead to reformulations that would dynamize that praxis.

3. A Minority. I think we must admit that the "activists in search of religious coherence" are a minority. And there are very few of them in the leading ranks, as direct initiators and animators of a revolutionary front. As a rule, they are newcomers to the causes and trenches of "nonbelievers" who went before them.

4. "Aggiornamento Reformulation." It would appear that there are fewer still of the "activists in search of religious coherence" who take the path of an "aggiornamento reformulation" proposed by books and journals that disseminate what I would call a pseudo theology of liberation. This theology (with its corresponding pastoral ministry) seems to be doing fairly well for activists from a traditional practice of Christianity who are embarking on the praxis of Marxist liberation. It is doing fairly well in removing the obstacle of anti-Marxism for many Christians and many hierarchies. It has helped many activists who practiced the faith from childhood, but who, upon entering the ranks of the revolution, soon abandoned it, to turn their attention again to religion. But this theology does not seem to have aided "activists in search of religious coherence" to retrieve and value their own vital experience in spending their lives and giving them up totally for the people's liberation as primary sources and bases for the understanding of life, of love, and of God. I have already stated why I do not think it has done so.

5. Spontaneous vs. Traditionalized Faith. When some "activists in search of religious coherence" are asked, as an exercise in methodology, to abstract from the beliefs and practices that they have pursued *because* they had had a certain education and had accepted a certain tradition, and to carefully seek within themselves what they themselves had discovered, grasped, verbalized, or created at the most intimate and ultimate levels of activist experience, it generally causes a great silence among them. They find a void, and undergo a certain vertigo, which seems not unrelated to the experience of many believing activists when they decided to abandon the "faith"—when they "lost the faith," as it is said. Wanting to continue "searching for religious coherence" may actually mean continuing to affirm and practice beliefs that conceal and stifle what would otherwise flow spontaneously from revolutionary praxis.

6. Relativization of the Absolute. What has been observed in the foregoing five points entails something that seems to me to be a very important step. Even among activists who continue with the patterns and language of biblical and traditional Christianity (reformulated to some degree, or not) there occurs a more or less conscious relativization of those patterns and that language—of that practice of religion. It remains something that is accepted and appreciated, but not "eternal," not "absolute." It is devalued in comparison with other dimensions of activism, precisely because no coherence with them is discernible.

7. The Unquestioned Majority. Activists who do not feel bound to the beliefs, symbols, and language of traditional religion—because they were never educated in it, or because they gave it up upon entering the Marxist environment (those of whom it is commonly said that "they lost the faith")—are not like virgin territory in which there is no preconceived or inculcated notion of, or no judgment at all about, the matter of God, or about the ultimate horizon of the human being in history. There are no neutral attitudes in this field. We are "condemned" to believe, to make a choice.

The men and women of the people, or allied with the people, who are waging the struggle for justice in today's world, and who do not act in accordance with the prescribed "obedience" or "fidelity" of a religious and ecclesiastical type, or use biblical patterns or language to interpret what is happening, constitute the most propitious territory that we have for detecting something of what is spontaneously emerging from the deepest strata of the revolutionary experience. What do they experience, hope for, and really and truly feel, in their deepest depths? Because, qualitatively, they are in the majority. They form, and have formed for some time, the vanguard and the mainstay of the proletarian revolution. From them come most of those assassinated for the cause of the people's liberation, and most of those exterminated in the anti-capitalist struggle. It is they who suffer the most hours of imprisonment and torture. If they do not seem to have found anything about the matter of God, or at least do not speak the traditional language of You or the Father, who else should be questioned to find out whether a mistake has been made, or something overlooked? Should the churches be asked, or "believers" as a whole? And these activists are often called "nonbelievers"!

8. From Activism to the Matter of God: An Untraveled Path. The fact that, in spite of the existence of Christian base communities *(comunidades de base),* Marxist Christians, the Christians for Socialism movement, and the like, there are very few "nonbelieving" Marxist activists who become enthusiastic about this type of religious faith and language, adopt it because it aids them in better interpreting their struggle, and seek to participate in those communities and organizations, gives us, I think, a very great deal to think about.

It appears that there is a rather well-traveled path from traditional Christianity to a Christianity in the style of the Christian base communities or Christians for Socialism (though from there it often leads to a long silence on the part of those who previously were very vocal). But there does not appear to have been any travel on the path that would lead from the activism that we usually call "nonbelieving" to participation in the base communities, Christians for Socialism, or similar movements. Can it be that there is here something of major importance that the revolutionary activist way of life holds within itself?

9. Unacceptable Explanations. It seems to me that to "explain" this phenomenon by saying that it may be because those activists are "closed" to the matter of God, that some "pride" prevents them from opening themselves to "the Other," or that, because of temperament or education, they are "negative" and "prejudiced" about religious matters, is no explanation.

Or to say that faith, after all, is a "gift," and that one either has it or not, is no explanation.

If individuals are open, selfless, and devoted to a neighbor who is exploited, would they not be the same toward a God whom they discovered in some way? And what is that faith that one has or does not have, because it is a gift? Could it not be the kind that consists in assenting to truths that someone else proposes as objective, and adhering to them with religious feeling? If the gift that one has or does not have is that of opting for "the poor, the orphan, the widow, the oppressed," they do indeed have that!

10. Authenticity or Authentification? In my opinion, the expressions of all kinds that those "nonbelieving" activists utter many times in their lives, voicing their most profound experiences and feeling, show a solidity, sincerity, creative newness, dynamic hope, and transcendence that compare favorably with the most sublime and dogmatically pondered sections of the Bible, or of the traditions of other religions. When those activists succeed in expressing themselves in the language perhaps best suited to this type of experience—the poetic—more attention is paid to them, and their contribution may perhaps be valued more. But when they do not achieve expression of a poetic nature, and instead express themselves in language that is dry, prosaic, unpolished, vague, or redolent of materialism or undomesticated self-initiative, almost no one pays them any attention or values them, particularly those who view or hear them from the "religious" camp.

But what is the mark of the "religious camp"? The concreteness of the "ultimate" that those activists experience, or the patterns and language learned from the traditional, *notional* religions? Is what is heard so often in Christian circles, including "progressive" ones of today, truly valid: either a personal God, Father, or nothing; either Christ, or nothing? What if there were something *more* than "*our* God" or "*our* Christ"?

11. Pure Gift. It matters little to those activists of whom we are speaking whether their expressions regarding what is ultimate and foundational are appreciated by others or not, rated as religious or not, or quoted in books on philosophy and mysticism or not. Their experiences are gratuitous—like shooting stars, a pure gift. Why have the expressions of Jesus of Nazareth changed from being a gift to being a dogma or rule?

12. The Realm of the Unexpected. Like shooting stars. . . . In the realm of the profound experience of life, love, freedom, hope, the matter of God, the same activist at one time expresses a thought, an impression, and, a little later, or the next day, turns in another direction, does not say the same thing, and may even appear to contradict something he or she said earlier. There are times when we would expect from a certain activist a great revelation, or a profound and brilliant observation, and all we get is a hasty or foolish gesture. At other times, we find a situation uninteresting and not at all likely for anything sublime, and the activist suddenly says something that is of tremendous value.

And let us keep in mind that it is not a matter of heeding and evaluating merely the phrase, the words, or the gesture emitted by the activist. It is also

necessary to consider the personal and communitarian process that prompted
the phrase or expression: the activist's personality, the surroundings, the internal and external circumstances. This places considerable limitations on the
possibilities of writing treaties on "revolutionary mysticism" or "the interior
life of activists in the proletarian struggle."

   13. Typological Features. I have left for the end a kind of typology of
the activists we have been reflecting on. They do not live bound to an "obedience based on faith" or "religious fidelity" to the thought patterns, ideas,
and language of the Bible, or of "religion" in general. Rather, they remain in
a living, dialectical relationship with those patterns and that language, which
allows them to serve as a stimulus, a provocation, and even a guide in discovering and bringing to light what lies in the innermost core of the activist
experience of struggle for human justice and freedom. The ones whom I have
typified as "searching for religious coherence" are somewhat different in this
respect. But what I have said about the unexpected occurs to a large extent
among them too. And therefore, after spending a day or a longer period of
time with them, one can detect features and expressions that can be associated with any of the twelve numbered sections above, as an approximation.

   After even a short time spent with Marxist activists, one detects in them an
extraordinary creativity in expressing "the ultimate," which I shall call an
"elucidation through abundance." I think that this "elucidation" also occurs among other activists—those who are "searching for religious coherence" and those who are "nonbelievers." But I think that it occurs far
more often and more clearly among Marxist activists. In addition, they often
express themselves in terms that hint at religious and biblical terminology.
Paying attention to this will make it possible to build better bridges of understanding, and to discover what, even in "religion," is a result of concrete
praxis, and not of a facile assent to dogmas or rules.

   Therefore, although it might be more interesting to study directly the experience and language of Marxist activists, I think that it would be a more
effective course of action to devote the remainder of this study to the subject
of the "elucidation" mentioned just above. Moreover, we have the advantage that there are, in my opinion, approximations to this type of activism
and this phenomenon of elucidation in passages from the articles, poems,
and books of activist authors such as Roger Garaudy, Ernesto Cardenal,
Xirinachs, Giulio Girardi, Alfonso C. Comín, and others. The opportunity
to quote them will facilitate my attempt at explanation.

ELUCIDATION THROUGH ABUNDANCE

Franz Hinkelammert writes:

> Paul of Tarsus realized that the image of God that the human being may
> have stems from the image of the liberated human being. Therefore, we
> have no source of learning what the true God is and what that God's will

is other than personal human liberation. God is the one who makes liberation possible, and the true God is related to the image of human liberation. If revelation does not reveal this, it reveals nothing else.[9]

That God proceeds at the same level and pace, neither higher nor lower, neither ahead of nor behind the progress of historical human liberation, is an intuition that is fairly common among the men and women who are struggling with and for the oppressed, and who *are* the oppressed in a stance of conscious, organized resistance.

And there are moments when those men and women experience the reality of their struggle, in one of its many aspects, with such solidity and fullness, with an overflowing brilliance and with such an absoluteness, that they spontaneously, poetically, and more than poetically—with the simplicity of children, but with the force of adults—divulge the reality that they are experiencing. It is both speakable and unspeakable; the much and the more than much; abundance glimpsed from this angle and that; the historical and what goes beyond it; the unpredictable that may be a reality tomorrow; the human and what exceeds that which we now grasp as human; the whole and even more; the horizon that attracts us along the way and the far side of that horizon, brighter still.

I heard a militant say: "My God is the people, comrade; alluring and demanding, like a god."

I also heard, in the front ranks of a people's struggle with oppressors, the comment: "The cry of the poor, in their poverty, awakened me, troubled me, dragged me out from where I was, and got me started. What is there inside that cry of the poor?"

Fragments like the following are abundant in the poetry of the combative proletariat:

> They killed him one day at dawn,
> But his voice resounds through the mountains.
> We shall keep on singing, we shall keep on dreaming,
> We shall keep on living with his Word.

> God is love? What I know is that love is God, comrade.

> Even though they may kill us, we shall keep on fighting.
> The people is immortal.

> Live!

> Tomorrow when I die
> Do not come to cry over me.
> I shall not be underground,
> I am a wind of freedom.

The latter was spoken by a militant for the freedom of the Basque people a few hours before he was assassinated, by a firing squad, under the Franco dictatorship. It does not matter whether or not he was the original author of those lines.

The examples of "elucidation through abundance" that we are discussing will probably be most plentiful along the path of the revolution that a people is carrying out, even though it may take centuries. The very expressions "new human person" and "reign of freedom" can be instances of this elucidation. In poetic and abrupt expressions—rooted in a gesture, a glance, a tear, a curse, an obscenity, or a shout—a people fighting for its freedom is asserting what we shall come to experience: something absolutely good, permanently valid, the ripe fruit, an astonishment that is unthinkable now but is to be enthusiastically awaited as we follow the path of the revolution; something that is not yet, but will be. What more can be said about that horizon where all limits disappear? There will be Life, everything will be Yes.

Let us repeat, what is essential is that there be a concrete praxis that announces this life from within itself, as a dialetical moment of itself. It is not a catechetical idea that has been learned and accepted religiously as a theoretical explanation of life and the universe.

Everything, on whatever level, that flows from the praxis of liberation is a dialectical part of it. We must attempt to express it, and in the best possible manner. Everyone who grasps something positive in any area of that praxis has an obligation to express it in some way, and to contribute it to the common table; to purify what they have found, make it shine, and share it with others. Failing to do so means betraying the revolution itself, and stealing from it; or at least unjustly withholding assets.

Because we are all still very deeply immersed in bourgeois culture, it has been very difficult for activists to find words and phrases for expressing the intense, profound moments in their experience. And when they succeed in doing so, the dominant culture readily considers their expressions its own—and reabsorbs and steals them—because they are necessarily expressed with elements of the prevailing, superimposed culture. The revolution's problems on the cultural level are serious.

Activists who have been brought up in a Western culture, and who turn to the Bible in order to better understand their own activism and to give it expression, easily (I think, often all too easily) make an "elucidation through abundance" in terms of a Person, a Someone, a You. It is the Yahweh of the Bible, and the Father of Jesus of Nazareth. This is an interesting elucidation, which could have some very dynamic and fruitful aspects, but which, as I have hinted several times throughout this study, also has its weak and problematic points. Its value should not prompt us to underestimate elucidations that are not in terms of a Someone, a You, considering them "faulty," or "of little value in comparison with our notions of God." For, in the long run, the touchstone for evaluating such matters should continue to be the praxis that precedes them and the efficacy that they have on subsequent praxis.

Perhaps we should regret that our languages lack terms that serve to designate entire, global realities (not only their features or types) without classifying them in one of the two usual categories of *person* or *thing,* that person or that thing, he, she, or it, someone or something. There are realities that are revealed and awaited as pertaining to the future. There are utopic horizons that are included among the possibilities of what is real, but we do not know what or how they will be; they could surpass all our expectations, classifications, and categorizations. Is what will be something, someone, or a reality that is even more surprising?

And what if, instead of calling the other side of the threshold between finitude and infinitude You, we were to call it All of Us? To some, this second expression may have more meaning, suggesting an abundance of justice and of friendship, a sense of dialogue, and a fullness of love and freedom.

Some have already warned that a personalistic view of the matter of God, as a unique individual with whom all human beings can be related on their own account (even though it may be "through" others), could, insidiously, lead to highly individualistic, closed, and anti-collective attitudes. Some others respond to this by pointing out that the Christian God is not a unique, solitary individual, but a community, a Trinity; that God is an intimate, loving communion among three Persons who have and are everything in common. But to this it can be objected that the personalistic warning is not heeded so long as there is an attempt to place apart from the human community—ahead of it, or over it, as an absolute focal point of admiration, love, and petition—one, two, three, or whatever number of divine persons who, regardless of any incarnation, are still considered to be fully existent and perfect in their own right outside the sphere of human life.

It is all very well for theologians to devise long explanations of the fact that God renounces omnipotence out of love, to become weak like the people, exploited with the people, and suffering what they suffer, in order to conclude that the people must seek and adore this God, that this God will save them, and that this is the only salvation. This approach presupposes that there is a Someone already known now, God the Father Almighty of the ancient creeds. This Someone renounces omnipotence (but has it if desired), wills to cease being powerful (but is powerful), and becomes one of us (precisely because of not being such). Everything follows from a Someone who, by definition taken in advance from the Bible and from church philosophers, is in all things absolutely superior, unique, and separate from collective humankind—the Absolutely Other.

This Someone, this You, to whom our churches pray and sing, is the one whom many activists do not find in the ultimate, shining depths of their experience. And it is not because they are "proud" or "closed off" to accepting something superior to themselves. It is because that alleged God is not the one emanating from, or present in, the community of free persons in the kingdom of freedom that they seek to create. That alleged God is not present in, and does not emanate from, the cry of the oppressed who are now demanding justice with all their strength (a justice that is not opposed to love).

At this point, some may claim (as stated in the quotation from Hinkelammert at the head of this section) that God is precisely the one who makes that kingdom of freedom possible. That may be; but then, because that complete freedom and that kingdom do not yet exist, we know nothing about God, except that God will be, because our freedom is bent on constructing that kingdom. And if God is not, but will be, we still know nothing: whether God is someone, something, or what mode of reality God is. Everything that we may say or imagine will be a distant, fragmentary, improvable approximation. The biblical confidence in speaking of You and Father is all well and good for the Bible, but it need not freeze the compass needle for all future humankind. The experiences of activists today, which, judging from the praxis in which they are rooted, are as substantive and profound as those of the biblical heroes—or more so—lead to a different vocabulary. Why could it not be better, superior?

At a meeting of activists, one of them, to explain his ideas, was making graphic designs on certain key points on which others would have put the word "Revolution" or the word "God," or some other word, whereas he simply put an exclamation point (!), in a heavy stroke of the chalk on the blackboard. Let us head in that direction. Sometimes the struggle or cry of the people is a great exclamation point, with no fixed, definable content.

As we have already noted, others talk about a total Yes, without any negativity about it. A yes is not a person or a thing; it is an affirmation based on something else. Based on the struggles of the people, an astonishingly transcendent, exhuberant Yes may be discerned.

A female activist talked about those "shining dots that go to the end of the line with which we represent the history of liberation." Shining dots. . . .

Others suddenly come out with the Omega Point, of the Bible and Teilhard, but arriving at it on a trek quite different from that of Teilhard, and hence at an Omega that is quite different as well.

Others speak of a Dynamism, an Event, a Task . . . words that, at diverse moments of activist experience, express and evoke as much as, or more than, talk about a personal God and Father.

I emphasize that this is not another recurrence of the famous "recovery of personnel" for the "faith" through the discovery of "anonymous Christians." Something quite the opposite is involved here. I am not claiming that those activists who speak of the Yes, the All of Us, and the Task are saying the same thing as the Bible but in different words, and therefore believe in the God of the Bible. I am claiming that what they say is valuable per se; it is perhaps the best thing that we can find now in the realm of "the ultimate," a guideline (although it may be temporary and variable). We must ascertain to what extent it is, or is not, the Bible that they are following "anonymously." If both "ultimates" are evoked on an equal basis, if they enlighten each other mutually, and supplement one another, fantastic! The same might be true of the Vedas, the Koran, and other religious writings. The path toward a new civilization is widened, the path toward a meeting of the universal proletariat.

Was the biblical movement (the origins of which are lost to us) that claims that God is the God-Demand for Justice and nothing else for the time being begun because some person received these ideas through enlightenment coming from elsewhere, from "God" who "spoke" to that person? Or was it begun because that person had such an intense experience of the demand for justice that he or she succeeded in elucidating it in its abundance, calling it God, Someone appearing in the torrent of that abundance? Of course, to call it God, or Someone, the person used ideas embedded in the culture and religions of the time. But the inherently creative, revelatory, and new aspect of the experience, that of a new God, the God-Demand for Justice, was a result of an elucidation—an elucidation of a human abundance that tends to exceed all bounds.

I think that Raúl Vidales hints at something of the sort when he writes:

> The phenomenon of a minority that took control of the economy of a certain area, and used the popular masses as a tool for work under enslaving conditions, will never be erased from either the living memory of, or the alternative plan produced by, the people of Israel. "Becoming a society of equals" as a collective plan will be expressed in many ways; one of the oldest is precisely that of making this plan appear as a design revealed by God per se.[10]

In the letters of Paul of Tarsus, there are times when he too appears to base himself on an elucidation of the abundance of certain experiences involving human creativity: "Agree with one another; live in peace; and the God of love and peace will be with you" (2 Cor. 13:11).

It is evident: as the struggle of the poor succeeds in constructing a society in which all of us will work for the achievement of true peace, we shall feel ourselves always projected toward something more, something that, in biblical categories, is stated by depicting a personal encounter with a personal God. It is the gusting of the abundance of friendship, love, and peace to which the struggle of the oppressed people, the lord of history, can lead us. That God does not yet exist.

Vox Populi, Vox Dei

There are increasing numbers of activists who, when asked about their faith and how they experience "religion," reply simply by describing their own lives, their own personal experience, and their participation in the praxis of liberation. They do not offer truths, assertions, or theories about God, or about the "next life," that have been believed and accepted by "faith." They explain their concrete action, their struggle, with its motivations, sentiments, and horizons, as if leaving to the reader the task, if desired, of discovering what data of a theoretical nature might underlie all of it.

It is Bishop Casaldáliga who, together with his listening and watching, utters a comment that may very well reflect the elusive dynamism of what happens to many activists, which I am calling here elucidation through abundance:

> Where you say peace, justice, love,
> I say God!
> Where you say God,
> I say freedom, justice, love![11]

The word "revolution," spoken or written, depending on where and when, may carry more force as a creative expression, and indicate a more ultimate quality in the human transcendent horizon, than other words that are usually categorized as "religious," or than the word "God" itself, if inserted in the same place. Nicaraguan Mario Cajina gives a good example:

> The Revolution is the meal,
> It is a table set with its pitcher of water
> and the knife and fork
> on the checkered tablecloth,
> with another place set,
> ready in case a visitor shows up.[12]

Could there be anything in the life of a contemporary earthling that would knock harder at the door, urge that person to give up comfort and selfishness, challenge the inmost recesses of that person's soul like a two-edged sword, and press that person (as a vocation) to take to the path of liberation than the cry of those two-thirds of humankind who are emarginated and crushed by a system based on the individual gain of those who have accumulated wealth? What can that cry of the poor contain? More than one activist has asked this question.

In my opinion the cry of the poor contains more than much of what is said in the Bible and other religious traditions about the "word of God." If anyone wants to call that cry for justice from the outcasts of the earth a "cry of God" or "word of God," so be it. When that cry is grasped and experienced in its essence, it really deserves such an elucidation; the cry itself causes it, although it is not the only possible cause. But anyone who elucidates in this way the cry for justice (outcry of the people = outcry of God) and the struggle that an oppressed people is waging should not later fall into the "religious trap" of preaching that God to us as one who is already known directly, as if a great deal were known about that God as Someone separate from the poor or distinguishable from them. The only thing that can be preached as a challenging word that urges trekking the path to build the new society and the new earth is the outcry of the enslaved. Anyone who turns an open ear to that outcry will be struck as if by the searing iron mentioned in some biblical texts.

There are too many persons who are "devoted to" or "very friendly with" that God whom they themselves (together with the Bible) must admit is real and possible to grasp only in one's neighbor, in the alienated and down-trodden—none other than the oppressed who knock at their doors. But, de-spite their undisguised devotion to and friendship with God, and their direct, intimate dialogue with God, their adherence to and union with God, they by no means live in solidarity or union with their neighbors, particularly if the latter are poor, "obnoxious," or persecuted by the forces of law and order.

The idea of a fetish easily comes to mind at this point. It cannot be denied that this living in "friendship with God," "in God's presence," and in "inti-mate dialogue with God" has been and is, for many believers, a source of even heroic dynamism, manifested in true acts of service to neighbor. But it is also evident that, at other times, it has been and is something very alienative, which dissociates them from overt, sincere, and risky contact with the prole-tariat and its organizations for struggle. Out of the expression "God," which was a common denominator of various experiences involving elucidation of abundance in activists' lives, there has been created an autonomous, separate reality absolutized outside time and space, to which everything else must be subordinated and subjected. It has been converted into a standard and cri-terion dominating everything else (even if very "lovingly"). It has become a fetish that evaluates the rest of reality, including human life (like the fetish of consumer goods), whereas the reality of oppression/liberation that the ac-tivist sees every day demands that the situation be reversed.

I mention all this because it seems to me that, even among those activists who have been the object of this study from the outset, intimate union and dialogue with a personal God is often an important key for maintaining the spirit of struggle and for recovering strength. It may be a good idea to use that key but, owing to the way in which it is often described, and the expressions used to publicize it, everyone identifies it with the traditional "God" of Christianity and of other religions, who is worshiped directly and easily in liturgies with ahistorical directionings. It is a "God" who nurtures the canonical religious life, whose members, in order to remain faithful to their vows, shun commitment to the liberation struggles. It is a "God" who can readily be manipulated and monopolized by the right wing, wherever it may be.

Many vowed religious are disenchanted on being told that their "mystical Spouse" does not exist, as Enrique Dussel has stated when addressing Latin American religious women.[13] This may entail the loss of a certain "apostolic" force because the psychological base that supported it is gone. Of course, we could continue to propose a You with whom religious can associate in addi-tion to, or apart from, associations with their flesh-and-blood neighbors—thus shoring up the alienating embankment of religion that we have lived with until the present.

But what about Christ? Did he not live in constant, intimate, direct dia-logue with his Father before he "approached" his neighbor? Is not Christ precisely the "Friend," the "Spouse," who calls upon us to love our neighbor and to sacrifice ourselves for the poor?

It is impossible to discuss this issue in depth here. It involves many aspects: what activists experience regarding Jesus of Nazareth and the Christ of the New Testament in general, or of the individual books that comprise it; a rereading of the gospel, ferreting out what it contains by way of "manipulation" and "fetishization" of the image of Jesus; an elucidation of the other/ Other relationship as it may be experienced at certain moments of dedication to the real, concrete other of history (the poor, the oppressed, the orphan, and the widow of whom the Bible speaks); and so forth.

We are touching here on the topic of the relationship of identification in the neighbor-Christ-God trinomial. And it appears that the gap mentioned by Gustavo Gutiérrez in his *Theology of Liberation*—a theology of the neighbor—is still a gap.

If God, if Christ, "is loved in the neighbor," as Gutiérrez also says,[14] what is the point of talking about a Christ and a God, with whom one deals directly (for example, in the Lord's Prayer), as someone who is there *in addition to* José, Isabel, Pedro, the neighbor woman, the laborer opposite us? I believe that there is something serious to be explained here, not as a theoretical problem for those fond of doctrinal hairsplitting, but rather as guidance for concrete, practical attitudes that have, it seems to me, direct influence on the course of the historical process of liberation.

If worship is dedicating oneself totally to something or someone, voluntarily subjecting oneself, and turning over to that something or someone all one's capacity for allegiance, admiration, love, and attentive, joyful dedication; if worship is recognizing something or someone as the definitive, absolute guide for our life—if worship is that, then perhaps the only one who must be worshiped is the neighbor facing us, particularly the one outside our place of security and establishment: the most oppressed, the one locked out of the prevailing system, or subjugated and exploited by it.

If this worship of neighbor, through an elucidation of abundance, prompts us to speak about the Neighbor-God, let us do so. But we must also understand this in the sense that it is not that there is not, at least yet, a God who calls us and sends us to the neighbor, but rather a Neighbor in whom we see and enjoy dimensions of God, a Neighbor who is God.

Ernesto Cardenal says:

> In reality, we have no God other than love, and love for neighbor, not love for God. For the Christian, there is no God other than the neighbor. We cannot have contact with God other than through our neighbor. That is why I have claimed that atheism is not a problem.[15]

What is strange is that Cardenal himself, shortly before making the statement that we have just quoted, gives the following answer to a question from an interviewer:

Interviewer: "You have said that contemplation is mystical union with God. What importance does that hold for you?"

Cardenal: "It is a personal relationship that I have, an intimate one, and I am given strength in the revolutionary struggle by that loving relationship with God, which is like a conjugal relationship. It is a very intimate, very personal thing. That is why I say that it is like the relationship of spouses, deeply personal. There is no way to explain it; it is accomplished through the medium of love, nothing else. Some mystics have reached the phase of mystical possession; but, generally speaking, it is comparable to human love, the love that we have for those who are absent and it makes us feel as if they were near."[16]

It seems that we are still far removed from rediscovering what some claim is a part of biblical tradition: that the precepts are reduced to just one: love one's neighbor.[17] Many others claim, in practice if not in theory, that there are two paths of love, two projectories, different, more or less parallel, and, in the end, one subordinate to the other: the neighbor and God. And if they are told that everything lies in the neighbor, they charge that this is an irresponsible "reduction" of what "Christian faith" is. But I think of it as a great and fruitful "expansion."

I take the liberty of citing a few more examples of the elucidation that comes from the overwhelming impact of certain activist experiences.

Sometimes it is the negative aspect, that of defeat and emptiness, that has such an intense impact. It is very obscure, and is spontaneously expressed in words that suggest a limitless expansion of what is immediately perceived. One militant whom I met repeated, with bitterness, this amusing old verse that is quite well known in Spain:

> When came here the Muslim hordes,
> we were slaughtered by their swords,
> for God with the evil stood,
> when they outnumbered the good.

Sometimes, rather than an outright elucidation of an abundance that has been experienced, the insight is injected into phrases that perfunctory routine has converted into ethereal music. One example might be this new reading of the first beatitude from Matthew:

Blessed are the poor who mobilize in the struggle against their oppressors, because they will not be deceived (as their parents were) by the kingdom of heaven.[18]

Even more interesting, it seems to me, is the following incident, which must be told with a certain amount of detail. It shows how the expression "inspired by the Holy Spirit" can be interpreted.

In February 1978, there was a chance meeting in Havana of Ernesto Cardenal, a revolutionary poet-priest; Sergio Méndez Arceo, the bishop of Cuernavaca, Mexico, animator of the Christians for Socialism movement; and Alfonso C. Comín, of the Central Committee of both the United Socialist Party of Catalonia and the Communist Party of Spain, and a Christian as well. All three agreed to draft a document dealing with the issue of Christianity and the church in the revolution. Comín drafted a preliminary text and, when he submitted it to Cardenal for criticism and corrections, the latter, after reading it carefully, told him that there was no correction or addition to be made. It is a text, he told him, "inspired by the Holy Spirit." Some time later, Comín put into writing his thoughts on Cardenal's remark:

> I am reflecting on what "inspired by the Holy Spirit" means to a believer. Simply this: in the solitude of a dwelling on the Isle of Pines, belonging to the island of youth [Cuba], the ancient Ciguanea, to the accompaniment of the sea, writing with love for the land of which one writes, with love for the church of which one writes, with love for the revolution of which one writes; with love and hope, indeed, despite all the imperfections of that revolution, despite the rationalistic positivism of which one is accused by those who have all their questions answered.[19]

Conclusions at the end of this study? None, so far as I am concerned. A path has been pointed out for traversing; nothing more. It would be like trying to draw harvest conclusions from the thrilling beauty of a plantation that is starting to bud in early springtime. Or drawing words from the braying of the she-ass of Balaam. No; conclusions will be provided by history, led by its lord: the oppressed people.

I am quite well aware of the fact that there are in this article repetitions, some more or less sudden changes, a disappearance and reappearance of themes, and little schematization, although in some parts I attempted to be schematic. I should not know how to deal with this type of subject matter without resorting to the kind of style that I might typify as "symphonic." In a musical symphony, there is usually a prelude in which the main themes are introduced with a certain indefiniteness. They subsequently appear in a variety of ways, sometimes clearly, sometimes intermingled; they disappear and emerge again, enveloped in different harmonies. Then a magnificent crescendo is cut off by a silence that is perhaps even more valuable. And so on, until a conclusion is reached, inspired by someone or something unknown.

It would perhaps be incorrect to call such a style scientific, in a written work. But that does not prove a lack of substance, logic, or coherence. They depend on other factors.

Late in the writing of these pages, I had an opportunity to read the study by Dr. Sergio Arce Martínez, "La teología y el ateismo contemporáneo," published in the book *Cristo vivo en Cuba—Reflexiones teológicas cu-*

banas.[20] His work exudes maturity; my own is still very rough at the edges. But I think that they have some (quite a few) features in common, with regard to proposals, concerns, and areas for searching; and I am very happy about those features in common.

NOTES

1. Ernesto Cardenal, *Oráculo sobre Managua* (Buenos Aires-Mexico City: Ed. Lohlé, 1973), p. 39 ff. Acahualinca is a slum area in the city of Managua.

2. R. Fernández Aldabalde, *Fetichismo y Religión* (Madrid: Ed. Zero, 1975), pp. 149 ff.

3. José Porfirio Miranda, *Marx y la Biblia* (Salamanca: Sígueme, 1972), Engl. trans., *Marx and the Bible,* John Eagleson, trans. (Maryknoll, N.Y.: Orbis, 1974), pp. 294–96.

4. Juan García Nieto, ''Reencuentro con 'Cristianos por el Socialismo,' '' in *Iglesia Viva,* 60 (Nov.–Dec. 1975): 509.

5. In the Basque magazine *Kristau Elkartean* (Otsaila, 1978), p. 8.

6. Ernesto Cardenal, *La santidad de la Revolución* (Salamanca: Sígueme, 1976), p. 48.

7. Franz Hinkelammert, *Las armas ideológicas de la muerte* (San José, Costa Rica: DEI-EDUCA, 1977).

8. Leader of the Chilean MIR (Revolutionary Left Movement), killed in October 1974.

9. Franz Hinkelammert, *Las armas,* p. 200.

10. Raúl Vidales, ''Vida-trabajo, binomio central del bien común en la tradición cristiana,'' in *Capitalismo: Violencia y anti-vida* (San José, Costa Rica: DEI-EDUCA, 1978), pp. 97 ff.

11. Pedro Casaldáliga, *Tierra nuestra, libertad* (Buenos Aires, 1974), p. 89.

12. *Agermanament* (Barcelona, 1978), no. 147, p. 68.

13. Enrique Dussel, *Teología de la liberación y ética* (Buenos Aires, 1974), pp. 128 ff.; Eng. trans.: *Ethics and the Theology of Liberation* (Maryknoll, N.Y.: Orbis Books, 1978).

14. *A Theology of Liberation* (Maryknoll, N.Y.: Orbis, 1973), p. 203. It would be well to read the entire section, ''Conversion to the Neighbor,'' pp. 194–203.

15. In the Basque magazine *Herria 2000 Eliza* (Maiatza, 1978), p. 28.

16. Ibid.

17. For example, Samuel Ruíz, in *Teología bíblica de la liberación* (Mexico City, 1975), pp. 73 ff.

18. Bernard Päschke, ''De la bienaventuranza a la lucha de los pobres,'' in *Liaisons Internationales* (Paris, August–September 1976), p. 9.

19. The magazine *La Calle* (Madrid, April 1978), no. 2.

20. San José, Costa Rica: DEI, 1978. See also Sergio Arce Martínez, *The Church and Socialism* (Maryknoll, N.Y.: Orbis Books, forthcoming).

VII

JAVIER JIMÉNEZ LIMÓN

Meditation on the God of the Poor

We cannot write about God without imposing a certain violence on ourselves, because we fear (and with reason) tampering with mystery, distorting or even perverting the good news. In most instances, casual talk about God is sickening: it blesses injustices, canonizes human policies, and ideologizes mundane realities. It extinguishes the fire, dulls the sword's edge, and makes love banal.

The difficulty is not due to the horizontalism or secularism that is in style on the theological market: they can be explained in terms of the inability to invoke God from a satisfied, apathetic abundance. Or they can be considered the effect of an enlightened, self-sufficient scientism that does not look for or even consider anything except what fits within strategy and tactics that can be planned.

Rather, one might expect that the difficulty in speaking about God is due to the awareness that God is always greater, and to the certainty that "it is better to be silent and be, than to talk and not be" (Ignatius of Antioch).

The difficulty increases if we attempt to speak expressly about the God of the poor, because this is the God of the oppressed, the mistreated, the despised, the exploited. What right do we have to be "the voice of the voiceless,'' perhaps distorting with polished words what they can better express in their cries, laments, and songs? If we theologize too hastily, shall we not simply find in the world of the poor an echo of the dominant ideology imposed on them by the powerful, so as to keep them impassive and resigned? If we reverently approach the poor, to listen to the voice of God, shall we not be mystifying a harsh and cruel reality, preventing it from reaching us with its primal outcry? Shall we not be bringing from outside a God of academia or poetry, not discovering the God already there, a more internal, more living, more biblical, and nearer God?

And yet, we must dare (at least occasionally) to stammer what we seem to hear concerning the only thing that is important in the long run: the God living in the faith, life, and death of the poor, who are the Body of God's Son.

But we must not do so without first asking Bishop Pedro Casaldáliga's wise question: "The living God of these poor people, is he ours, Teófilo?"[1]

I have two strong reasons for speaking, in spite of the dangers. The first is the joy and responsibility of the good news: God appears again, surprising us, offering hope, inhabiting the struggles and faith of the oppressed. When the gospel reaches the wretched of this world, the living God of the Bible takes life and comes close. This is the first, and the more important reason. The second is more human, but is also serious: many are afraid that, if we take the poor seriously, we shall no longer take God seriously; we shall become worldly, horizontal, unbelieving. When we do not have the credentials of a prophet, and we have had this same fear ourselves, there is no use cursing those fears. We should have the confidence to say: "Have no fear, brothers and sisters, the only way to take God seriously is to take the poor seriously. Have fear, rather, that God without the poor will become an idol for you." The atheism of the concerned is preferable to the idolatry of the complacent. And, in any event, the good news is possible (almost connatural) only in the midst of the sufferings, struggles, and hopes of the poor.

Hence I offer these conjectures or meditations, in the hope that a comment of mine might communicate something of the spark that is lighting the hearts of many of the poor. May it ignite a desire and hope for burning and destroying, for illuminating and building, and for continuing to be (and not in the last place) the servant of Yahweh through suffering, unwelcome like all suffering, but warmed by solidarity and the struggle for the kingdom of God.

Only the God of the Poor Exists

First, a brief explanation. When talking about the God of the poor, we are talking about the only God who exists, according to the Christian Bible. There is no neutral, transcendent god, pure in metaphysical essence and in metahistorical inaccessibility, a god lacking relationships with creatures, and specifically with the poor. Such a god is an abstraction. And metaphysical ecstasies are not transcendent; they encompass a void that can be filled *ad libitum* with all manner of human desires and fears. The only possible transcendence comes to us in the gift and the appeal of the God of Israel and of Jesus, the God of the exodus and the exile, of the beatitudes and the cross.

Nor is there a God of the church who is more catholic, more universal, than the God of the poor. The only God who convokes the church and who is its Lord is the God of the oppressed. We are not engaging in religious sociology, analyzing the God of one sector of the population, to be compared with the God of other sectors; we are simply reading the good news of God. Let us not try to be more catholic than God: God's universality and catholicity are compatible with partiality in favor of the poor. The Father of all human beings is the God of the poor.

The true God of Christians who are not poor is the God of the poor. All believers, regardless of their socio-economic origin, receive the mandate and the gift to opt for the poor.

Nor do the poor always accept their true God. They too can be, and in fact have been, idolatrous. In most instances, however, they have been driven to it by the idols imposed on them by their oppressors (a materialization of the power of sin that overreaches social classes, but is evident in them).

Nor are we discovering a new God, although God always appears new. The deep current of the Bible and Christian tradition, which has often followed a subterranean course, now seems to us to be surfacing, powerfully and openly. God knows the times; who could be God's adviser? But God always appears with the signs that were made manifest in Jesus; God is the God of the poor.

If I appear dogmatic, it is because the most elementary teachings in the Bible have been kept hidden and captive on the outer edges of our historical tyranny. We had better read the Bible again. We are so ideologized that talking about the God of the poor seems to us an ideologization! "I bless you, Father, because you have revealed these things to the lowly, and have concealed them from the wise and cautious."

God Is Joy

The Quechuan sacristan in José María Arguedas's novel *Todas las sangres* is opposed to the ideological God proposed to him by the *padrecito*: someone who is the same everywhere. "Was God in the heart of those who destroyed the body of the innocent teacher Bellido? Is God in the engineers who are despoiling the Esmeralda mine, or in the official who took away from its owners the cornfield in which the Virgin used to play with her little Son every harvesttime? Don't make me cry, *padrecito*." And he proposes his own intuitive definition of God to him: "God is hope, God is joy, God is spirit. . . . [A man] came, with yellow skin, ragged, sick, and bent over; he left robust, healthy, like an eagle. He went back with the same clothes, but in his eye there was God. . . ."

It may seem paradoxical that, in talking about the God of the poor, we begin by talking about joy. It would appear more fitting to talk about grief, anger, and indignation. But the paradox of the beatitudes is at play here, the messianic joy that pervades the gospels (especially that of Luke), and that invades the hearts of the poor and sings through the lips of Mary. It is a joy related to hope for liberation, and courage for struggle. But it starts at a deeper level, in the joyous surprise of knowing that one's dignity is recognized by God: "Tell out, my soul, the greatness of the Lord, rejoice, rejoice, my spirit, in God my savior; so tenderly has he looked upon his servant" (Luke 1:46–48). This is the experience that transforms the one who arrived "sick and bent over" into someone "robust and healthy."

It is a joy that is subversive, but no revolutionary strategy can engender or express it, a joy against which the entire capitalist ideology is fighting, disdaining the poor as lazy, drunken, malodorous, and dangerous. It is a joy that has often been squelched by institutionalized religion and a false evangelization that has brought to the poor a moralistic, castigating God.

It is a joy that persons need, and that encourages and nurtures them on the long journey through social changes. It is the clear joy proclaimed by the prophets to the poor. Read Deutero-Isaiah again to rediscover all the cries of jubilation, rejoicing, and happiness: Yahweh remembers his people, taking away their fears and inhibitions, reminding them of his creative love (Yahweh, your liberator, who created you from within), shepherding them, taking the lambs in his arms.

This joy remained buried in "evangelization," because those who approached the poor did so from an ethical perspective, motivated more by compassion than by the good news: the news that arouses the active dignity of the poor, their will to live, and the surprise of being children of God in freedom. The paternalistic church is incapable of arousing this joy among the poor; it can be achieved only by the church of the poor, in which they are recognized as the privileged members of the church, against all "wise and prudent" evaluations to the contrary.

I cannot resist the temptation to quote in this context a criticism made by Karl Marx of what he perceived as the social principles of Christianity:

> The social principles of Christianity preach cowardice, self-deprecia-
> tion, debasement, subjection, and humility; in short, all the attributes
> of the rabble. The proletariat, who refuse to allow themselves to be
> treated as rabble, need their courage, their self-respect, their pride, and
> their taste for independence, more than they need bread.

How could there be a factual basis for this perception, in such obvious contradiction to the entire teaching and practice of Jesus?

There must be no fear to associate the foundational Christian message with the active dignity of the poor—a dignity so necessary to the revolution. It does not lie only in the God-given creativity of humankind and its call to stewardship of the world and political liberation. It lies in the beatitudes: in the plenary freedom of God who wants to be the God of the poor; in the justification that is manifested in deeds, especially by bringing dignity to those who are despised; in the joy of knowing oneself to be recognized as an individual, and as a member of a poor family, in the all-embracing fatherhood of God. No revolutionary ideology could penetrate so deeply; and only such a deep joy can prove itself real by giving birth to a revolution.

I have seldom felt the deep sadness of the oppressed so well spelled out as in the following autobiographical passage by the Indian Gregorio Cóndori, who had been orphaned:

> I always wanted to return to Acopía. My parents were dead, but I had some aunts and uncles there whom I wanted to talk to. With this thought, which had grown in my heart for years, I went to Acopía. Because I was very young when I had last been there, none of my aunts and uncles recognized me. Of course, I did not recognize them either, nor did I know how many there were; but still I wanted them to recognize me. And for that reason, I sat from the early morning hours at the foot of the cross in the square, all day, hoping to be recognized. Townsfolk kept passing by, and some commented: "There is a stranger sitting beside the cross." I remained motionless, sitting there that entire day. Then it was late; the cattle were returning from where they had gone to graze; and I remained sitting there.

How can the joy of the poor fail to erupt happily and clearly when the beatitudes are presented, not as a consoling doctrine, but as a surprising, even scandalous, statement of the fatherhood of the God of Jesus? In this joy there is subversion that triggers historical revolutions aimed beyond the present.

In this joy, the poor evangelize those of us who are not poor but who struggle with them, because they dispossess us in favor of the "pure joy" that animated Francis of Assisi. It is the joy that, without softening the mandate for struggle (rather, providing grounds for it), can assuage that nervous, Pelagian seriousness that many Christians of bourgeois extraction bring to it.

Let it be clear: we are not wafting beautiful, innocuous poetry. This joy can be announced only by repeating the deeds of Jesus. And there will then come the disillusionment and the anger of the older brother in the parable, of the inveterate Pharisees, of the sated and satisfied, and of the rich and powerful. "He stirs up the mob, and restrains the payment of taxes."

God Is the Courage to Struggle

The love of the Father that brings dignity to the poor and breaks out in messianic joy is a creative love relating essentially to the kingdom: "How blessed are you who are poor; the kingdom of God is yours" (Luke 6:20). It is not a consoling love that brings only personalistic affection, but rather a creative love that brings justice and transformation.

We are so accustomed to considering the poor a passive object of God's love that it is difficult for us to perceive their active dignity. The religiosity of compassion, resignation, and fatalism prevents the poor from sharing in the liberating praxis of God. It would appear that only the resigned, suffering poor could mediate God. But the truth is exactly the opposite: the God of the kingdom appears in our respect for the active dignity of the poor. The otherness of God appears when the poor struggle for a world worthy of God: for the kingdom. Otherwise, we remain in the closed circle of the unregenerated world.

Mary's joy does not derive only from the fact that her God looked upon the humility of his handmaiden, but also from the fact that God toppled the mighty from their thrones and raised up the poor. That is why the gospel proclaims, "Stand upright and hold your heads high, because your liberation is near" (Luke 21:28).

It is true that a widespread understanding of the leading role to be played by the poor in historical liberation will entail a complex process of maturation, and it is precisely in this newness that the ancient gospel assumes timeliness, as a means and requirement for salvation. The God of the Bible is not a dead relic, but the one who today gives courage to the poor to assume, responsibly, their historical empowerment:

Fear nothing, for I am with you; be not afraid, for I am your God. I strengthen you, I help you, I support you with my victorious right hand. . . . You shall thresh the mountains and crush them, and reduce the hills to chaff [Isa. 41:10–15].

Young men may grow weary and faint, even in their prime they may stumble and fall; but those who look to the Lord will win new strength, they will grow wings like eagles; they will run and not be weary, they will march on and never grow faint [Isa. 40:30–31].

The active dignity of the poor may often be dormant, crushed, violated, and, in extreme cases, even dead; but it arises powerful and aggressive upon contact with the good news. A Venezuelan document on the church born of the people has expressed this magnificently:

Primarily, we announce a gospel, good news: it is possible to live in opposition [to the prevailing system]. We do not rely on the will of our oppressors. We can dissociate ourselves from their organizations, pay no heed to their slogans, ignore their styles, and disregard their leaders. They have decreed political death for us, but we are alive. We work in their factories, their fields, their offices, their hospitals, their schools, and their universities, but not as slaves; rather, learning to run what will some day belong to everyone. This system was presented to us as a god capable of offering life and death. . . . Recognition and submission was required of us. Today, we are atheists of that god, and we are still living.

This is our good news. We have discovered the limits of this system: it is not all-powerful. And the power that will overthrow it in the future has now germinated. We have experienced this new power as a power that liberates us from the fear of dying. Because of that fear, we used to spend our lives as slaves. Now we know that our poverty can enrich others, and that in our weakness there is shown the force of God as salvation for every person who dares to become dissociated from these powers of death, to live on our hope.[2]

This God-spirit causes the people to emerge as responsible subjects. It is not a politico-religious messianism wherein the poor surrender their responsibility as a result of a blind, emotional, alienating hope. Such is the temptation of the poor when they are not with the God who gives spirit, offering responsibility and freedom. That was the paternalistic, comfortable messiah that the Galilean masses wanted. Jesus raised up the poor, without excusing them from involvement, without transforming them magically, but inviting them to the responsibility of discipleship and struggle—without deceiving them with the image of a paradise within easy reach:

This is our good news. We do not say: "If all of us were to agree to build a just, dynamic, social system, I would gladly leave my comforts to embark upon that shared life." That is an unrealistic proposal. We say: "It is in the midst of this discriminatory society that the struggle to build a new and different one takes place." That struggle has a social cost, a price. The sin of the world will be taken away only by the love based on service that bears the burden of the sin of the world. . . . Our good news is the proclamation that one can live out the storm. It is only with that accepted risk that solidarity can be created as a fruitful union of free human beings.[3]

The poor filled with spirit and infrahistorical power are no longer the tameable "poor little things" who are the object of false charity. They are united, free, brothers and sisters, aware of their dignity. The God of consolation and fear has become, for them, the God of spirit and hope. Those of us who have approached them with paternalism sometimes sense, with bewilderment, that God has become more demanding of us, has restored us to our true status as brothers and sisters, and has made us share more tellingly their risks, their weaknesses, and the responsibility of solidarity. And God has given us the gospel of a power not created from heroic self-sufficiency, but rather from a commitment shared in solidarity.

God Is Hope against All Hope

If the poor maintain messianic joy and a liberating spirit, it is not because oppression and pain have disappeared, but because God is for them a strong, persistent hope. God is not resigned because of his love: this is a God of the living, who wants abundant life for his children. The secret of hope lies in the unconditional nature of love.

In the popular understanding and practice of religion, the poor do what they can to seek meaning in their incomprehensible suffering. And they usually show it in an impassive resignation, with a trace of ineffectual protest. Gregorio Cóndori, whom we have already quoted, reflects in his autobiography:

> I question whether this is the fate of those of us who have been thrown into this world to suffer. In this way—they claim—we poor heal the wounds of God. And when these wounds are completely healed, suffering will disappear from this world. We were told that once by a corporal, and we privates said to him: "Damn it, those wounds must be big if they haven't disappeared with so much suffering." And he answered: "Don't be heretics, damn it! Fall in!" Now, as I think about it, I would say that there is more suffering than before. This life is no longer bearable. This life is heavier than the load on my shoulders [he is a stevedore].

This daily, incomprehensible suffering is the unremitting life experience of the poor. It becomes even worse when the oppression is combined with repression of their legitimate struggles and organizations. Therefore, for the poor, hope against hope is not a matter of privileged moments in spectacular crises, but rather their daily bread.

Upon discovering the living God, the poor are liberated from resignation and fatalism; they know their protest is accompanied by the protest of God; and their hope is nurtured on small achievements, solidarity, and organization. However, the great hope, that of community and justice, the hope that goes beyond bare subsistence, has no other ultimate nourishment than to walk with Jesus in his struggle, his passion, and his resurrection.

A God Just Beginning to Appear

The poor are only just starting to speak out in the church, in the midst of their liberation struggles. We are discerning only the first signs of this change. Not everything is going to be bright and transparent, unsullied. Even in the Bible there is mention of the failings, temptations, and sins of the poor. But we have a premonition that the joy, the strength, and the mysterious weakness of God will continue taking shape in the faith, hope, and love of the poor. And, in any event, we know that God is close by, and that the danger is not unbelieving worldliness, but apathetic resignation and indifference toward our brothers and sisters.

To express it in the metaphor of Bishop Pedro Casaldáliga of Brazil, I have spoken about the God of the poor as singing in the joy, the spirit, and the hope of the oppressed. But it must not be forgotten that this same song (which is that of the conversion demanded by the poor) must sound like a shout and a demand in the ears of the oppressors, the satisfied, and the indifferent.

I should like to conclude these reflections with a portion of Casaldáliga's poem, "These Raucous Roosters Answer You":

> You ask me about my faith. . . .
> Shall I answer you by asking impertinently? . . .
> The living God of these poor people,
>   is he ours, oh Teófilo?
> These roosters that persist, into the night, shrill clarion calls,
> piercing the darkness, challenging the stars and the stock markets;
> rigid sentinels, braced against sleep, as often as is needed;
> these roosters born and alive and always on duty
> so that nobody will sleep, foreign to the testimony,
> if he did not previously make his alliance
> with the night and with the dawn.
>
> These roosters (that crow to us) are the roosters of the guilt of Saint
>   Peter.
> These roosters (that call to us) are the roosters of Mary's vigil.
> These roosters (that sing to us) are the roosters of the sepulcher,
> *mane prima sabbati!!!*[4]

NOTES

1. Teófilo Cabestrero, *Mystic of Liberation* (Maryknoll, N.Y.: Orbis, 1981), p. 7.
2. *Iglesia que nace del pueblo, una buena noticia* (Mexico City: Ed. CRT, 1978), pp. 26–27.
3. Ibid., p. 27.
4. Cabestrero, *Mystic of Liberation,* pp. 7–8.

VIII

FREI BETTO

God Bursts Forth in the Experience of Life

Activism and the Experience of God: A Change in the Quality of Faith

I shall begin with how my activism intensified my lived experience of God.

I had a long period of activism in Brazil, dating back to my student days, which is why I was jailed twice: in 1964 (fifteen days) and 1969 (four years).

Obviously, there was a change in the quality of my faith during this process; faith as the point of contact of my existence with the existence of God. This is where I locate the change in quality of my faith.

Until I entered the Dominican novitiate (1965), I had a far more doctrinal faith. It was a faith that was made up of, and nurtured on, catechetical memorization and Bible readings. It was a very sensitive faith, very much aimed at sensitive stimulation. Therefore, wherever there was an absence of sensitive stimulation (or we might even call it an idolatrous relic relating to what is sacred), there might be a danger of losing faith. In the religious life, idolatrous relics were everywhere. The halls were filled with statues, pictures, pho-

These reflections originate from an interview held with Frei Betto in Puebla, Mexico, on February 7, 1979.

159

tographs, and posters, for the purpose of creating an environment that would stimulate one's faith.

But, strangely enough, in my case the opposite occurred. When I entered the Dominican order, when I remained for a year cloistered in the novitiate, coming from an experience of complete political activism at the university, instead of finding the environment a stimulus to my faith, there was a loss. I felt as if all my religious associations had been dispelled, and I began to find the prayers and the Eucharist meaningless. And I found the things that faith professes, especially the Eucharist and the presence of the Holy Spirit, absurd.

There was a time when I was certain that I was losing faith; that I no longer had faith. I began preparing to leave the religious life. But a priest helped me a lot when he told me something very simple: "If you were lost in the night, in a forest, and the battery in your flashlight had gone dead on you, would you stop walking, or would you continue on your journey?" Then I said to him: "Well, obviously if I were in a forest at night, without light, I would wait for the dawn." "Then wait for the dawn," he told me. That was what I did; I waited for the dawn.

During that wait, I discovered that I had not lost my faith, but rather that I had undergone a change of quality in my faith. I had moved from an experience of sensitive, rational faith to an experience of faith itself—in other words, that of a very intimate relationship with the love of God, and of acceptance of the life of God in my life. I believe that there are only two ways of having this experience: in what we call the mystical experience, that intimate, personal relationship with God; and when two persons are deeply in love. I believe that it is only in these instances that such experience occurs, and there is the possibility of possessing the other person and of being possessed by the other person in oneself.

That is the experience of intense human love—when the other person takes up a stronger presence in my life than I do myself. That is the experience of deep human love and that is the mystical experience.

After that, the idolatrous God, or the deified idols, lost meaning for me, and more than ever I gained a sense of God the person, the God who becomes known in the experience of love and in the experience of the liberation struggle. This is why I think that those who set up a dichotomy between God and that struggle are attempting to reduce to a single human realm—that of the rationale of political design—other human dimensions that are far more extensive, such as the dimension of the spirit, the dimension of generosity, the dimension of gratuitousness. These dimensions are not confined to the dimension of political design or its rationale. But I do think that the issue should be based on something that makes sense—namely, the experience of love.

While in prison I had an experience that also helped me to re-pose the question of God in my life. It came in my discovery that God is the negation of self—in other words, God is the ultimate depth of human experience. I would say that I moved from a medieval, Thomistic conception of God (the omnipotent, omnipresent, omniscient God; the God so great, so wonderful, so powerful that I feel like an abject sinner, I feel like a condemned culprit, and I cannot do anything worthwhile in the presence of that God) to a discovery of something very important: that God is revealed in the negation of God. We learn this when we come in contact with the one who reveals God to us: Jesus Christ. What is it that we encounter? Someone omnipotent? No, he let himself be apprehended and led away without a struggle. Someone omniscient? No, the threat of death came unexpectedly; he was afraid, he was not prepared for it. Someone all-powerful? No, he had to yield to, and be crushed by, the Roman and Jewish authorities.

In Jesus Christ there is not only an identification with the lowliest of human beings—with the oppressed, with those who are crushed by power, with those who are tortured, with those who are persecuted—but a solidarity with those who feel abandoned by God: "Father, Father, why have you forsaken me?" In other words, God provokes the experience of self-negation.

This is profoundly dialectical, and difficult to explain, but it goes something like this: God is self-negated—negating the medieval image that we have of God—in the event of Jesus. And God enters into solidarity with, and hence offers salvation to, those who feel abandoned by God.

But God does not stop there. God proceeds to a third phase, the article of faith that we profess in the Apsotles' Creed: "on the third day, he descended into hell." In Jesus, before the resurrection, God is in solidarity with those who feel condemned by God. This datum of Christian faith—that Jesus descended into hell—is very important. Why do we not descend into hell? Hell, the gate of hell, is the limit of our faith. When I discovered that God exists in God's absence, all the idolatry of the ruling classes ended for me—that is, all identification of the image of God with power, with the bourgeoisie, with bourgeois morality, and with all the correct, acceptable niceties. It all ended there.

I discovered that God exists in God's negation when I came to understand the experience of God among my imprisoned comrades, persons who had been there for seventeen, twenty, or twenty-five years, or were to be there all the days of their lives. Their bodies had been reduced to mere shells of what they once had been, but they had inside them a profound capacity to love, to be open toward, and in solidarity with, their comrades. It was then that I realized that they are saved, not by professing a faith, or because they are capable of performing deeds of love that we consider exemplary. They are saved by something deeper and simpler. They are the ones who are identified in history with the passion of Christ. They are themselves the personal extension of that passion.

Since then, I have found it inconceivable to make a distinction between the divine and the human, or between the experience of what is divine and the experience of what is human. I believe that it is through the experience of what is human, in its deepest aspects, that one encounters the experience of what is divine. In my opinion, that was the experience of the Hebrews. It was when they were under the harshest oppression that they perceived the liberating presence of Yahweh. When the situation was a little more relaxed and calm, they sought out idols.

What is the experience of God? The experience of God is what makes transcendence possible. That transcendence is a very personal thing. For me, that transcendence and that personal experience are rooted in what I believe has come from Christian revelation through the living tradition of the church.

We move from an idolatrous God to the discovery of a God who is self-negated in Jesus Christ. If I want to find God, if I want to find a person, I must go where that person is, and I must allow that person to be revealed to me. I cannot know you unless you talk to me, and tell me who you are. Therefore, I can know God only where God talks to me and tells me who God is, historically, in the experience of Jesus and in the experience of the poor—the extension of Jesus' experience.

The Personal Experience of God in the Basic Christian Community

I believe that Jesus is the revelation of God. God is not a creation of the oppressed mentality of the proletariat, the alienated, the wretched of the earth. Although it is true that religion can serve as an escape valve and lead to alienation among the masses, the same thing can hold true of political manipulation. There are many factors in alienation and escape valves that are not proper to religion. To blame religion for all of them is a deception. Even religion as Marx regarded it shows two aspects: it may be the opium of the people, but at the same time it shows an aspect of constructive protest: "to be the heart of a world without a heart." It is a form of protest of the oppressed who have no other language, no other way of expressing themselves except through religion.

Intellectuals who have intellectualist and colonialist eyes do not understand the liberating dimension of popular religion. I have never heard any theologian talk about "episcopal religion." There is always talk of "popular religion," as a rather pejorative term, as if the people had no true religion. The masses have a smattering of religion, and it is commonly called religiosity. But why not "the religiosity of bishops," or "religiosity of priests and pastors"? Because we are incapable of perceiving the entire religious depth of the people's faith. Why? Owing to a very simple fact: because we do not live with the people. I cannot understand the idiosyncrasies of Germans if I have never lived in Germany. I must live with the people in order to understand the people.

The theologians of liberation have this commitment to the popular classes, but there are also those who are "theoretical" theologians, who rehash half a dozen books into another book, and know that others, in turn, will blend their book with six others into still another book, and so on, in geometric progression.

The basic communities were very important to me, in that they offered me contact with the people, and forced me into a certain cultural revolution. I had to reshuffle a series of intellectual patterns that I have developed, which were analytical projections over and beyond the people. And I perceived the great discrepancy between my analytical projections and the reality of the people's life.

The reality is completely different from the analysis that many make. For example, many believe that the proletariat is waiting for someone to appear, someone incorporating its aspirations, and then it will rise up. This is a deception. There is an entire learning process of injection, dialogue, openness, and transformation of consciousness that the proletariat is carrying out (and we are not).

Now we can help the proletariat to create conditions for that change. But as we approach it, and try to help it create these conditions, we too are challenged by it, we too are evangelized by it.

Something else important occurred in my experience with the basic ecclesial communities: I perceived that the personal experience of God there was different from the personal experience of God that I had known until then. Theirs is a God who eats; a God who breathes; a God with experience in sex; a God in whom the freedom of life is lived; a God to whom one weeps, cries, protests, makes demands; a God with whom one struggles. There is not the slightest difference between that God and the human persons in the people's life.

This made a very great impact on me, as I perceived to what extent, and how, God is present in their lives, and they are present in God's life; and how they perceive this presence in the lives of others.

In Brazil, when two persons bid farewell, the one says to the other, "Go with God." There is not that dissociation between spirit and body. The masses pray with their bodies. They do not know how to say a prayer of silence, or an abstract prayer. I have never heard it said that a group of them ever managed to remain an hour before the tabernacle, worshiping. This is because they pray with their bodies. They need to kneel, light candles, walk, make pilgrimages, hold festivals, sing, and dance: that is the prayer of the people. It is a prayer that does not divide body and spirit. It is a prayer that is said with all the forms of expression that they use in everyday life.

On the one hand, the religious mentality of the masses is, in fact, alienating, to the extent that they transfer to God the responsibility for solving their concrete problems. But, on the other hand, as a process of conscientization and politicization unfolds, there is also a change in their image of God, not a rejection.

In that respect, the masses have a far greater wisdom than ours as intellectuals, who are always changing ideas or changing concepts, just as we would change our clothes. Does the proletariat undergo a change with every new book, every new experience? No. It seems to me that the popular classes have the opportunity for a greater integration of their personally experienced cultural heritage with the new discoveries that they make. I sense this in connection with the popular struggles in Brazil. There, there is no strong religious emphasis, such as there is in the struggles in Mexican history, in which the Virgin of Guadalupe is always present. But neither is there opposition between the struggle and faith. I mean that, in a way, faith goes beyond the struggle, and the struggle, in turn, influences the view of faith. I sensed this in prison, when some communists came to tell me, in strict confidence, "Look, it would not be good for the others to know. . . . I am in the party. . . . I took courses in the Soviet Union . . . but I never stopped believing in God." To me, it is not a matter of ceasing to believe in God; it would be impossible. But someone might say, "That is alienation." Why is it alienation?

They do not have a theological projection of God; they do not have an intellectual description of God. To them, God is something as concrete and as identified with their lives as is the experience of love, the experience of struggle.

There does not exist, I repeat, that dissociation that we make when we argue about God, about an intellectual category. We put God on the chemical analysis table, and we dissect, divide, and analyze God. In the basic community, this is impossible. God is the air they breathe, and the very experience of their own lives.

I believe that the same thing holds true of biblical experience—I mean that it reveals a flesh-and-blood God, a God who bursts forth in the very experience of life itself. The systemization of that experience takes place later. An example would be the experience of the exodus; its literary systemization came centuries after the people's experience. This experience, like our own personal and group experiences, is always greater than our capacity for systemizing it literally.

Therein lies the importance of the balance that we (who concern ourselves with theology in Latin America) should strike between intellectual endeavor and findings based on personal experience, on concrete experience and concrete commitment. It is only in this dialectical relationship that we shall avoid ideological constructs that would keep us apart from the life of the people.

IX

FRANZ HINKELAMMERT

The Economic Roots of Idolatry: Entrepreneurial Metaphysics

At first glance, it must surely be surprising that mention is made of entrepreneurial metaphysics. Although there is such a metaphysics, and it has spread to all parts of our bourgeois world, it is very seldom perceived for what it is. It often appears as nothing more than a candid description of reality, or it takes on the appearance of a set of widely accepted slogans. Nevertheless, it is omnipresent, and religious dicta, particularly those of the Christian tradition, abound in it. Capitalist entrepreneurs are devotees of this metaphysics, treating it as the framework of their religion. And those among them who claim to have no religion subscribe to this same metaphysics.

Entrepreneurial metaphysics is a metaphysics of commodities, money, marketing, and capital. Since the beginning of the bourgeois world, the thinking of the bourgeoisie has had a metaphysical perception of these mat-

165

ters, and has not given it up, even today. It is present in all the ethics and morality of the capitalist undertaking, and constitutes the essence of the legitimacy of the power of capital. It is expressed in all the outlets of bourgeois society: in the newspapers, the magazines, the speeches of politicians, and, most especially, in everything said and done by entrepreneurs. And, concurrently, there is a vast advertising effort aimed at transforming this entrepreneurial metaphysics into the common thinking of the entire populace.

However, this entrepreneurial metaphysics does not appear only in the advertising of the bourgeois society. It is also evident among that society's leading theoreticians. They speak to and live in the world of commodities, money, marketing, and capital, as the great object of their devotion; a pseudo-divine world towers over human beings, and dictates their laws to them.

The first theoretician of this persuasion emerged at the beginning of bourgeois society. He was Thomas Hobbes, who perceived this superworld (genuine nature) to be simultaneously promising and threatening. He called it Leviathan. Leviathan is bourgeois society itself, and Hobbes called it, at the same time, the mortal God living under the eternal God, and expressing that God's legitimacy and absolute right to repress human beings, in the figure of a sovereign.

Hobbes observed that money is the blood of this Great Leviathan. From Hobbes's time onward, the machinery of bourgeois society has continued to be the great object of devotion in bourgeois social science. Locke still thought in terms of Leviathan. Hegel began talking about the Absolute, the Idea. Adam Smith made an important change: the object of devotion appeared as the "invisible hand" of the social machinery. However, a major new change has occurred in present-day thinking. Max Weber complements the "invisible hand" with its formal rationality—namely, the "rationality of the West." This involves an eternal struggle, which is "destiny." The Trilateral Commission terms it "interdependence."

Whether it be Leviathan, the Idea, the "invisible hand," "destiny," or "interdependence," there always appears in bourgeois thinking a central object of devotion identified with the machinery: goods, money, market, and capital. The forms of expression and words change, but the content never changes.

Bourgeois thinking derives its ethics and morality from this object of devotion. Hence, the values and rules of the market (made legitimate by the object of devotion) appear as paths of virtue or, in the event of their absence, as paths of sin. Thus, there are virtues of the market, just as there are sins against the market. There is also one virtue that is absolutely preeminent: humility. To subject oneself to this great object of devotion, and never rebel, is a requirement of this humility.

Therefore, there is no bourgeois theoretician of the social sciences who does not preach this preeminent virtue of humility. Hayek is only one example, when he states: "The basic orientation of true individualism consists of humility with respect to the procedures [of buying and selling]."[1] This concept of devotion, not surprisingly, aligns its virtues with the great idea of compensation. It leads from repentance to amendment and, finally, the great compensation. In this pseudo-mystical world, the supreme expression of compensation is the "economic miracle." It is considered to be a result of this key humility, which is the gateway to freedom.

Bourgeois freedom is the counterpart of bourgeois humility, which accepts the domination of commerce above all else—a domination primarily viewed as freedom of prices. Human beings act freely (in the shadow of their humility) insofar as they free price curbs, businesses, and markets, and are subject to their indices.

In fact, entrepreneurial virtue in bourgeois thought is nothing but subjection to market fluctuations, and hence it can be very closely associated with humility. Bourgeois thought perceives this type of conduct as "natural" or, according to Max Weber, "rational." The human being is free so long as the dollar is free. This is "nature" to the bourgeois mind.

The enemy of the bourgeois is as metaphysical as the bourgeois itself. In bourgeois thinking, the image of this enemy is constructed from an inversion of what the bourgeois perceives as natural. The primal enemy of the bourgeois appears as the great rebel against God, God being nothing but another term for the main object of devotion that the bourgeois ideology has created. Therefore, anyone who rises up against the bourgeois society is rising up against God. At the same time, that person is also rising up against "nature," which is God's creation.

Although these specifically religious terms are not always used, some derivative of them is always used. What is involved is a negation of humility, as interpreted by bourgeois thought. Hence, to refuse to subject oneself to the market and its indices is the chief sin against the market, and an overt negation of humility. Thus, an image of the enemy of bourgeois society emerges, and that society sees it in any attempt to oppose the main human values championed by the bourgeois philosophy. The enemy's chief characteristics would be hubris, arrogance, and pride.

While the bourgeoisie humbly adheres to the virtues of the market, giving thanks to its great object of devotion, the enemy of bourgeois society arrogantly follows the path of sins against the market. The enemy neither experiences repentance nor makes amends. Logically, the bourgeois receives compensation in the form of an "economic miracle," but the enemy produces only chaos. The enemy of the bourgeois society acts under the protection of the lord of chaos. And because the lord of chaos is Lucifer, the enemy of the bourgeois society is called a utopian. The enemy's way leads to the "path of slavery," because it denies the freedom of prices. It is a perversion of nature, as the bourgeois understands it.

This dual metaphysics (that of the bourgeois order and that of the chaos of any alternative to the bourgeois order) lies at the root of the extremely violent nature of bourgeois thinking. Whether overt or covert, bourgeois thinking entails an unlimited justification of violence, and of the violation of human rights. Bourgeois thinking leads to the most unrestricted legitimizing of the violation of human rights when confronted with any group capable of replacing the bourgeois society. There is no atrocity that cannot be committed in the name of this entrepreneurial metaphysics. One need only consider the types of treatment that Locke recommends for the opponents of the bourgeois society. There are three in particular: torture, slavery, and death. This explains why there has not been in human history such a brazen legitimizing of slavery as that in the liberal thought of John Locke, or such a crude affirmation of the violation of human rights in all respects as is found precisely in this author. He considers opponents to be "brutes," "beasts," and "wild animals," and repeatedly recommends treating them as such.

Based on the metaphysical image of the bourgeois society itself, and hence of its opponents as well, the primary constant in bourgeois action and ideology is the affirmation of the violation of human rights of those opponents; certainly not the defense of their human rights. The proclamation of human rights is, rather, the exception. Hence, the treatment that is currently administered to the opponents of the bourgeois society in many places is nothing new. It is the treatment that has been practiced and recommended ever since Locke, one to which there have been very few exceptions.

On the following pages we shall attempt to demonstrate the way in which this entrepreneurial metaphysics is present in the contemporary mass media. It is impossible here to present a scientifically complete analysis. Ours does not claim representativity according to the canons of strict methodology. Nor do we think that such representativity is necessary, inasmuch as the concepts that we shall cite are virtually omnipresent. We shall base our analysis mainly on comments from newspapers and magazines, and on statements made by politicians and entrepreneurs.

THE CAPITALIST ENTERPRISE
IN THE COMMERCIAL WORLD

When viewed from a business perspective, the economic world is extremely odd. Commodities seem to be little devils moving in and out of all kinds of interrelationships. They seem to exhibit human behavior. The location of their moves is the market, especially the stock exchange. There commodities rise and fall, gain ground and lose ground, have victories and suffer, spin upward and fall. Among them, there appear enmities and friendships; there are mergers and commitments. And many conflicts arise among them. "The dollar underwent a slight decline yesterday . . . it lost ground on other markets." "Where will the downward trend of the dollar end?" "The dollar is plummeting." "With the weakness of the American dollar, the market for European currency is flourishing."

What is said about the dollar is said about every commodity. Coffee advances on the stock exchange when there is a frost in Brazil. Oil wins over coal, and synthetic sodium nitrate over natural sodium nitrate. Japanese electronic products flood the United States market, and French wines dominate the European wine market. Oil wins over coal, but causes an energy crisis. Atomic energy has come to save us from it.

The economic world of business is not inhabited by human beings, but by commodities. The commodities take action, and human beings run after them. The basic agent in this world is a commodity that is moving and carrying out social action. Following the commodities, the business firms appear. In this world of business, firms too engage in action—not to be confused with human action. All the social relationships that entrepreneurs discover in commodities, they rediscover in business firms. Entrepreneurs do not view themselves as the prime movers. From their standpoint, the business firm is the prime mover; they are nothing but the leading employee of the business firm.

Nevertheless, in the social relationships among business firms, entrepreneurs see warfare, and see themselves as combatants at war. The president of Kaiser Resources, Ltd., comments: "The American coal mining companies are old companies that have done nothing new in fifty years. We are killing them."[2] *Business Week* describes this as "superaggressive marketing." In another reference, it notes: "Betamax had too much success. Suddenly, it brought the heavy caliber guns into the business."[3] Concerning another type of competition, it says, "These are terrorist tactics of the corporations, a declaration of war."[4] "In the hard-fighting steel markets . . . higher prices cannot be imposed. . . . The competition is too stiff. . . . The Japanese are entering the arena with export subsidies."[5] "VEBA is fighting for its future on two fronts. . . . However, a contract . . . received the blessing of the VEBA board of directors on Monday."

But it should not be thought that everything is a struggle. Business firms also marry, make commitments, and sometimes get divorced. One failed marriage is commented on in these terms: "It was impossible to consummate the marriage between the two firms, which was planned seven years ago and postponed for seven years. In the end, Corona-Holding, which is the superior associate, decided to dissolve the commitment."[6]

Just like the commodity, the business firm too is converted into an entity with a personality of its own, which operates independently from the concrete lives of concrete persons. Just as the commodity is converted into an active subject, the business firm becomes an active subject as well. It becomes the favorite child of the entrepreneur. An astrologer, discussing his relationship with entrepreneurs, comments:

[Astrology] has a farflung market, an extensive area for work, because the astrologer's knowledge can be useful in medicine, sociology, and psychology, as also to business firms, and to the like. Many firms request our advice when their status is critical. *We study their incorpora-*

tion papers, taking into account the day, place, and time at which they were signed. Once we have studied this information, we advise the firm as to what it should or should not do in order to achieve positive results.[7]

The business firm is converted into a personality, a legal person, and now seeks attention. Hence it is not surprising that business firms have a code of morality. Mention is made of "the morality of the corporations" and "business firms with acknowledged ethical solvency."[8] This is not the same thing as the morality or ethics of entrepreneurs, but of the behavior of their firms. The norms that some would like to impose on the multinational corporations are of this same type. There can be no questioning of the moral conduct of entrepreneurs, but rather that of the business firms.

The most common social relationship between commodities and business firms is perceived and described by entrepreneurs as that of a war. They claim that it is a healthy, wholesome war, but it is not a matter of "catch as catch can." It is a war with goals and with rules. That is why the business firms that do not abide by them are accused of being terrorists: "the corporations' terrorist tactics," says *Business Week*. But the war is waged among gentlemen, noblemen.

Entrepreneurs perceive goals and rules in their firms' behavior. The perception of goals is something we can see very clearly in a speech by the president of the Bank of Nicaragua, published in Managua's *La Prensa*. This is a highly significant statement regarding the entrepreneur's perception of the emergence of goals in the economic process. He discusses the economic history of Nicaragua following World War II:

Fortunately, there appeared intrepid, unprejudiced, vigorous, and capable individuals who plowed the uncultivated land and, like *great captains,* led an unprecedented movement of national transformation. Without the *dynamism of cotton* that whitens our fertile fields at the end of every calendar year, we would not have achieved the *change of mentality* that was required to shake off the lethargy of our calm, bucolic life. The fact is that *growing cotton* is a *challenge that forces the producer* to use the most advanced techniques, to combat the pests that could destroy the crops, and to seek the maximum yield in order to assure profits. *The cotton grower cannot be an average person.* He must be resolute and daring, and hence he has been the inspiration for a *production mystique that has generated optimism and faith in the future.*[9]

This is a perfect self-portrait of capitalist entrepreneurs. But the real actor is not the entrepreneur; it is the commodity that entrepreneurs produce. The commodity seeks them out with its "cotton dynamism." This cotton dynamism is a "challenge that forces the producer" and brings about the necessary "change of mentality." By accepting this binding challenge, the cotton growers become "great captains" who are the "inspiration for a production mystique that has generated optimism and faith in the future."

Entrepreneurs (great captains; nay, generals) sense the dynamism of commodities, and know how to accept their challenge. In this way, they can be more than average: resolute and daring. The business firm is the environment wherein they respond to the challenge, piloting it. By acting resolutely and daringly, they generate optimism and faith in the future. For this reason, entrepreneurs feel that they are the leading employees of their firms, taking the firm as an environment for accepting the challenges that stem from the dynamism of commodities. As great captains, they steer their ships that are driven by a far greater force than they—namely, the market, the great object of devotion.

Entrepreneurs obey this great force, and it is this obedience that makes them *great* entrepreneurs. Hence the conviction of entrepreneurs that they are ideally humble and truly exemplary persons. The maximizing of profits appears to them as an act in the public service they render, and it gives them compensation commensurate with their devotion. Even if they are not churchgoers, entrepreneurs are deeply religious persons, who preach to the entire world the good news of subjugation to the anonymous machinery of the markets, wherein a Supreme Being issues them challenges.

From the great goals to which entrepreneurs are dedicated in the service of their firms, their rules of behavior are derived. This is the origin of the great capitalistic ascesis that imbues the entrepreneur's entire behavior. Such ascesis is by no means a prerogative limited to Puritan entrepreneurs à la Schumpeter or Max Weber. The Puritan entrepreneur is only one particular example of this ascesis. It involves transforming the entrepreneur, and the whole of society, so as to enable them to accept, efficiently, the challenges stemming from the dynamism of commodities. "The world of business establishes its own rules."[10] Its basic rule is to make the focal point of the entrepreneur's life the "production mystique," which is simply a phantasmagoric reflection of the unending search for profit. The rules imposed by the world of business require that the entrepreneur do everything on behalf of better service to the firm.

Hence this ascesis is difficult. It entails a "total impoverishment" of the entrepreneur as a concrete person, so as to be able to become rich as an entrepreneur. It is an austerity that entrepreneurs impose on themselves (and on society as well), in search of the amassing of wealth for their firms, in whose profits entrepreneurs share. A German banker describes this capitalistic ascesis in perfect (and hence ludicrous) terms:

> Entrepreneurs, especially bankers, should not engage in artistic activities. They should not even play music, or compose; and they should

never paint, much less be a poet; because otherwise they stand to lose their good reputation, and damage both themselves and their businesses.[11]

This is the most striking expression of the way they torment themselves, seeking to respond to the challenge issued to their companies by the dynamism of commodities.

This type of personality is, however, much older than bourgeois society itself. St. Paul mentions it: "The love of money is the root of all evil things, and there are some who in reaching for it have wandered from the faith and spiked themselves on many thorny griefs" (1 Tim. 6:10). What is new about bourgeois society is that it has converted this type of behavior into the very root of society. This was the origin of a new metaphysics around which the entire bourgeois society revolves.

Bourgeois entrepreneurs call the aggregation of rules whereby they form their own personalities and that of their entire society freedom. And, inasmuch as all these rules stem from the challenge posed by the dynamism of commodities, to which entrepreneurs, together with the whole of their society, strive to respond, bourgeois freedom also stems from this basic datum.

If the commodity is to be able to exercise its dynamism, the commodity must be free. If the commodity is to be free, its price must be free. When they are free in this way, commodities can make their challenge.

If the entrepreneurs are to respond to the challenge, the firm must be free. The firm is free when the prices of the commodities it produces are free.

With all commodities and all business firms free, by virtue of their freedom all entrepreneurs are also free, and society is free as well.

However, as we have already observed, that freedom is not license. The world of business establishes its own rules. Compliance with its laws is what makes one free. They are laws of freedom itself, which transform both the entrepreneur and society in such a way as to enable them to respond to the challenge emanating from the dynamism of commodities. When the price controls on basic consumer goods were repealed in Costa Rica, the explanation was given: "The minister of the economy has announced that a number of items would be left free, so that the laws of the market, rather than bothersome state controls, might have their effect."[12]

In enterpreneurial metaphysics, this freedom is basic and, in the final analysis, the only freedom. Human rights, for example, are purely incidental. With commodities free, business firms are free; therefore, entrepreneurs are free, and the entire society is free. From the standpoint of entrepreneurial metaphysics (and this holds true for John Locke who, in addition to being a philosopher, was also a businessman, having invested his capital in the slave trade), the most absolute tyranny could be the site of freedom; because, according to this metaphysics, the human being is free in the degree to which commodities are free.

THE CAPITALIST BUSINESS FIRM AND MONEY

Commodities and business firms do not exist separate from one another. They form a combination. According to entrepreneurial metaphysics, money is the link connecting all of them.

The assemblage of business firms united by money appears as a great organism. Hobbes has already termed this organism Leviathan, and money, the blood of Leviathan. Entrepreneurial metaphysics also perceives money as the blood of the economy. When the comment was made that "The bloodshed of Vietnam . . . converted the dollar into the weakest and the most vulnerable currency of all the currencies in the developed nations,"[13] the writer was not deploring the human bloodshed in Vietnam. The bloodshed that figures in entrepreneurial metaphysics is of a different kind. It is the money that was spent on that war. In entrepreneurial metaphysics, even though there might have been far more deaths, there would have been no bloodshed in Vietnam if the dollar had strengthened.

From the standpoint of entrepreneurial metaphysics, there is no blood other than money. Inflation is a "fever," and *Newsweek* once carried the headline "Taking the Pulse of Inflation." New investments are "infusions of income"; a financial crisis is a cardiac arrest:

> The crisis is not a cyclical, but rather a structural phenomenon—a kind of industrial arthritis in the advanced economies. The GATT economists caution against the expectations of being able to cure the economic ills of the present by means of the traditional stimuli to demand.[14]

Success is expected when "money is pumped into the area's industry."[15] Mention is made of the "fever of prices," a fever that can be purifying: "A high price index is not a bad index so long as it reflects the process of recovery in the health of the economy."[16]

This Leviathan's blood—money—even has a eucharistic aspect in entrepreneurial metaphysics: "The Italian stock exchange resembles a church without worshipers, which is visited occasionally by a priest or chaplain, to keep the eternal flame burning."[17]

In this context, reports of monetary problems such as inflation resemble those in medical bulletins: "The pound sterling spent a calm day"; "the fever returned"; "infarction was prevented."

But, when curbing inflation is involved, the reports resemble military briefings: "The dollar, which was previously strong, lost ground on a broad front." The search for weapons with which to combat inflation and save the dollar begins. Entrepreneurs never come to save human beings; they come to save the dollar, and to remove price controls. The dollar is defended, and the banks have the ammunition with which to defend it. Politicians concerned about inflation are called "inflation fighters." "The White House inflation fighters appear in the ring"; "Jimmy Carter declared inflation the number one enemy."[18]

Just as, in precapitalist society, money was perceived as the force corroding society, inflation is now so perceived:

> Inflation takes its toll of the *nation's morality; like the Chinese water torture, it eliminates the social contract*. . . . The feasibility of planning the future erodes. What is upset is the foundation on which the people lead their daily lives . . . a kind of *fraud committed by everyone against everyone*. It is a world in which *no one keeps his word.*[19]

Hence, with the appearance of the corrosion of money (the key to the social contract itself and the boundary between order and the war of everyone against everyone), the sacred, dependable gold comes to the rescue. "Unlike oil, a nonrenewable resource, almost all the gold ever produced still exists in one form or another."[20] "Gold, the traditional refuge of money at times when political upheaval becomes intensified."[21] Gold glitters even in the garbage heap: "When Anglo perfected a process for extracting the last tiny remnant of gold and uranium from waste, a new world opened up for the gold extraction industry. . . . finally, the work process does not involve intensive labor. It will not be necessary to find the thousands of persons required for a new conventional gold mine."[22]

For others, the new world has not opened up so much; but they still have a sure remedy—prayer: "But Lawrence Hercules goes a little further, in view of the new changes in the dollar. 'We pray a great deal,' he says."[23]

THE CAPITALIST BUSINESS FIRM AND CAPITAL

Entrepreneurs feel that they are at war: a war among business firms and a war against inflation. Although peace may at times prevail among business firms, the war among them is what is paramount. Their peace is really a continuation of warfare, employing different methods. By means of these wars the accumulation of capital progresses and, with it (at least this is what entrepreneurs think), the progress of all humankind.

Nevertheless, when they discuss their struggles and wars, they do so in the manner of the historian Ranke. These are wars in which only the captains and generals count. Although foot soldiers have to do the actual fighting, they do not appear in this history: neither their lives, nor their poverty, nor their deaths. These wars have rules (euphemistically called "rules of the game"), which also apply to the generals.

For the industrial armies, the economic wars among business firms are as devastating as any other war: they wreak the same destruction, death, and disease, and they distort human destinies. But this war of business firms does not affect only human beings; it destroys nature. It is a war that leaves scorched earth behind it.

The history of the Third World is a history of such wars; they have devastated one country after another, and one people after another. The captains of cotton, whom the president of the Bank of Nicaragua during Somoza's regime described above, pursued the challenge of dynamic cotton with such zest that now the land on which they planted it has become a desert. So that the captains could flaunt their derring-do, the inhabitants lost their land, and became poorly paid laborers. They will soon become inhabitants of a deserted land, lacking all means of making a living.

When artificial sodium nitrate won out over natural sodium nitrate in Chile, a population numbering in the hundreds of thousands had to leave their homes and wander about the country, living from beggary. The entire region now looks as if it had been the target of a major bombing. The same sort of thing occurred in the Amazon region, when artificial rubber won out over natural rubber. During the final decades of the nineteenth century, when the dynamism of coffee imposed its challenge on the daring, resolute captains of El Salvador and Guatemala, they introduced so-called liberal reforms, the main effect of which was the introduction of forced labor for dispossessed Indians. At the present time, throughout the Third World, there are gigantic projects underway for felling timber, using large armies of workers who were, a few years ago, ousted from their own land, which has now become a desert. The famines in the Sahel region and Ethiopia were the first results of this scorched earth tactic of embattled capitalist business firms.

A reporter from the *New York Times* who traveled through Bangladesh during the time of the great famine remarked: "Large areas of Bangladesh look like Bergen-Belsen" (one of the major Nazi concentration camps). If he had traveled through other Third World countries, he would have discovered that there is not one in which such living conditions do not exist for a large portion of the population. The entire Third World is covered with enormous stretches that differ from Bergen-Belsen only in that they are not surrounded by barbed wire. But that does not mean that there are no police surrounding them.

More and more regimes have come into existence with the main objective of keeping these populations—numbering some 800 million—in a state of oppression. They are suffering from unemployment, hunger, and the total absence of any prospects for the future. And, while they suffer from these conditions, their countries, with their natural resources, are being despoiled, destroyed, and plundered, depriving them of the very foundation on which they might become integrated into a reorganized, rational economy in the future.

Hence, when entrepreneurs talk about war among business firms, they are not really using an allegory. The war is real. However, entrepreneurs treat it as a war among generals, and therefore there is little talk about casualties.

When speaking about the war against inflation, again there is no equivocation. The battlers of inflation and their weapons are truly warlike and fearsome.

It begins with instilling confidence in business firms. "The White House inflation fighters are increasingly convinced that business confidence is the key to maintaining economic growth."[24] However, this confidence makes its own demands.

> As might be predicted, the conservative economists tend to view the remedy rather in Calvinist terms. "No one wants recession," says Fellner. "The government must show that it is ready to restore stability, and to stop fooling people. That might mean a 7 percent unemployment for up to three years"; but, he claims, "There is no other solution."[25]

Next, what is chiefly responsible for the situation gets blamed: the government's expenditures for social services, and the demands of labor unions. The entrepreneur is among the innocent:

> The process of creating money is the heart of inflation. . . . Therefore, the economy can be kept sound simply by restricting the money supply. . . . The government is meeting with *increased difficulty in curbing its spending, because more and more of it consists of transfers of income to* citizens who cannot be eliminated: *the elderly, the poor, and the sick.* . . . But the greatest challenge to Carter's appeal for restriction . . . is posed by the unions, which must be persuaded to accept wage increases that are below average, at least from a relative standpoint. "We shall have to bite the bullet."[26]

It is important to stress that the opinion expressed in this commentary is false. The largest share of U.S. government spending does not go to social services, which are on the decline, but rather to military ("defense") costs, which are on the incline. However, the inflation fighters are concerned about something else:

> In brief, the stagflation is no reflection of our ineptness, but rather of our commitment to social values, and the relative political force of these values in comparison with our interest in the "sound dollar" and our inclination to trust more in the government than in the market.[27]

In entrepreneurial metaphysics, the conflict between "sound growth" and inflation is, in fact, the conflict between the "sound dollar" and what are termed "social values." Essentially, in entrepreneurial metaphysics, inflation is just another term for the commitment to social values. The commitment is seen on two levels: (1) government spending for "the elderly, the poor, and the sick"; and (2) the demands of labor unions. And commitment to the "sound dollar" makes demands that go counter to social values: "sound" growth, law and order.

Hence, when entrepreneurs say that inflation undermines the "morality of the nation," "voids the social contract," is a "fraud committed by everyone against everyone," and creates a world in which "no one keeps his word," they imply (although they dare not say it expressly) that it all results from commitment to these "social values."

"Social values" appear as the great corrosive force of the modern capitalist society. Commitment to them is viewed as a breaking of the "social contract," and its conversion into a "fraud committed by everyone against everyone else"—in other words, a kind of commitment to the war of everyone against everyone else, which, in the liberal tradition in which this thinking has evolved, signals the most absolute perversion.

The entire liberal tradition agrees that any measure is legitimate when threatened with a return to a state of war of everyone against everyone else, breaking the social contract. In this instance, Locke says that opponents must be treated like "brutes," "beasts," "wild animals." For this reason, accusations of "breaking the social contract" are, in the liberal language, a dreadful threat. Using such terms, everything is declared legitimate vis-à-vis opponents.

Obviously, they would not dare carry out such threats in the United States. Organized labor is too strong to be treated in that fashion. The very existence of organized labor makes it difficult (although by no means impossible) to reduce social services to "the elderly, the poor, and the sick."

It is different when the inflation fighters become specialists of the International Monetary Fund (IMF) and are members of IMF missions to Third World countries. There they impose what they have not yet been able to impose in the United States.

IMF missions are one of the major influences in the current subjugation of Third World countries. Inasmuch as all these countries have debts that they cannot pay, they have no alternative except to break off from the capitalist system—and remain in debt. So long as they have bourgeois governments, a breakoff is precluded. Hence, they have to continue their indebtedness and their subjection to the blackmail of the developed countries. The IMF missions are the go-betweens for this blackmail.

The IMF missions come on behalf of the battle against inflation. They never study the concrete status of any country. Their advice is already prepared before they arrive, and it is monotonously the same, regardless of where they go. They espouse the most absolute dogmatism. Their requirements are always the same: (1) cut the government's spending on "the elderly, the poor, and the sick"; and (2) destroy labor organization.

Taking the advice of the IMF mission, the respective country's "social" spending is reduced considerably, and labor organizations are emasculated. The poverty, death rate, and hunger are evidence that a war has been lost.

However, neither government spending nor the inflation rate is reduced, with very rare exceptions. "Social" spending is diverted to military and police spending. Those who broke the "social contract" are treated as Locke recommended. With the lost war, an occupation force appears.

But there is one area in which the IMF mission takes a positive interest in a given country. It examines very carefully what can be extracted. Then its advice contains demands regarding deliveries of raw materials and concessions for export assembly industries. The forests are doomed to die, and other raw materials to be plundered.

The IMF missions plot the destruction of the human being and of nature, nature being the future life of humans. Hence, they leave a trail of blood behind them: the blood of the poor, which they convert into money, which is the blood of their economy, the blood of the Leviathan. The sound of the dollar becomes a cry of terror.

With the war lost, inflation remains the same. But that is of no concern to the IMF, or to the inflation fighters. "A high price index is not a bad index provided it reflects the recovery of the health of the economy."[28] With the spending on "the elderly, the poor, and the sick" eliminated, and the labor unions dismantled, inflation remains the same. But now it reflects the "recovery of the health of the economy." It is no longer a threat. In Brazil it has reflected that kind of "health" ever since 1965.

The inflation fighters prefer an economy without inflation to one with inflation; but inflation is not, in fact, their chief concern. Their chief concern is to win another war: the war against the people.

What the inflation fighters intend and achieve is something different from what they claim. It is a change in the conditions for the accumulation of capital on a worldwide scale. It is the accumulation of capital for the multinational corporations.

NATURE: REPENTANCE, AMENDS, AND COMPENSATION

Mother Nature . . . gives preeminence to the species which prove to have her in their favor: in particular, survival in the Darwinian struggle for existence [Paul A. Samuelson].[29]

From the standpoint of entrepreneurial metaphysics, when the "sound dollar" is confronted with "social values," nature comes in confrontation with anti-nature, with what is artificial and depraved.

Entrepreneurial metaphysics has a concept of nature that is exactly the opposite of nature as viewed in the Aristotelian-Thomistic tradition. In this tradition, what is natural is that human beings have the means to live and work for what they have. A mercantile orientation of human activities is unnatural.

Aristotelian-Thomistic metaphysics represents a transcendence of physical nature, but in accord with a natural order. That is why Thomas Aquinas stresses that "higher" values must never be achieved to the detriment of "lower" values, the latter being the values associated with concrete life, and work for a decent living. This viewpoint sets a limit to its own worst excesses. Even in the legitimation of slavery, neither Aquinas nor Aristotle grants the master of a slave absolute rights over the life of the slave.

In entrepreneurial metaphysics, "nature" is the opposite. It is a strictly mercantile nature, for which physical nature is a mere vehicle, utterly deprived of rights. The laws governing that nature are the laws of the response to the dynamism of commodities; a nature wherein freedom is the freedom of prices and business firms. The values of concrete life are virtually nonexistent in it; they are unnatural. Therefore, when this liberal thinking proceeds to legitimize slavery, as Locke does (and in his tradition, the major trends of bourgeois thought until the twentieth century), it does so in the most merciless terms imaginable.

To the entrepreneur, nature is strictly metaphysical. It does not transcend physical nature, but is opposed to it. It is pure metaphysics, and hence it is a nature that is completely invisible. Prices, commodities, and business firms are the elements comprising it, whereas the elements comprising concrete nature are human beings and the values they cherish.

However, entrepreneurial metaphysics conceives of nature in terms analogous to those of physical nature. Just as a house collapses if it is not built in accordance with the law of gravity, the economy collapses if it is not built in accordance with the laws of entrepreneurial metaphysics. The laws emerging from the response to the challenge of dynamic commodities are perceived as laws produced by events, by this mercantile nature. This nature enforces them, even by the collapse of an economy that does not abide by them.

When food is scarce, according to this law, prices should increase. This means that some will be left without food, and consequently will die. According to entrepreneurial metaphysics, they die as a result of a dictate of nature. If, on the contrary, prices and distribution of food are controlled, everyone would survive. But, according to entrepreneurial metaphysics, that would be an act against nature: the law of nature calls for increased prices. Price control was an unnatural, depraved act, breaking the social contract, and, in the end, an act against humankind. Freedom was lost, and what is life worth without freedom?

When lumber is scarce, the dynamism of that commodity issues a challenge, to which the entrepreneur responds by felling woods, and converting nature into a desert. According to entrepreneurial metaphysics, it is done in compliance with a dictate from nature. Following this dictate of their "nature," entrepreneurs are destroying the Third World, but not the Rocky Mountains or the Black Forest.

When peoples defend themselves and care for nature as their basis for living, they commit an "act against nature," and the IMF will blackmail them until they make their countries available for plundering. And the IMF defends nature against anti-nature, depravity, and the breaking of the social contract. It defends humankind and freedom, even though it does so without mercy. And when entrepreneurial metaphysics stops talking about "nature," it talks, with Max Weber, about the "rationality" required by precisely everything that "nature" required previously.

From the entrepreneurial standpoint, the major victims of this battle between two natures (the nature of the "sound dollar" and the anti-nature of "social values") are not the impoverished, the destroyed, and the unemployed. The victims are the entrepreneurs themselves:

> The entrepreneurial sector in our countries *suffers* almost constantly from this battle between the situations and interests of the politicians and of certain social groups.[30]

And if they are Christians, they will identify themselves in their sufferings with Christ crucified. The poor will be accused of being the crucifiers.

Thus, all the values, guidelines, and conditions of entrepreneurial behavior are converted into "laws of nature" that cannot be broken. Entrepreneurial metaphysics turns the "behavioral logic" of the market into a law of nature.

The entrepreneur is the one who lives this real logic. When a product is in short supply, price control is troublesome and inefficient. Entrepreneurs argue that the price must be increased, leaving without supplies those who cannot pay. The market and God are to blame. The alternative—reorganizing the distribution system and the distribution of income—either does not occur to them or they reject it.

Entrepreneurs follow the same logic when they dismiss a worker or refuse someone a job. They neither hire nor fire arbitrarily, and could not do so. When workers protest, entrepreneurs refer to the market situation, claiming that it is the market—not they—that has forced the layoff. As entrepreneurs, they would very gladly provide jobs. But the market does not allow it. Once again, the market and God are to blame; the entrepreneur is not involved. And, once more, the entrepreneur avoids or precludes discussion of an alternative systemization of production, wherein no market would necessitate leaving anyone jobless.

By refusing any other alternative, the entrepreneur converts the logic of the market into a law of nature. If there is no alternative, everything must remain as it is, and entrepreneurs are the ones who suffer from any conflict, with no remedy other than to affirm nature. They are the mainstays and workhorses of the business firm. As the head of the businessmen's association of El Salvador once remarked: ". . . the splendid human team that comprises the *mainstay of free enterprise* in El Salvador."[31]

Entrepreneurial metaphysics mouths the most thorough-going irresponsibility, in the name of nature:

> In the running of a business firm, profits must be generated. . . . To wish otherwise is *utopian*. It means going *against the nature* of human beings and of society.
>
> What we mean to say is that certain basic principles in an economy must be faithfully upheld and must not be subject to the judgment of politicians, public officials in office, or any individual.
>
> There are rules that must be obeyed. They are the premise for *sound development*.

Controls and restrictions often have a "boomerang" effect on consumers, not only with respect to prices, but also with respect to the quality of products and other important factors.

In the economy, as in nature, contrivance never brings good dividends. . . .

Contrivance is a sign of evasion and laziness.[32]

In this nature, it is a law that business firms accrue profits, although human beings have no right to live. To live or not is a matter of "values," not natural laws. To accrue profits for a business firm is not a matter of values, but "natural law" or "rationality" (Max Weber). Anyone who protests against a natural law is a utopian. Protesting against the natural laws of the market is as foolish as protesting against the law of gravity. It is madness. The utopian is someone searching for a contrivance to override the law of gravity.

Repentance

For the entrepreneur there is a *duty* to obey the laws of this "nature." This is the origin of an entire ethic, with repentance, amends, and compensation. If the natural laws are disobeyed, repentance is called for:

Sooner or later, the economy of a country *clashes with reality*—that is, with economic science, which cannot be divorced from the facts. Political theories and sentiments then dissolve, giving way to the *humble rule of everyday reality*. It is a time, to quote the *biblical phrase, for the gnashing of teeth,* when there is a yearning for the opportunities that were available at the outset, when there was sufficient time to make headway on the *right path, even though it might not have been to the liking of certain groups.*[33]

With "nature" or "rationality" established, entrepreneurial metaphysics begins preaching and delivering sermons. The economy that did not abide by the natural laws clashes with "reality." This clash necessitates repentance, owing to the opportunities that were missed, and the improper steps that were taken. Reality, with its laws and obligations, imposes itself. The resultant subjugation reflects the humility that is a counterpart of and requisite for true repentance. The way is paved for "the humble rule of everyday reality," and hence for the repentance of "gnashing teeth," which entrepreneurial metaphysics perceives as in perfect agreement with the Bible. The improper steps (breaking the laws of the market for the sake of "social values") disappear with repentance, and the "right path" appears. This right path is right, although it may not be "to the liking of certain social groups." These social groups are, once again, the ones already held blameworthy for inflation: "the elderly, the poor, and the sick," and the labor unions and agrarian leagues.

Amends

The move to the right path does not come to an end with biblical repentance. It also requires amends. There must be explicit recognition of the laws of the market as a duty and a virtue, by individuals and by society as a whole. In the speech by the president of the Bank of Nicaragua under Somoza, cited earlier, the role of amendment is touched on:

> There is a dangerous economic stagnation, and there are no dynamic elements in sight that would prompt a reactivation. *Confidence* has been lost, and it cannot be restored except on the basis of *constructive actions and amends.* Private investment is at a standstill, and the *money that we need so badly for our development is escaping* in considerable amounts.[34]

The improper steps that were taken destroyed confidence, and with confidence lost, money flees. As banker Abs has said, "Money is as timid as a deer." But money is required, and it cannot be retrieved except through "constructive actions and amends." Mere repentance does not suffice.

However, the president of the Bank of Nicaragua also has a political factor in mind: "It would appear that the basic reason for this state of uncertainty and dissatisfaction is the continuance of the same personalist regime for a long period of time."[35]

But the entrepreneurial logic is still the same: there is no dynamic commodity in sight that could make the necessary challenge that would make the entrepreneur feel summoned. Money has fled, and confidence has declined. The reason why commodities cannot make their dynamic challenge lies now in the political situation: Somoza's personalist regime. Therefore the bank president becomes anti-Somoza. The Nicaraguan bourgeoisie feels constrained by Somoza's arbitrary actions. The economy has ceased to be calculable, and therefore Somoza appears to be a tyrant. The bourgeoisie needs a bourgeois regime, which does not necessarily mean a parliamentary regime. But it has to be an impersonal regime, which abides by the laws of the market.

However, it should be noted that this confrontation of the bourgeoisie with personalist regimes is not typical. It was so to a certain extent at the beginning of bourgeois society, which explains the bourgeoisie's support of human rights. What is now normally asked for, as amends based on the laws of the market, is the elimination of labor unions and of social services, neither of which existed at the beginning of the bourgeois era.

This combination of clashes with reality, and the resultant humility, with the repentance and amends needed to reverse false moves, so as to find the "right path," has led to the creation of a complex entrepreneurial ethic. It is an ethic of the "truth of prices," of the virtues of the market, and of the sins against the market. The right path includes the truth of prices and the virtues of the market:

The comment was made about the head of the Bordeaux region grape growers: ". . . He has defended himself against the charge of having scrapped the 'virtues of the market econony,' plus having created a kind of social security for the grape-growing industry."[36]

On the contrary, he himself claims to have defended himself from the "specter of speculation." "We think that we have exorcised some demons."[37]

But there are also sins against the market. In the name of the "virtues of the market economy," we are summoned to a crusade to counter the sins committed against that economy. It was once remarked, concerning an international banking congress: "On that occasion, there was injected into human hearts the notion of a crusade to fight inflation, a cause wherein the state plays a critical role."[38]

But unlike so many other sins, sins against the market economy are not punished in the next life. At least that is the belief of institutes of economic analysis in West Germany:

It sounds like a trial at which the *greatest sins* in the area of wage and economic policy are punished: the five independent economic analysis institutes in Germany announce in their joint spring report that the total economic growth this year [1978] will reach only 2.5 percent, and this was on the assumption that all those responsible for the economy would do what they should. . . .

The reasons would have to be sought in a deep *lack of confidence* in business firms, for which the *labor unions would bear the main responsibility.* . . .

The *penalty* for this reckless behavior . . . is severe.[39]

Compensation

The market punishes those who sin against the market. Although this punishment cannot be obviated by humility, repentance, and amends, there is nevertheless the possibility of some recompense in the future. When the Begin government in Israel finally rid itself of the desire to liberate human beings, and dedicated itself instead to the liberation of prices, Milton Friedman commented:

Israel's economic policy measures . . . show the same combination of daring, cleverness, and courage as the *six-day war, or the liberation of the hostages* at Entebbe. And they should be no less important to the future of Israel. Twenty-nine years of socialist domination, . . . all that has changed. For the first time since the founding of the Israeli state, *the citizens can now buy and sell dollars freely,* without a permit stamp from some bureaucrat. . . . *In essence, now they are no longer treated as wards of the state, but rather as a free people,* who can control their own lives by themselves . . . away from socialism, toward the free market, and toward capitalism. They promise more personal freedom . . . they promise a better, healthier, and stronger society.

If this takeoff by Israel toward freedom is successful, then *(I predict) there will occur the same economic miracle* that a comparable advancement in Germany caused in 1948. . . . As matters stand in Israel, this *miracle will benefit in particular the less privileged groups* of the population. . . . And, furthermore, *the freer* economic and political system *will attract more money and immigrants* from the developed Western countries.[40]

This prophet's voice announces the miracle, which now appears as compensation for the repentance and amends. Just as punishment is fitting for the sins against the market economy, compensation (the economic miracle) is fitting for the virtues of the market. In this instance, the supreme act of virtue of the market is the liberation of the dollar.

It is no coincidence that Friedman compares this economic measure to a war, on the one hand, and to a "liberation of hostages," on the other. Just as, at Entebbe, a group of persons had been kidnaped, in "socialist" Israel the dollar was kidnaped. It had lost its freedom, and was a hostage in the hands of the kidnaping "socialist" regime. The measures of the new government, however, freed it. With the dollar freed, all the citizens were freed, for the simple reason that the freedom of the dollar is freedom in its true essence. Therefore, according to entrepreneurial metaphysics, the moral requirement for "freeing captives" relates to the supreme virtue of "freeing the dollar and prices."

It is insidious for the prophet Friedman to say that this "miracle will benefit in particular the less privileged groups of the population." However, apart from being insidious, it is an allusion to the reign of justice to which the entire entrepreneurial metaphysics is committed. This reign of justice will stem directly from the freeing of prices and the search for profits:

Investing means not only contributing to the *creation of wealth and employment,* and thereby cooperating in the *reign of social justice* and in the soundness of the economy, but also having opportunities to *accrue profits.*[41]

The entrepreneurial metaphysician views the business firm as a creator of employment, and overlooks the fact that employment is the requisite for the creation of wealth on the part of the business firm. It is claimed, on the contrary, that investment creates wealth and employment. Therefore, it is presented as a path to social justice, the only kind of social justice that the entrepreneurial metaphysician understands: the kind that does not break the law of profitability.

In the pursuit of this "reign of social justice," entrepreneurial metaphysicians can accept any social demand, and they affirm all of them. However, they affirm them not in utopian terms, but in "realistic" terms, according to the laws of "nature." Better standard of living, higher wages, better education and health, the elimination of extreme poverty in the world, full employment . . . entrepreneurs are in agreement with them all. But, realists that they are, they know very well that all this cannot be accomplished overnight.

Abiding by the laws of nature (the entrepreneurial metaphysical nature), they also know that, in order to arrive at the "reign of social justice" an incentive must be given to business firms, whose mainstays and workhorses are the entrepreneurs. But business firms live on profits, just as a work animal lives on food. The more the effort, the more profits they need. And reaching the reign of social justice is a colossal effort, which the business firm cannot expend without colossal profits. This is the law of gravity of entrepreneurial nature.

Therefore, it says yes to everything: a higher level of wages, education, and health, full employment and the elimination of extreme poverty, yes. But yes also to the only "sound" means of achieving it all: greater profits. Because today's profits are tomorrow's investment, and the day after tomorrow's employment and growth. But greater profits also mean lower wages, less education, poorer health, more poverty, and often also more unemployment. Thus, one arrives at the "accursed dialectics" of entrepreneurial metaphysics: to reach the "reign of social justice" there must be an increase in the "reign of social injustice," precisely. The more we foster injustice, the more quickly we attain justice. From the entrepreneurial standpoint, injustice itself is the "right path" to justice.

In this regard, entrepreneurial metaphysics performs a fantastic sleight of hand. It takes the concrete fact of an objective link between standard of living and standard of production forces and transforms it into an abstract fact related to (its metaphysical) nature. It transforms the great goals of social justice into objectives of economic growth and the process of capital accumulation. In this transformation the possibility of justice appears limited by a "shortage of capital." Capitalization based on maximizing profits is seen as the path toward achieving those objectives. The "reign of social justice" becomes a task of Sisyphus, and the glitter of capital appears as the sheen of justice.

In fact, the accomplishment of justice depends very little on the level of production forces. Full employment simply has nothing to do with capital shortage or the level of productivity. Full employment would result from a better systemization of the economy, and unemployment is a result of the enshrinement of the logic of the market as a natural law.

Moreover, a decent standard of living for all would be attained by an equitable distribution of existing products, not of products that will be available only in the future. A rise in the standard of living is commonly associated with the development of production forces, whereas the decent standard of life has to do with the distribution of what is available in such a way that everyone can live. Education and health depend on production forces only in the degree to which they relate to the use of certain techniques, but as social services they have no such dependence.

Therefore, from a concrete, responsible view of the facts, capital is an obstacle to social justice. In the view of the entrepreneur, however, it is the light in the shadows, the morning star.

When the entrepreneur becomes an advocate of social justice, the desire for justice is converted into a vehicle for the accumulation of capital. When injustice is made to appear as justice, the desire for justice is converted into a driving force for injustice itself. Even if demolishing entire populations and nature itself, the accumulation of capital is interpreted as a contribution to the "reign of social justice."

Milton Friedman summarizes the social programs that must disappear so that there may be justice:

> . . . agricultural programs, old age benefits, minimum wage laws, legislation favoring labor unions, import duties, regulations for granting licenses for trades and professions, and so on, in what appears to be an endless series.[42]

In this way, justice is replaced by "sound" economic growth. It is nothing but the accumulation of capital itself. Its aggressiveness is legitimized by reference to social justice. When G. William Miller was appointed to the U.S. Federal Reserve Bank, the comment was made:

> Chairman Miller is learning the hard way that it is quite easy to talk against inflation; on the other hand, balancing the needs of a real economic growth over the short term against the attempt to fight inflation is a task that he has just begun to perceive. May heaven help him in this task.[43]

As everyone knows, fighting inflation is fighting for a reduction in the government's social spending and for the weakening of labor unions. This battle must be aligned with the need for real growth. And, because it is a matter of an injustice committed in the pursuit of justice, which is imagined to be the product of such growth, it is fitting to call upon heaven. God (an obvious sublimation of the market and capital) will help in this difficult task.

Sound economic growth as a result of the accumulation of capital and the denial of the requirements of justice is converted into the dynamic myth of entrepreneurial metaphysics. The metaphysical conceptualization of nature is a prerequisite. On the basis of this concept of nature, any social catastrophe can be viewed as a natural catastrophe. Economic crisis, underdevelopment, and low wages now are like earthquakes, hurricanes, and blizzards. There is no exploitation: a hurricane does not exploit anyone. The law of gravity is in effect, and the law of the market.

Inasmuch as there is no alternative to the law of the market, there is no alternative to the accumulation of capital and "sound" economic growth.

The goals of justice are therefore converted into products that are anticipated from the accumulation of capital.

There arises as a problem related to the legitimacy of bourgeois society the need to convince the urban and rural working classes, whether by intimidation or persuasion, that there is no justice other than this. As they cease to be guided by socialist plans, these classes have no way of avoiding attraction toward the accumulation of capital whether they actively accept it or are simply left making demands with no way of having them fulfilled.

However, bourgeois society seeks affirmative acceptance from the working class, which leads to conflicts between the virtues of the market economy (freeing of prices, reduction in social spending, weakness of labor organization) and its needs for legitimacy beyond the entrepreneurial class. This conflict is resolved through a compromise.

The compromise consists in the unbounded exportation of the virtues of the market economy to the economically weak countries, where governments use force to supply for their lack of legitimacy. These governments are backed by the highly developed countries, which, internally, maintain their legitimacy on the basis of a relatively high regard for the labor force and for social policy.

This is why the IMF never imposes on First World countries programs so catastrophically extremist as those that it usually imposes on the Third World. Although the guidelines based on the virtues of the market are the same in all countries, the radical manner of their entrenchment is quite different. The stronger countries necessitate that broader base of legitimacy in order to justify their backing of governments in the Third World, which for their part could not uphold the virtues of the market without external assistance.

In the legitimation of bourgeois society in First World countries, the linkage between accumulation of capital, economic growth, and social justice becomes more and more important. If labor organizations can be brought to adopt this outlook, they can then look favorably on the accumulation of capital, and become accomplices—with all the aggressiveness that accompanies that accumulation.

Concern over unemployment plays a leading role in this regard. From the socialist standpoint, the solution to unemployment is sought in a change in the social relationships of production. In the degree to which the capitalist outlook prevails, the search for full employment entails an acceleration of the accumulation of capital and of growth rates. The labor organization that accepts this second alternative continues to talk about the need for full employment, but now identifies it with the policy of economic growth and the accumulation of capital. The labor organizations in the United States and West Germany, in particular, have adopted this outlook.

Now, from this standpoint, any obstacle to the accumulation of capital appears as a threat to employment. Therefore, in the name of justice, the labor organizations can be used as a shock force against the social groups that hamper the accumulation of capital. For such labor organizations are now awaiting the solution to their social problems and the bettering of their living standard in an absolutely unlimited accumulation of capital.

In this way, workers' interests have been submitted to a narcissistic logic, contrary to the logic of international solidarity that prevails with the socialist outlook. True, it is limited to certain capitalist countries, but it operates there with great power. It backs the aggressive accumulation of capital along two lines in particular: against the Third World countries and their liberation movements, and against the social movements that are fighting to protect the environment.

The following quotation serves to demonstrate this type of logic relating to the protection of the environment and the limits on economic growth:

> Whereas today there is almost no one left who would not call for increased growth in economic output to solve the problem of full employment, just a few years ago economic growth was considered the work of the devil. . . .
>
> Economic growth was made to appear more and more as something morally questionable and dangerous to all humankind . . . but the "limits of growth" were discovered to be a mirage: it dissolves into nothing when one approaches it.
>
> Reduced economic growth does not concern only those who are not indifferent to the fate of the unemployed. . . . Slight economic growth or, what is even worse, zero growth, as it spread a few years ago, could, together with technical change, lead to a socially explosive situation. Because if growth is not sufficient to create jobs for all those who have lost their jobs in offices or factories as a result of technical progress, the number of the unemployed could skyrocket.[44]

With the problem of employment dissociated from the social relationships of production in this way, and associated with the speed and aggressiveness of the accumulation of capital, the following type of propaganda is possible:

> After the congress of the [German] Social Democratic Party, the chancellor emphasized that the citizens must not allow their jobs to be destroyed under the pretext of protecting the environment, much less because of the action of "well-intentioned individualists" or "certain intellectual circles." He received resounding applause from the trade unions, which have proclaimed themselves, not without some justification, "the greatest citizens' initiative in the country."[45]

This type of argument can be readily applied to relationships with Third World countries. If jobs are to be created, there must be cheap raw materials. And there must be markets in countries where capital enjoys "confidence." Liberation movements in Third World countries may even appear as a threat to social gains in First World countries. In Latin America, the AFL-CIO has, through ORIT, become an arm of multinational capital from the United States. The exploitation of the Third World and the plundering of its natural resources could thereby become the condition for guaranteeing the social gains of labor movements in First World countries.

The circle is completed in this way. The accumulation of capital creates privileged islands within an exploited world—islands on which the most unrestrained accumulation is associated with high wages and generous social spending by First World governments. Pressure from unemployment serves constantly to force the population to continue ahead, increasing the rate of accumulation and combating the obstacles to that accumulation, which, in its view, is the guarantee of employment. The accumulation of capital is given free reign over large, impoverished regions. The population and nature are exploited, in subjection to capital. And the modern islands in that vast impoverished world are willingly subject to capital, seeing it as a bearer of the "reign of social justice."

Only in this way can the legitimacy of these developed islands be established on a broad enough base to enable some of them to maintain parliamentary governments. Elsewhere recourse is made to governments based on force, which could not survive without the backing that First World countries (which are democratically legitimized) give them. Inasmuch as such governments do not have a sufficient basis for legitimacy on their own, they are the most dependent governments imaginable. Hence, they have no option but to turn over their populations and natural resources for exploitation and plunder by the capital in First World countries.

Only this multilevel analytical picture explains why capital in the First World appears in the guise of social justice and democracy.

OPPOSITION TO ENTREPRENEURIAL METAPHYSICS

Entrepreneurial metaphysics views its opponents in the same metaphysical terms in which it views itself. But, for this purpose, it reverses the terms.

Inasmuch as its opponents are opposed to freedom of prices and of business firms, they are viewed as enemies of freedom. Inasmuch as they counter the metaphysical nature of the mercantile world with the concrete, material nature of concrete human beings with their right to work, food, and housing, they are materialistic. Inasmuch as they reject subjugation to the higher forces of the market, they are the personification of hubris, arrogance, and pride. Inasmuch as they are attempting to build a society without using the law of value as the law of the economy's gravity, they are utopians. Inasmuch as they proclaim their right to defend real life, they are violent.

Entrepreneurs view themselves as free, idealistic, humble, realistic, and peaceful. They view their opponents as enemies of freedom, materialistic, proud, utopian, and violent. Entrepreneurs represent order and justice; their opponents represent terrorism and anarchy.

And because, from the standpoint of all entrepreneurial metaphysics, world history is a final judgment, its opponents receive the bitter fruit that reality itself offers them. To entrepreneurs, with market virtues, nature offers economic miracles. It offers their opponents chaos.

In the view of entrepreneurial metaphysics, this chaos is as metaphysical as is the economic miracle. Just as the economic miracle is a secularization of the religious heaven, chaos is the secularization of the hell of religious tradition. Therefore, entrepreneurs act under the protection of God, and their opponents under the protection of the devil. When entrepreneurs confront their opponents, it is a confrontation between God and Satan.

That is why entrepreneurial metaphysicians speak in such absolute terms when referring to their opponents:

> It has been our fate to live during a time when the entire world is embroiled in an open battle between order, legality, and justice, on the one hand, and terrorism, anarchy, and the most inhuman sentiments, on the other.[46]

They associate the extreme of terrorism—anarchy—and the most inhuman sentiments with what is utopian: ". . . demagogic voices that *offer our workers paradises that are impossible to attain,* and induce them to *disrupt social peace through violent means.*"[47]

They denounce their opponents as "hordes seeking to take the workers to their own destruction," "upsetters of order," and "making violence their way of life." "It is obvious that freedom would be annihilated by an oppressive, collectivist regime that pompously terms itself a 'new world' or a 'new society.' "[48]

From this sheer Manicheism, the metaphysical perception of the opponent can proceed to the charge of reverse blasphemy:

> . . . overtly challenging human authorities and clearly disrespecting and violating our political constitution and other laws, *going so far as to give theological interpretations of human laws.*[49]

These human laws, to which "theological interpretations" are given— thereby constituting blasphemy in the view of entrepreneurial metaphysics— are the laws that are called natural in the Aristotelian-Thomistic tradition. They relate to the fulfillment of basic needs as a right of the human being.

Entrepreneurial metaphysics envisages a different nature, that of commodities, money, and capital. It obviously interprets this in theological terms as a truly divine nature. Entrepreneurial metaphysics does not consider this "nature" a human product, or its laws human laws. Hence, it feels completely justified in making them divine. They constitute its great object of devotion.

On the other hand, that concrete, material nature in which the concrete human being lives and which the human being has to protect in order to live in it, is viewed by entrepreneurial metaphysics as an area of human laws, the theological interpretation of which is scandal and blasphemy.

The criticism that we cite is aimed at liberation theology. The scandal perceived by entrepreneurial metaphysics is seen in the fact that the liberation of prices and business firms is replaced by the liberation of human beings. Hence, there appears again the charge of pride and rebellion not only against "human authorities," but against God.

From the standpoint of entrepreneurial metaphysics, anyone who rises up against the mercantile relationships of money and capital, and hence anyone who upholds the concrete human being with the right to work, food, and housing, is rising up against God. God and capital on the one hand, and the concrete, needy human being and the devil, on the other—this is the supreme vision of entrepreneurial metaphysics.

In this metaphysical polarity, the reaction of entrepreneurs is easy to predict. They rise up against the "contemporary Cains," who are "a living example of the stupidity and lack of human sentiments of those who *attempt to take refuge in rights that they themselves trample upon and destroy.*"[50]

No freedom for the enemies of freedom; no human rights for the enemies of human rights. Anyone who does not want the freedom of prices or of business firms does not want either human freedom or human rights. Therefore, they obtain exactly what they want when refusing freedom and the recognition of human rights. And when you have what you want, you are free.

Those who do not want freedom (the freedom derived from the freeing of prices) obtain what they want when freedom is taken away. Hence, in bourgeois society everyone is free, both the respected and the persecuted, both the rich and the poor. This invocation of freedom (a genuine "call of the wild") incites the entrepreneurial metaphysician to leave "the illusory realm of conversation and arrive at the field of action. . . . Let us prove with facts that the free enterprise system knows how to respond to the challenge of the unrest of the times in which we live."[51]

ENTREPRENEURIAL IDOLATRY

Except in the view of entrepreneurial metaphysics itself, it is quite clear that such metaphysics is idolatry, in the very sense in which this term is used in biblical tradition. Marx calls it fetishism. It is the subjugation of the human being and of human life to a product of human labor, with the consequent destruction of the human being per se through the relationship that is established with an idol. Every idol is, in this respect, a Moloch that devours the human being. The idol is a "god" associated with oppression.

Nevertheless, there is an important new element. Entrepreneurial metaphysics is related to an object of devotion that is certainly a human product. But, and this is the difference from the idolatry known in the Bible, such a human product transformed into an object of devotion is an *unintentional* human product. It is not, in the literal sense, a product of *action*, but rather of human *interaction*. It is a way of interrelating human beings.

The idol of entrepreneurial metaphysics is invisible, distinguishing it from the biblical idol, which is made of elements of concrete nature, and is therefore visible. It is a concrete image. In its form as an unintentional product of human interaction, the entrepreneurial idol is a fetish.

In view of this invisible and unintentional nature, entrepreneurial idolatry has been able to absorb many key elements of the Christian tradition, converting them into elements of fetishism. In its combined ramifications, it even gives the impression of a genuine inversion of Christianity.

On the basis of entrepreneurial metaphysics, there emerges a concept of nature the only obstacle to which is the human being who expresses needs and who claims concrete nature as an environment and requisite for concrete life. This concrete human being appears as the great antithesis of the divinity of entrepreneurial metaphysics, which is nothing but the sublimation of the market, money, and capital, on behalf of which the business firm operates: a god of the powerful, who subjugates human beings.

This fetish must be opposed by the biblical criticism of idolatry and the discernment of gods. In biblical tradition, the true God is the one whose will is that the concrete human being, with concrete needs, be the center of society and of history. In competing with the human being, the idol competes with God. It sets itself up as God as it converts the human being into a depraved being, whose misery is the foil of God's grandeur. The biblical God, on the other hand, lives where society and history revolve around the concrete human being and the fulfillment of human needs.

NOTES

1. Friedrich von Hayek, *Individualismus und wirtschaftliche Ordnung* (Zurich, 1952), p. 115, Engl. trans., *Individualism and Economic Order* (Chicago: Regnery, 1972), p. 32. See also p. 22: "We must face the fact that the preservation of individual freedom is incompatible with a full satisfaction of our views of distributive justice."

2. *Business Week,* May 12, 1977, p. 131.
3. *Business Week,* March 13, 1978, p. 32.
4. Ibid., p. 30.
5. Frankfurt, *Die Zeit,* Dec. 23, 1977.
6. Ibid.
7. San Salvador, *La Crónica,* July 22, 1978; italics added.
8. San José, *La Nación,* May 25, 1978.
9. Managua, *La Prensa,* April 30, 1978; italics added.
10. *La Nación,* June 1, 1978.
11. *Die Zeit,* Jan. 6, 1978.
12. *La Nación,* May 25, 1978.
13. *Die Zeit,* March 24, 1978.
14. *Business Week,* Nov. 21, 1977, p. 138.
15. *Business Week,* Dec. 5, 1977, p. 41.
16. *Die Zeit,* May 5, 1978.

17. *Die Zeit,* Dec. 30, 1977.

18. *Newsweek,* May 29, 1978, p. 68.

19. Ibid.; italics added.

20. *Business Week,* Dec. 5, 1977, p. 19.

21. Ibid.

22. *Business Week,* Nov. 21, 1977, p. 44.

23. *Business Week,* Aug. 29, 1977, p. 68.

24. *U.S. News and World Report,* April 11, 1977.

25. *Newsweek,* May 29, 1978, p. 69.

26. Ibid., p. 72; italics added.

27. *Business Week,* Feb. 27, 1978, p. 18.

28. *Die Zeit,* May 5, 1978.

29. *Newsweek,* May 26, 1975, p. 41.

30. *La Nación,* May 24, 1978; italics added.

31. San Salvador, *La Prensa Gráfica,* May 20, 1978; italics added.

32. *La Nación,* May 24, 1978; italics added.

33. Ibid.; italics added.

34. *La Prensa,* April 30, 1978; italics added.

35. Ibid.

36. *Die Zeit,* Dec. 16, 1977, p. 23; italics added.

37. Ibid.

38. *Die Zeit,* May 5, 1978.

39. Ibid.; italics added.

40. *Newsweek,* based on *Die Zeit,* Jan. 6, 1978; italics added.

41. *La Nación,* May 24, 1978; italics added.

42. Milton Friedman, *Capitalism and Freedom* (Chicago: University of Chicago Press, 1962), p. 35.

43. *Newsweek,* May 29, 1978.

44. *Die Zeit,* May 5, 1978.

45. *Die Zeit,* Jan. 31, 1978.

46. *La Prensa Gráfica,* May 20, 1978.

47. Ibid.; italics added.

48. Ibid.

49. Ibid.; italics added.

50. Ibid.; italics added.

51. Ibid.

HUGO ASSMANN

The Faith of the Poor in Their Struggle with Idols

Proem

This chapter consists of fragments of meditation on the surprises that we are given by ordinary believers when they have started moving and fighting for their liberation. It is an unpretentious putting into writing of a few of the many things that one learns in conversations with male and female comrades in the struggle, when there is a willingness to take seriously what the Final Document from Puebla terms "the evangelizing potential of the poor." It is a learning based on dialogue and dialectics. Making a myth of an idealized, abstract "people" has no place in it. No one gives final lessons, but rather it is up to everyone to move from action to reflection, and to turn from reflection back to action. And it is, in particular, a learning that is always open and inconclusive, although it is conclusive as to the necessity of taking in turn every step along the way.

Part One (following these preliminary sections) presents a series of inconclusive "border scenes"—scenes, from different angles, of things that are known more than halfway, but find expression in our speech only halfway. Part Two presents a mosaic of revolutionary poems—or at least poems composed by revolutionaries—relating explicitly to the matter of God. I have my own comments to make on each poem, attempting to ascertain its popular validity—that is, its capacity to express the mind of the believers who are struggling for their liberation. And I try to bring out their ability to identify and denounce the idolatrous nature of their oppressors' alleged faith.

The Backdrop: Nicaragua

It should be explained, at the outset, that these writings, including the metaphorical aspect of their language in certain instances, must be read against a background of concrete experiences, particularly the ones most closely related to the struggle and victory—and now to the continued struggle for reconstitution—of the heroic people of Nicaragua. What has happened and is still happening in the Sandinista revolution offers us more than does an ordinary *locus theologicus*. The explosive creativity of the people, and its unified view of life, will keep us learning for a long time to come. Their demand for the right to work, food, housing, health, and education is combined with unrestrainable outbursts of poetry, song, dance, tenderness, and love, linking the bitterest sacrifices with popular celebration.

The participation of Christians in the Nicaraguan revolution—an unconditional participation for the majority of Christian militants and part of the Christian people—involved something new in the history of revolutions. The attempt to capitalize on this participation, in the interests of power-sharing, as certain ecclesiastics tried to do, especially the last-minute enlistees, ran counter to the essence of that participation. It was a violation of the authentic, historical essence of a Christian faith that knew how to work out its materialization in acts of struggle rooted in love and hope.

But we must not isolate the fact of Christian participation in the revolutionary struggle from the other impactive lessons of the Nicaraguan process as a whole. They include the lesson of a unity that is at once strainful and secure—the lesson expressed in the marvelous union of people/youth/people's vanguard (the Sandinista National Liberation Front), bursting forth from those whose very existence was threatened and attacked by the Somoza dictatorship. Another beautiful and enlightening lesson is the impressive quantitative and qualitative participation of women.

Situating the participation of Christians in this broader context will help preclude a superficial treatment of isolated events. It was an entire people, the majority of whom were Christian, that set forth to make a revolution without affixing Christian adjectives on it.

There, in the spontaneous naturalness of that massive Christian presence in a revolutionary process, lies the major datum that must not be distorted or manipulated on behalf of outdated designs of Christianity. At least one pastoral letter from the Nicaraguan bishops warned against any attempt at that type of manipulation. But let no one be deceived: the old ties of certain sectors of the church with certain sectors of the ruling classes call for constant vigilance to thwart any resumption of manipulation of the Christian faith against the forward march of the revolution.

Needless to say, the entire "church born of the people," throughout our part of the Americas, is part of the backdrop for our fragments of meditation. Illusory and overly optimistic generalizations have no place in this theater. But ignorance of an entire, very extensive process of forging new realities for our peoples and for the church itself would also be inappropriate.

Steps Leading to the Stage

The Faith of the Poor. "The faith of the poor" is included in the title of this chapter. This expression is used for a definite purpose. We wish to meditate precisely on that faith of the people which, when it actively materializes love and hope, does so through references to God, Christ, the Virgin, the saints, and religious symbols in general, even when the symbols appear in ostensibly secular language. Many ecclesiastics are fond of talking about the "deep religiosity" of the people, the people's "Christian traditions," and the like. This magnanimous granting of a "Christian" ID card to the people veils, in many instances, a "reserved judgment" on the "quality" of faith in that religiosity.

In this regard, I do not deny the alienating aspects of many forms of the popular practice of religion. I do not intend to magnify popular religiosity indiscriminately, as if to suggest that it is, in all instances and always, a fitting expression of Christian faith. We are talking about concrete matters involving a people in its struggle for liberation. The Nicaraguan people called upon God, the Virgin, and their saints—St. Sebastian and St. Dominic, for example—praying that "the boys" would win over Somoza. When Nicaraguans engaged in the most dangerous acts of struggle or support for the struggle, they transformed the very structure of their worship and liturgy in many instances. After the victory, Radio Sandino and the Sandinista Television Network included religious hymns (especially excerpts from the Nicaraguan Peasants' Mass and Carlos Mejía Godoy's "The Christ of Palacagüina") in revolutionary programs. In mass demonstrations, with the National Reconstruction Government Junta and in the presence of high-ranking officials of the FSLN (*Frente Sandinista de Liberación Nacional,* Sandinista National Liberation Front), they shout out announcements of Masses of thanksgiving and Masses in memory of heroes and martyrs who died in the struggle against the dictatorship.

Sometimes there are humorous incidents, such as during the reception for General Torrijos on the Plaza de la Revolución. A speaker, who was of high rank in the FSLN, was interrupted by noise coming from the plaza. He was told that someone keeping a religious vow was dragging a huge statue of St. Dominic in a procession. The speaker's spontaneous reaction was to suggest that the saint's image be brought to the center of the reception ceremony— "because the saint may be exhausted."

At a public ceremony in Masaya, on July 22, 1979, while awaiting the arrival of government officials, someone read out lists of heroes and martyrs from both the people and the liberation movement. At a certain point, and with great naturalness, there was included the announcement that Señor X, father of two militants who had been killed, invited everyone to a Mass of thanksgiving marking the death of Somoza.

What right do ecclesiastics and theologians have to dispute the nature of the faith of those who speak of God when they are expressing and materializing their love and hope? In the most traditional and sound Christian theology, no one has faith because of the mere *claim* of belief in God. From the biblical perspective, the question of whether or not one has faith is not resolved in the rectory or seminary, but rather in the realm of action where the collective love and hope of human beings materialize. It is a preeminently practical matter. The verbal husk of the orthodox creeds is worth as much as, or less than, the verbal husk of the most routine Lord's Prayer recited by someone while sleepwalking. It all depends on the mediating role that this or that religious formula, or this or that recourse to religious symbology, plays in putting love and hope into practice in a social, organic manner.

The church, in all its institutional forms, has no "mission" (if its nature as a "sacrament" and its "missionary nature" are to be taken seriously) other than that of channeling the motivations and actions of human beings toward the path of materializing love and hope. This obviously cannot be accepted by those who conceive of love for God as something so spiritual that it is not required to materialize in social, organized love for one's neighbor, and in the construction of a more comradely society, because they do not understand it. It cannot be understood by the theologians who talk about hope as if it were a bundle tied to one's back—an obligation—and not the decision to risk testing the limits of the possible, and to resolve that the only real, genuine thing for those with hope is to strive so that what is not yet real (work, food, housing, and joy for everyone) will come into existence as a tangible reality and a collective benefit.

For all these reasons, the first thing that we wish to establish is that there is a wrong way of judging the "rather primitive" or "alienating" nature of the religiosity of the masses. This wrong way usually comes from the "upper realm" of theology, which conceives of faith as a code illustrated with theoretical clarifications. Or it comes from the "upper realm" of a levitical mentality, which conceives of faith as orthodoxy in relation to a creed, and fidelity in relation to prescribed rituals. Or it even comes from the other "upper realm" of some self-styled Marxists who conceive of actions and practices associated with the struggle as infrastructural when they are nurtured from an irreligious stimulus, but as superstructural from the time when religious motivations go into effect. Of course, the "lower realm"—"down there"— for all these schools of manipulation is the people.

A Favorable Historical Context. The second step leading to our stage relates to the historical conditions of a struggle by an entire people—the conditions needed so that the forms of religiosity of that people can be changed, can be converted into forms of faith that seek materialization in deeds of love and horizons of hope. Obviously, a favorable historical context is needed. The church too, inasmuch as it is a set of institutions with historical influence, is faced with the same problem—with the difference that the masses tend to "detonate" their religiosity in acts of hopeful love long before ecclesiastical institutions do so. It is not usually the masses who lag behind in historical breakthroughs.

The Latin American masses believe in God, and refer to God at many vital times in their individual and collective existence. This is a fact. The historical circumstances surrounding this fact (something that we shall discuss later) do not negate the reality of the fact. When studying it, we are certainly correct to identify the many obviously alienating aspects of this popular religiosity that cause apathy—in other words, the ways in which it truly is "opium." But very closely related to the "opium" aspects are the aspects of protest, clearly recognized in the classic Marxist theory on religion. It is not unlikely that features of protest can be discovered in the frequent association of popular religious expressions with the deprivation and unfulfillment that the masses suffer with regard to their most fundamental human rights: work, food, housing, health, education, security, and structural freedom.

What needs to be emphasized here is that these two aspects—apathy and protest—do not exhaust the practical essence of the masses' faith in God. They do not, as such, highlight the feature that I regard as most fundamental from the political perspective. To the masses, the fact of believing in God and being able to express that faith is a substantial part of their ability to struggle. It is part of their practical language about love and hope, in which faith is historically materialized (in sound Christian theology). Hence we are returning here, both theologically and politically, to the sphere of faith as such, beyond symbolic, ritualistic, linguistic, and other trappings. It is, fundamentally, a matter of understanding how essential it is for Latin Americans to be able to do something concrete, in terms of practical love and hopeful struggle, in their own expressions of religious faith.

I am not claiming that this is the only way or method that persons have to be effective in the realm of love and hope. There are other channels: some in the arts, others directly related to secular politics, and still others on the level of material and corporal subsistence. Nor is it a matter of giving privilege of place to religious expression as the only dynamo of action. The question is one of knowing how to evaluate it in its proper dimensions, as an existing and common expression for extensive population blocs. Theologically, this implies not refusing to put faith where it most belongs: in the practice of a loving fellowship, arising in ever new hope for a more comradely world. Politically, it involves something far more serious than merely the respect owed to the people: it entails major levels of efficacy in political action.

It is true that Latin America is "circumstantially" Christian. But this is not at the heart of the concrete situation from the pastoral and political view-point. The Christian circumstantiality of Latin America is a real and present fact, and hence it must be taken into account. A closer analysis of the historico-genetic features of this circumstantiality (for example, the situation of a Christianity imposed colonially and transmitted more by way of biology than by radical evangelization) could certainly shed considerable light on the high degree of consciousness of domination aided by Christian symbols in the mind of the dominated. It would not be unwise for the theologian who is somewhat proud of the fact that Latin America carries so much weight, and increasingly so, at least quantitatively, within worldwide Christianity, to reflect on the truly historical and circumstantial nature of that fact, so as not to toy with "theologies of grace" or "theologies of salvation" dissociated from facts that are, historically, contingent. The rage of medieval Europe in its wars against Islam did not allow the Iberian peninsula to remain in the hands of the Muslims, and that is why Latin America is not Muslim today. It does not make much sense to conjecture on whether a colonization of another provenance would have saved the lives of several million Indians, in view of the catastrophe perpetrated by Christian evangelization. It provided an ideological justification of the atrocities committed by the Spanish and Portuguese colonizers. A sound "catholic" (*kata holon*) theology, embracing the entire universe, would have to readjust its teaching on the action of God in history to the reality and circumstantiality of the "geography of religions" in the present-day world. And, going back further, its teachings on grace and salvation would have to be realigned with everything that has taken place throughout the million and a half or more years of human existence on earth.

However, all this is secondary to the issue that is of central concern to us here. Latin America, "made Christian" by circumstances that are not relevant now, presents a pastoral and political scene where the fact of asserting faith in the God of Jesus Christ is both an obstacle to the liberation struggle *and* a source of motivation and inspiration for that struggle. In other words, a really liberating revolution of the masses will be extremely difficult in this part of the world if there is not an eruption, from within this "Christian" conditioning, of a positive dialectics of the faith that, in biblical terms, is real only when it finds materialization in acts of love and shimmerings of hope.

The momentous events in Nicaragua, together with other significant events that have been taking place throughout Latin America, seem to suggest that the faith of the oppressed is, beyond apathy and protest, also a font and vehicle of constructive acts of organic fellowship demanded by new forms of societal organization. These events, at the same time, reveal that the potential for a "theological faith" latent in popular religiosity cannot be activated except under historical conditions for struggle based on very concrete liberation causes. Such struggle could be experimental, noncoercive struggle with problems tangentially related to oppression, which nevertheless prepares the people for qualitative leaps when its faith is incarnated into a more extensive liberation cause, with all its political and organizational implications.

Expropriation of the Means of Symbolic Productivity. This is the third and final step leading to the stage.

If, in an objective evaluation of reality, we are confident that the oppressed who believe in God can achieve a significant expropriation of the means of symbolic productivity held by the ruling classes and the portion of the clergy associated with them, then we must extract some theoretical and practical consequences from that confidence. On the theoretical plane, which is not of preeminent concern to us now, there emerges the challenge of a fundamental restatement of the classic Marxist theory on religion. It will be necessary to assess the epistemological strength of all the infrastructural practices in which love and hope become effective for human beings, in the activation of the religious resources of a believing people.

Such a theoretical restatement would have to take into account the revolutionary importance of two concrete aspects of the activation of religious faith. The one is related to the capacity to act effectively here and now (the materialization that we call love, in the Nicaraguan-style songs and poems that are currently in the streets, such as the one that rejoices that "dawn is no longer a temptation"). The other is the capacity for keeping alive the collective desires for what is "not yet possible" but is perceived as a real promise for tomorrow (the open horizon that we call hope).

A corollary of the hope aspect—a corollary that has immediate pastoral and political repercussions—is that to "deactivate" the God of the poor, in the sense of imposing irreligious slogans on a revolutionary but believing people, could mean that part of the "historical dynamism of the poor" would be deactivated. True, there is nothing to be gained by pursuing vague desires and hazy depictions of the dialectical potential of a people's faith— desires and depictions that are not borne out in fact. However, this matter is of such practical importance that the mere positive suspicion that such a dynamism is at work forces us to consider it an area of not only tactical, but strategic relevance. And I think that, in the events referred to, there are grounds for more than merely a suspicion.

In the search for clear, transparent expressions, the essential challenge can be formulated as follows. Amid the very complex web of a people's religious language it is possible to discover (under certain historical conditions) a symbology and a religious self-expression that are intrinsically, not accidentally, revolutionary. That intrinsically revolutionary impulse stems from the political essence of the practice of struggle for liberation that has materialized through such religious self-expression. In a confrontation with the religion of the dominator, an oppressed people, by expressing its faith linked with historical action, carries out a process of expropriating the means of symbolic production held by the oppressors. This expropriation process entails the exposure of the contradiction that exists between the uses of the same religious symbols in a society comprised of opposing classes.

PART ONE: THE GOD OF THE RICH AND THE GOD OF THE POOR

(Scenes, from different angles,
of things that are known more than halfway,
but find expression in our speech only halfway)

Prelude

Let us not be told afterward
   that there are no minerals
     because they appear only in impure gangue;
   that the reality is always there,
     available and transparent,
     and that it is useless to try to unveil hidden things;
   that to engage in science is to classify
     what is evident to everyone,
     and that it is a waste of time
     to probe opacity;
   that there is no truth in
     what cannot be generalized.
Because praxis establishes its consistency
     in the cradle of the particular,
     and, multiplying differences,
     it destroys the identity
     of the perpetual state of affairs.

Entrance Scene: The Roots of Idolatry

Concern with Atheism as a Matter of Geography

The rich countries of the world,
their churches and doctors,
and their allies in our midst,
go about very busily
and do not spare zeal
in publicizing, as something profound,
the danger of atheism
and of crass materialism
(of communism, in other words).

And while they dispute
over faith threatened
by too much politics,

we fire our criticism:
it is in the best interests
of the poor to discuss
the roots of idolatry
in a particular economy.
(Can it be a matter of geography?)

The God of the Rich and the God
of the Poor Are Not the Same God

The gods have been battling
   since very ancient times.
The gods of some were winning,
   and those of others were losing.
This was the state of things,
   in the midst of polytheisms
   and attempts at monotheism;
   the matter was not settled.
Because when they began to believe
   that there was only one God,
   one God of the whole world,
   it turned out that the Jews
   wanted to monopolize that God
   (they who had fought
   in a lengthy war
   against the many gods
   of the many oppressors,
   while slaves in Egypt;
   unfurling the banner
      of the one God
      who takes the side of,
      and convokes the struggle of,
      the oppressed).

But it so happens that this history
     of Jewish monotheism
   is not always told correctly,
   because right there in Israel
   the one God,
     the God of liberation for slaves,
   again became a rallying point
     of oppressors against oppressed
   (and only now and then
     of the oppressed against oppressors).

At this point God is thought to have reasoned:
  "They did not understand that time,
  they have not yet understood the side that I took.
  So, I shall take sides
    once and for all,
    definitively."

And God became incarnate in Jesus Christ,
  a person like everyone else,
  a true human being.
    ("Christ was born in Palacagüina
    of Chepe Pavón and a certain María;
    she goes very humbly to iron
    the clothes cherished by the beautiful wife
    of the landowner.")[1]

When everything seemed clear,
    clarified once and for all,
when everything seemed better,
    definitively,
  some theologians arrived,
  protected by some clerics
  and allied with some politicians
    (sometimes without realizing it, poor things),
and they invented the story
  about God's having been made a human being in general,
                    an abstract human being,
                    a single-mold human being,
                    a human being patterning
                      everyone.
(Just imagine!
an abstract, single-mold human being
patterning each and every SOB oppressor!)

It also turned out that those magicians
  subjected God, with the passage of time,
  to a lot of plastic surgery
  (blond Christs born of blond Marys,
  Josephs with the face of a veteran
  of imperialist wars),
  whereas every poor person knows that Christ
    was like a Bolivian miner,
    like a black slave,
    like any oppressed person.

So, the job of being God
   is not all that pleasant,
    because there is no way to escape
    the games of the counterfeiters
     and their borrowed idols.
God has been pulled from one side to the other,
    God was the last of the Roman emperors,
     and the first and last of the medieval kings,
    and, much later, a captive of capitalism,
     eventually playing the role of the god of
     "in God we trust."
But the oppressed of all the centuries,
   when they set out to struggle,
   always discovered many things
   about the identity of the counterfeiters,
   and the reasons for the counterfeiting.
No one can any longer deceive
   the poor of our America about this:
     the god of the rich
     and the God of the poor
     are not the same divinity!

Modern Idolatry

The stories that they told us when we were children
    about primitive peoples being idolatrous,
    about the gods of the pagans being idols,
    were certainly not innocent stories
    (despite the innocent narrators);
   they were stories told for a reason.

And the more recent stories,
    about the State-idol of those who care for everyone,
    about the Material-idol of those who struggle for bread,
    about the Body-idol of those who know about tenderness
    (with less innocent narrators)
   are stories told for a reason.

The true idolatry
   is not that of nonbelievers,
   is not that of atheists
    (who are often those who
    destroy idols
    and are fighting against idols).

Idols are
   the gods of oppression.
Idols are
   the shining fetishes
   with divine names
   and broad smiles,
     with creeds,
     with worship,
     with prayers,
     with laws,
     with sacred and divine power,
                power to oppress,
                power to exploit,
                power to kill.

The dominators,
the idolatrous,
   will never make the mistake
     of declaring themselves atheists
     (of their idols)—
God, Homeland, and Family,
Tradition, Family, and Property.
The family that prays together stays together
     without work,
     without food,
     without housing,
     without good health.
In God we Trust. Amen.

The Idols of Security

The oppressive system
   does not allow heresies,
   does not tolerate apostasies,
   of its only god:
     its god!—
     its true god of "true reality,"
     its providence-god who demands "freedom,"
     its god!

Otherwise,
   how could it defend the "equality of opportunity"
     that guarantees so many opportunities to the rich?

How could it ensure the continuation
   of the "social construction of appearances,"
      the indispensable fetishism of capital?

But this only true god
     (a captive of the truth of this single system)
   is an idol with a thousand faces,
   multiplied in all the commodities
      (there is nothing more religious
     than the objects of piety
     called commodities),
   present in every mercantile relationship
      (no religion has so many rituals and gestures
     as that "religion of daily life,"
     as Marx described capitalism).

The many facets of the true god of capital,
the many functions, with comings and goings, of the god of farce,
   are worth little, are worth much,
   are valuable today and tomorrow,
   are always valuable, are worth everything;
     and the fetishism of capital,
     the omnipresent god,
     becomes everything in all things;
       is everywhere,
       but, obviously, cannot
       be on everyone's side.
Lesser here, greater there,
fleeting here, present there,
something now, everything later,
a spare part, a mounted assembly.

Sometimes the idols become nervous.
When their physico-metaphysical system
     (concrete things
     compound fetishes)
  is threatened
  with being torn asunder,
    the idol defends its integrity
    (the physical and the metaphysical)
      with nails,
      with rifles,
      with bombs,
      with prayers,
      with worship,
      with creeds.

No one has ever seen the idol more faithful,
   more exact, imposing, and cruel,
   than at those solemn times
   when it must play the enormous role
      of guardian of everything,
      of guardian of all for all,
      of guardian of all at one time,
      of guardian of the clear-cut boundaries.

At such solemn times,
   when everything is at stake,
   when everything is threatened,
   when the end of the system is threatening it,
      the phalanxes of idolaters
      unfurl their creed,
      and demand that everyone
      pay tribute to the "true god,"
      the one that secures everything.

And in the name of the divine doctrine of security,
   everyone is assured
      that the idol is God,
      that the Beast is God.

Culinary Preferences of the Idols

When a historical product
born of human hands,
of useful human toil,
to be of value by having a use,
geared to human needs,
   when this useful thing
   takes the "death leap" into the stock market,
      and begins functioning
      as an exchange value,
you cannot imagine how the idols relish it!

Their mouths start watering,
they shiver convulsively with pleasure,
and purr in "strange tongues"
   (because publicity must be aroused).

The idols relish
   the seasoning value
   of the mortal leap
   of the useful thing to a commodity

(mortal, because it is the origin of
the metaphysics of death,
the necrophilia,
of the capitalist system).

The idols demand a spiritual extract
of this mortal leap
in all their meals.

Needless to say, all the worship offered
to the fetish by the entire system,
to the one and only divine guarantor,
is a liturgy of deaths,
of immolations,
with robbery, slaughter, pillage,
and the veins of the people bled dry.

The prescribed ritual for this necrophilic banquet
is governed by a criterion that does not brook violations,
and, unveiled as "the law of profitability"
to a very few clerics and no capitalists,
requisitions the blood and corpses that the Beast devours.

Interior Scene I: Forms

The Perfect Workmanship of the Idols

Ah,
the perfect workmanship
of the god of the rich!

It is not easy to explain
with words or gestures
how, out of smoke, and vapors, and daylight,
and scraps of spirituality,
such soundness could be achieved,
such consistency.

The god of the rich never sleeps,
is never distracted from its lofty mission.
Its wakefulness inspires confidence.
One notes immediately
that it is a god that governs,
a provident god.

If we add to this
  its clear-cut doctrines,
  its steadfast values
  and exact functions,
 to whom would it occur to doubt
   that it is coherent,
   that it says everything,
   that it is absolute,
      absolutely opposed to chaos,
      functional to the order of all things?

Eternal praise
to reliable gods!

God, Statued and Unstatued

The God of the poor
  seems incapable of obeying
    the command "Attention!"
    or "About face, march!"

They have made many statues of that God
    but God escapes from all of them.
God lacks the rigidity
    of perfect things.
God's artistry is supple, subtle,
    relaxed, winding and unwinding,
  making things and disappearing,
  with forms, gestures, and actions
    as unpredictable
    as the flowing movement
    of an African's body.
      (They are researching God's tropical origin.)

No one has ever been able to explain
    how God summons multitudes
    from shadow, silhouette, and lightning flash.

With the odor of sweat and earth,
    redolent of the *animal* in *animal rationale*,
    with some once-in-a-whiles
    that are a little more spiritual,
those who are learned in such subjects
    say that it is a provisional God,

an interim God,
a tentative God,
an unfinished God,
a not-yet God,
a relative God.

But the poor continue to claim
    that they find him everywhere,
    that they find him
    in every oppressed person.

Interior Scene II: Uses

The Ethereal Purity of Idols

Let no one doubt
that the god of the rich
is unsullied transcendence.
It has its residence
    in the kingdom of "other values"
        totally spiritual.

To arrive at a strained image
of that kingdom of absolute purity,
    let us imagine the pure number,
                the clear number,
                the hard number,
                of the pure "value."
That pure-value number
dances across satellites
        (the pure soul of commerce,
        with nothing material about it)
untouched by dirty hands
in the great
totally metaphysical transactions
of the stock exchange.
    It is the *divinum commercium*
    that can exist only
        among entities
        that are totally spiritual:
    the pure number,
    the clear number,
    the hard number,
    the pure "value"
        of the pure exchange value.

And what if it were possible to raise
to this transcendent level
the relationships among human beings?
   A totally spiritual sexuality,
    family, work, nation,
       and, of course, love of neighbor,
         without prejudice or conflicts,
    all unsullied by history—
ah, it would be the perfect morality,
   of perfect relationships,
     with perfect grace,
       with no admixture of hormones.

This is the proposal
of the god of the dominator.

The Useful God

The God of the poor goes about
involved in earthly things.
A God who is not within range,
apart from being useful in history.
   That God is in active human hands,
   in the struggle that wagers on life,
   in work and in food,
   in the today that demands a tomorrow,
   in embrace and in dance,
   in the tenderness that kindles hope—
     the God of savor,
     the God of love,
   the God of this world of Jesus Christ.
The wise know nothing of this God
      (they have ideas in their head
      but no thrills in their heart)
   but the poor delight in that God.
Because it is no lie
   that this is a God who eats.
     (Sometimes the God of the poor is accused
     of spreading materialistic ideas.)

The God so linked with the necessities
of the social reproduction of life
   is sought in the faith
     that shapes the present,
       procreating the future.

Interior Scene III: Pleasures

The Splendors of the Heaven of the Rich

The heaven invented by the rich
   is magnificent, olympian, splendid.

Celestial relationships
   will be a pure interchange
   among metaphysical entities.

There, there will be no squandering on food.
There, there will be no extravagance on drink.
There, there will be no sweaty embraces
   or anything similar
      of a pleasurable, dialectical nature.
         (They say this is why
         the poor invent songs
         that speak of an ultimate embrace
         here, below,
            possibly in the grave).

It has not yet been studied in depth
   why the rich invented this kind of heaven.
Some suspect that it was
   so that all those without bread
      (who therefore do not enjoy love either,
      but only accumulate sins)
   would come to understand
      and appreciate that there is
      nourishment in heaven
      with an exquisite taste
   (having nothing to do with proteins and vitamins).

The Joy of the Fiesta

To show everyone
   how pleased they are
      with God,
         the poor put on a fiesta.

(And to show that their love
   also includes priests,
      they offer supplications
      and make novenas.)

One must observe
  very closely
how the fireworks and rockets
    emerge sparkling and exploding
    from within their hearts.

They also take the saints' statues out to the street
  to get a breath of air,
    and open their eyes,
    and see the people,
    and escape from inside
    those statues,
    and find their rightful place
    in the common struggle.

      (Others say that it is done
        so that they may escape the insipidness
        of the bourgeois heaven.)

Interior Scene IV: Devotions

The Sublime Supplications of the Rich

Let no one say that when the rich pray
  they ask for petty things,
    and only for themselves.
Their supplication is sublime,
and has objectives that break the molds
of all the varieties of selfishness:
    they pray thinking of everyone,
    they pray for order and peace.

Any economist can prove to them
that what they ask,
in addition to being realistic,
    makes sense
    for the benefit of all:
    that love may exist in homes,
    and order throughout the country;
    that cooperation may exist
    in the interdependent world;
    and, especially, that there be no lack of
      economic miracles,
      political stability,
      and unending accumulation

(and, that all criticism may cease,
    because accumulation is for the good of everyone).
Even so, there are some who claim
    that "the verb 'to have'
    is the death of God."[2]

The Trifles That the Poor Entrust to God

Because the God of the poor
goes about the world,
along streets, highways, and country paths,
    it is not surprising that the poor
    ask that God for small favors,
    and entrust that God with small errands
        (perhaps thinking
        that, by involving God in all this,
        they are revealing truths to God),
    things that we all know about:
    that the husband may find work,
    that the children's bread not be lacking,
    that we all have better health
            (routine trifles).

And because the God of the poor
is apparently not concerned about morality
        (bourgeois morality),
    prostitutes
    and even thieves
    make requests to God and the saints
    that it would be better not to mention.

And when they mix politics
in their prayers and Masses
        they even bring
        subversion
        to the Hail Mary
    ("Blessed is the woman
    who gave birth
    to a Sandinista child").[3]

The unimaginable
    also happens:
        the distinction is erased
        between blasphemy and prayer.

(I ask you, honorable reader, to permit me
to narrate to you, honestly,
something dreadful that was heard,
in these very words, in Panama:
    "If we do not win this strike,
    I'll shit on Christ's holy balls.")

Lately, some exotic theories have emerged
    on this intimacy of the poor with God:
    it is said that the poor,
        upon requesting something concrete,
    destroy in themselves
        the law of destiny
            (and in God it would destroy
            his holy will).
    And so, gradually, one would discover
        that the human being has no destiny,
        but has only hands,
        and what is achieved with them
            in the common struggle
            of many brothers and sisters.

Final Scene: Horizons

Why the Poor Invent Resurrections

The rich take death very seriously,
    so seriously that it suits them to accept
    the unavoidable death,
    the necessary death.

Because, to the rich, death is not
    mere normal death,
    natural death.
No, ladies and gentlemen
    do not be deceived:
    it is the destiny-death
        (the death that is part
        of the economy of salvation
        —*economia salutis*—
        decreed forever
        by the god-capital),
    the indispensable death,
    the necessary death.

(How could the capitalist system operate
without the millions of deaths each year
from hunger and malnutrition?)

The poor invented the resurrection.
Accustomed to hunger and death,
    they invent resurrection
    so that their dead,
    and especially their heroes and martyrs,
    will not die completely.
        ("Carlos Fonseca Amador." "Present!"
        And we are present, with Carlos present.)

For Sandino
    (San Dino, the most miraculous saint in Latin America)
they invented,
from the 1930s to date,
    a constant, resolute, insurrectional presence
        and infinite miracles
    (Sandino removing roofs from houses
    . . . and a landholder dies,
    Sandino who was seen as a shadow at night
    . . . and a colonel dies).

And in Mexico
    (where Zapata is still riding horseback)
who knows what hidden threats there may be
        behind the skulls,
        behind the skeletons,
    that the people's art displays
        at fiestas
        and other celebrations
        of struggle.

It is simply fantastic,
simply incredible,
    the people's experience
    of the dead who will not stay dead
        (they die neither in this world,
        nor in the other, of course).

("The grave of the guerrilla fighter,
where, where, where is it?—
all are asking.
Some day they will know [. . .].

They refused to tell us the place
where you are,
and therefore your grave is
all our territory.
In every stretch of my Nicaragua,
there you are.'')[4]

(''Sharpshooter Juancito [. . .]
your sweet blood was shed by
the bullet of a coward;
the iguanas mourned
when evening fell.
Now that no one any longer
restricts your freedom,
you practice by night
your vast marksmanship.
You shoot down stars;
they fall into the river,
and then you put them,
when dry, into your pocket.'')[5]

As you can see,
    the poor have
        unmanageable dead!

Addendum for Pastors and Theologians

In their struggle, the masses
prove to us that it is not impossible
    to clothe new truths
    in age-old symbols.
They demonstrate that it is possible
    to experience in action,
      as something real,
      the victory
      that has not yet taken place.
The masses chart the future,
    and live it as something secure.

It is up to the theologian and the pastor
    to be there,
      to remain there,
      together and within,
    grasping what happens when a revolutionary act
    makes religious symbols burst inside out.

What is it that is happening,
what is it that could happen,
    when the masses fire with skilful marksmanship
    the event of their God into the face of the idol?

PART TWO: REVOLUTIONARIES WRITING ABOUT GOD

I begin this collection of verse with a challenge-poem by a Brazilian com-
rade (unfortunately, I must maintain his anonymity). It is a poem that I in-
cluded in the Introduction to one of my books.[6] This poem, or excerpts from
it, was quoted in many reviews of the book, and even apart from references to
the book. This attests to its impact. I am now of the opinion that, in essence,
the position expressed in the poem reflects a typical stage in the journey of the
petty bourgeoisie, when radicalized in its difficult approach to the reality of
the people. However, this does not detract validity or force from it.

The Right to Give God a Name

On the day when you succeed in transforming
    your many abstract nouns
    into a few concrete nouns
        with substance verified in experience,
perhaps it will again make sense
    for us to talk about Christ and God.
On the day when it becomes a truth
        utterable because verified
        —Justice "pitched its tent in our midst"
    and Love "dwells with us"—
perhaps there may exist a basis of experience
    for what in your Bible
        is called "the name of God."

Following is a poem by Ernesto Che Guevara. In my opinion, it has enor-
mous force, and it is also very beautiful from a literary standpoint. His em-
phasis on the rejection of the "harsh god" is a demand for radical apostasy
from the "opium-gods." This does not mean that the "atheist"—or, to put it
more aptly, the anti-idolatrous position—must necessarily be at odds with
the practical position of Christian faith from the biblical perspective. The
poem, together with a few other well-known ones by Che, is taken from a
book devoted entirely to revolutionary poets who died in the struggle.[7]

Old María, You Are Going to Die

Old María,
you are going to die;
I want to talk to you seriously.

Your life was a 15-decade rosary of agony;
there was no husband, or health, or money,
only hunger to be shared.
I want to talk about your hope,
about the three different hopes
that your daughter forged without knowing how.

Take my hand, which seems like that of a child,
in yours, polished with yellow soap.
Rub your hard calluses and pure knuckles
on the soft shame of my hospital hands.

Listen, proletarian grandmother:
you believe in the new humankind that is coming,
you believe in a future that you will never see.

Do not pray to the harsh god
who belied your hope for an entire lifetime;
do not ask kindness of death
to see your dark caresses grow;
the heavens are deaf and the darkness is summoning you;
you will have a red revenge on everything,
I swear it by the exact dimensions of my ideals.
All your grandchildren will experience the dawn;
die in peace,
old fighter.

Old María,
you are going to die;
thirty shroud designs
will say good-bye with a glance,
one of these days, when you depart.

Old María,
you are going to die;
the walls of the room will remain mute
when death joins with asthma
and they consummate their love in your throat.

Those three caresses fashioned of bronze
(the only light that brightens your night),
those three grandchildren clothed in hunger,
will miss the calluses of the old fingers
where they always used to find a smile.
It will all be over,
old María.

Your life was a rosary of frail agonies,
there was no husband, or health, or joy,
only hunger to be shared;
yours was a sad life,
old María.

When the announcement of eternal rest
clouds the pain of your pupils,
when your hands of perpetual scrubbing
feel the last youthful caress,
think of them . . . and weep,
poor old María.

No,
do not pray to the lazy god
who belied your hope for an entire lifetime,
do not ask kindness of death.
Your life was wretchedly clothed in hunger,
and is ending clothed in asthma.

But I want to announce to you,
in a low and virile voice of hope,
the reddest and most virile revenge,
I want to swear it by the exact
dimensions of my ideals.

Take this man's hand, which seems like that of a child,
in yours, polished with yellow soap.
Rub your hard calluses and pure knuckles
on the soft shame of my hospital hands.

Rest in peace, old María,
rest in peace, old fighter,
all your grandchildren will see the dawn.
I SWEAR IT.

Following is a poem by the Guatemalan poet-martyr Otto René Castillo, born in 1936. After very active participation in student politics, and in the youthful artistic creativity of his country, and following travel in many other countries, including the socialist ones, he joined the FAR (Revolutionary Armed Forces) guerrillas. Wounded in combat in March 1967, he was captured and taken to the Zacapa military base, where he was tortured, mutilated, and burned alive. His captors did not succeed in their attempt to make him betray his friends. His poetic work is permeated with hopes and certainties—something that, in the Guatemala of his time and of the present, says a great deal. The poem that I have chosen shares with Che's in its radical denunciation, although it does not offer radical hope with the same force.[8]

The Grave of God

Such strange
things happen
in my small country
that if, in fact,
there were Christians,
they would believe
    doubtless
in the real death
of God.

A person,
for example,
is impelled
by violent
personal hunger,
and steals,
because one has
to steal.
Then that person
is sentenced
to twenty years
in jail.
    Think
for a moment what it costs
to satisfy hunger:
twenty years
confined within
sixteen square yards
of space!

But the principal
stockholders
of the banks
who transact
business deals
and reap applause,
walk calmly
along the streets.

Think
for another moment:
where does
so much wealth come from?
Have they made it
        perhaps
with the sweat
of their brow
and the calluses
on their hands?

You answer
the question.

The leading businessman
of the city,
who goes to Mass
at eight o'clock,
and looks for a bar
at eleven,
shows,
after a pious
"Bless you!"
his ticket to enter
heaven,
if he happens to die
suddenly.
        Stubbornly
he shows the signature
of the pope
and adds, demandingly:
"It cost me
five hundred prostitutes!"

I say only:
they still have
half of the world
to travel and to prostitute.
But the leading
hungry person
in my town
will be left
without heaven
if the bomb
comes by surprise
at work.

One thing is certain.
Camels will never
pass through the eye of the needle,
but the rich
have already
bought the kingdom
of their heaven
without denying it.

In fact, I think
that if there were Christians
in my small country,
where such horrendous things
happen,
they would believe
in the certain death
of their god,
        without any doubt.

False Christians,
the grave of any god
lies in you!

The following poem, with a dreadful closeness to real life, is by the Nicaraguan poet Fernando Gordillo (1940–1967). A student leader from a very early age, he was, together with Sergio Ramírez, a member of the National Reconstruction Government Junta, a political leader, and a very influential artist in the Ventana group. The poem recommends shelving the problem of God (a clearly anti-idolatrous gesture) until basic human problems are solved, with human hands. This liberal legacy, which is unconscious in many revolutionaries of bourgeois background, prompts very serious questions regarding communication with the masses who are struggling without having to experience abstract radicalization.[9]

What Do I Know about God?

What do I know about God?
And, after all, what does it matter to me?
I see the powerful giving a kick in the pants
to whomever they please, because
        the idea occurs to them.
There are dogs that eat better than humans.
And I see anxious faces peering over garbage cans,
faces expecting to find the treasure of Sinbad.
And the powerful come to me talking about God,
as if they had put God in their hip pocket.
        Don't bother!

Talk to me about my friend Pedro who,
for two pesos that any of you spend
to come and see me,
to talk to me about God,
could not put his son
in the hospital,
the little one whom we had christened Pijulito,
and after crying all night,
he was finally quiet,
     dead quiet.
Or María, Crecencio Guido's wife.
     Don't you know him?
He was in the newspapers the day he fell
     from the scaffolding
and broke his spine, and since then
he has lived on a cot,
with a pillow at his side,
eating there, when he eats;
and there had had two children by María,
and he defecates there,
and remains all day with the excrement
    until María returns,
and cleans him;
and the cot is by now rotted from so much filth,
and Crecencio lives thinking that the cot is going to collapse,
and that he will fall to the floor and contract consumption.

Ah, but you fill your mouths saying: God, God, God. . . .
But you do not fill the belly, the black, wrinkled stomach
of old Justina Plazaola,
or of any of her four grandchildren
who beg with her near the Shanghai Bar, or thereabouts.
They threw her into jail two weeks ago,
because, indeed,
she was giving the town a bad appearance,
and dared
to sleep on a sidewalk at your Holy Cathedral,
and her grandchildren were left alone;
and Juan Roberto, the oldest one, aged eight,
gave three-year-old Quico a beating,
because "he is a pig
who never stops crying."
And with all that,
the first thing that the old woman did when she got out
was to light a candle to Saint Jude Thaddeus,
the advocate of the poor.

What does God matter to me?
I don't know; at best it is of some concern to me,
but let us not talk nonsense;
don't talk nonsense to me. . . .
If you knew . . . Tinita Salazar—
she remembers that
the year before last
she earned at least thirty pesos a night,
and now they won't go with her even for ten,
because she caught pneumonia one night on a spree
    when she swam naked in the sea.
God has punished me, she says,
and there are weeks when she does not earn even ten pesos,
and they don't want her in any brothel,
and she doesn't know what to do,
because she has spent eight of her twenty-seven years that way.

Where? Where is God?
In the weeping of Pedro's son,
the one we used to call Pijulito;
or in Crecencio's fear that the cot will break
and he will become consumptive from lying in dampness all day;
or in the hunger of old Justina who,
when she sees a policeman at night,
urinates from fear,
and her grandchildren make fun of her;
or in the old prostitute's ugliness that Tina Salazar took on
after the pneumonia—
    where?
    Where?
Don't talk nonsense to me!

Let us see how all this can be put together,
and later, later
we shall talk about God,
or whatever. Meanwhile,
    Don't bother!

The following poem is by the Costa Rican poet Jorge Debravo (1938–1967), a Communist Party militant who was killed in an accident. His poetic talent was just in the phase of maturing when he died. One of his books is entitled Recados a Cristo al Comenzar el Año *("New Year's Greetings to Christ"). The religious issue, and particularly the theme of hope in the meaning of the struggle of the oppressed, runs through many of his works. The poem offered here is, in my opinion, a real literary gem and a salutary lesson to Christians.*[10]

The Good Mass

Let us celebrate
the Mass of love this morning.
We shall make a host
of corn meal, flour, and hope.
On a rocky ledge,
in the bowels of a hill,
we shall consecrate the host of life
and the wine of right.

> *(Those who do not come,*
> *the enemies,*
> *will only fall*
> *into bad rivers.)*

None of us
shall pray kneeling;
We shall pray standing up,
ready for life,
with eyes peering.

> *(The knee bends*
> *when the hands*
> *are crushed*
> *in defeat.)*

By night we shall arrive at our altar, united,
mingled in an embrace,
reciting the prayer of joy,
with the kiss of the free on our lips.

> *(When we embrace,*
> *saying brother and sister,*
> *those who do not embrace*
> *will be found wanting.)*

We shall all be priests, all,
the high and the low.
And we shall all eat the host of love
like warm animals.
We shall invite everyone to the Mass:
children, the aged, prisoners,
pilots and mechanics,
archbishops and laborers.

(When prayers are said
standing and singing,
those on their knees
are the pagans.)

    Just as the preceding poem had the theme of life and hope at its center, the following is a "wager on life." The poet makes the wager directly with Christ. Both come out relatively well in the end, because it is clear that both were betting on the same thing. The poet, Roberto Obregón, a Guatemalan born in 1940, was of the generation of Otto René Castillo. A fighter committed to the cause of the oppressed, he was captured in June 1970, and his whereabouts has never since been learned.[11]

Resurrection

Christ got rid of the wooden beam.
The nails and thorns were still protruding
from his hands and forehead.
He returned strengthened from crimes and legends,
miracles and threats of destruction and accession.
Right there we sat down to play dice.
"I bet on life," he said calmly;
and I, "Why shouldn't I bet on life?" I replied.
(I smiled maliciously, as if I had an advantage over him.)
I threw: "You *claimed* to be the way, the truth and the life,
but your way was unrealistic; you hadn't reckoned on cruelty;
at the first clash, you turned the other cheek,
although, in certain matters, of course, you were right.
And to top it off for your friends, you chose death."
We took our positions, and I pointed out the cross to him.
"Then let's play, and bet with the eternal currency,
before I descend and hurl myself into Golgotha."
"Heads," I hastened to say; and all he could say was "tails,"
when suddenly an abyss separated the two of us.
He was there on the shore, and I was shouting from here,
"I myself chose this world, and I will stay here.
No one sent me to be a hermit."
The wind, only the wind there in the background,
was tearing earth from the foundations of the allegory.

I no longer want to know anything, anything, anything.
I left with the pain and dreams of human clay,
and the unabridged history of someone named John or Mary.

When, after three days had elapsed, the mist was dispelled,
the cross emerged stripped, just as before, from the symbol,
fresh and fragrant, to a tree casting shade.

"Adam went to his head," the press reported,
and they spread the rumor by teletype among the multitudes.

In less time than a cock's crow,
in the broad realms of Jehovah,
a guerrilla center commanded by the son of a carpenter
blew up right in his face.

It is no exaggeration to say that the "Nicaraguan Peasant Mass" ranks among the best, most successful, and most concrete (from the standpoint of expressing real situations experienced by the people and communication with the people) of all that liberation theology has produced in Latin America. Here, that theology assumes the most consistent and concrete forms. Hence, to conclude this brief anthology, let us take a text from that Mass,[12] *one that speaks of the God of the people.*

Entrance Song

You are the God of the poor,
the human, unassuming God,
the God who sweats in the street,
the God with a weathered countenance.
That is why I speak to you,
as my people speaks,
because you are God the laborer,
Christ the worker.

You go hand in hand with my people,
you struggle in the countryside and the city,
you line up there in the camp
so that they will pay you your day's wages.
You eat, scratching there in the park,
with Eusebio, Pancho, and Juan José,
and you complain about the syrup
when they don't put much molasses in it.

I have seen you in a grocery store,
sitting on a stand;
I have seen you selling lottery tickets,
without being ashamed of that job.
I have seen you in the gas stations,
checking the tires on a truck,
and even patrolling highways,
with leather gloves and overalls.

Let me recall once again, at the conclusion, the essential idea of this entire collection of texts, from my own at the beginning to the culmination in better writing by others. The essential idea or suspicion is that it is possible, in concrete praxis with the people, to "repack" religious symbology so that it will aid in dynamizing a "church born of the people." It is possible—and more: it is a tremendous challenge to pastors and theologians. The "evangelizing potential of the poor" must be taken seriously.

NOTES

1. From the song "El Cristo de Palacagüina," by Carlos Mejía Godoy, in his *El son nuestro de cada día*.
2. See "Ladainha homem mundo Deus," by Moacyr Félix, Brazilian poet, in his *Invenção de crença e descrença* (Rio de Janeiro: Ed. Civilização Brasileira, 1978), p. 66.
3. Inscription running the entire length of one wall of the church of Our Lady of Fatima, in Colonia Centroamérica, Managua, Nicaragua.
4. From the song by Carlos Mejía Godoy, text by Ernesto Cardenal, "La tumba del guerrillero," in *La nueva milpa*.
5. From the song "Juancito Tiradora," by Carlos Mejía Godoy, in *El son nuestro de cada día*.
6. Hugo Assmann, *Teología desde la praxis de la liberación* (Salamanca: Sígueme, 2nd ed., 1976), Engl. trans of Part I: *Theology for a Nomad Church* (Maryknoll, N.Y.: Orbis, 1976).
7. Mario Benedetti, ed., *Poesía trunca* (Havana, 1977), pp. 13 ff.
8. Otto René Castillo, "Informe de una injusticia," in *Antología poética* (San José: EDUCA, 1975), pp. 222–25.
9. Ernesto Cardenal, *Poesía Nicaragüense* (Managua: Ed. El Pez y la Serpiente, 1975), pp. 430–32.
10. Jorge Debravo, *Nosotros los hombres* (San José: Ed. Costa Rica, 1974), pp. 17 ff.
11. Benedetti, *Poesía trunca*, pp. 216 ff.
12. The "Misa Campesina Nicaragüense," resulting from an extensive research effort. From *Carlos Mejía Godoy y el Taller de Sonido Popular*. Various recordings of it are available.

Index

Compiled by William E. Jerman

231